Flannery
  O'Connor

and the Mystery of Love

RICHARD GIANNONE

Flannery O'Connor

and the Mystery of Love

University of Illinois Press   URBANA AND CHICAGO

This book is printed on acid-free paper.

Library of Congress Cataloging-in-Publication Data

Giannone, Richard.
    Flannery O'Connor and the mystery of love / Richard Giannone.
        p. cm.
    Bibliography: p.
    Includes index.
    ISBN 0-252-01606-8 (alk. paper)
    1. O'Connor, Flannery—Criticism and interpretation. 2. Love
(Theology) in literature. 3. Mysticism in literature. I. Title.
    PS3565.C57Z679 1989
    813'.54—dc19   88-30130
                                                              CIP

To Francis Samuel D'Andrea

Here we contemplate the art which so much love adorns,
and we discern the good by reason of which the world
below again becomes the world above.

Paradiso IX 106–8

Contents

Acknowledgments

I wish to thank Robert Giroux for permission to quote from manuscripts in the Flannery O'Connor Collection at Georgia College. The National Endowment for the Humanities and the Mellon Faculty Development Fund at Fordham University provided grants for trips to the collection, and I am grateful for the courtesy extended by the staff of the Ina Dillard Russell Library in Milledgeville. I would also like to thank the American Academy in Rome for its hospitality when I began writing the book, and Fordham University for awarding me a faculty fellowship to complete my work.

Parts of this book have appeared in different form in *The Flannery O'Connor Bulletin, Since Flannery O'Connor: Essays on the Contemporary American Short Story, Studies in Short Fiction,* and *Thought* 49 No. 235 (Copyright © 1984 by Fordham University). I am grateful to the editors for permission to publish the material here.

Many friends and colleagues helped me at various stages of preparation of this study. Thanks go to a Cistercian monk of Spencer, Alfonse Cinotti, Kathleen Cinotti, Gary Ciuba, Mary Erler, Martin Geller, John Edward Hardy, Anne-Marie Mallon, Gerard Reedy, S.J., Joseph Sendry, and Philip Sicker for their encouragement and criticism. I am especially indebted to Arthur Kinney, who carefully read the manuscript for the University of Illinois Press and put the entire project in perspective for me, and to Rose Adrienne Gallo, who answered all my calls for help.

Years after her death I draw upon the gentle teaching of my mother, Nellie Giannone.

The dedication attempts to acknowledge my greatest debt.

Note on Texts

Citations from Flannery O'Connor's writings refer to the following editions:

The Complete Stories. New York: Farrar, Straus and Giroux, 1971.

Everything That Rises Must Converge. Introduction by Robert Fitzgerald. New York: Farrar, Straus and Giroux, 1965. New York: Noonday Press edition, Farrar, Straus and Giroux, 1968.

A Good Man Is Hard to Find and Other Stories. New York: Harcourt, Brace, 1955. New York: Harvest edition, Harcourt, Brace, 1977.

The Habit of Being: Letters of Flannery O'Connor. Selected and edited by Sally Fitzgerald. New York: Farrar, Straus and Giroux, 1979.

Mystery and Manners: Occasional Prose. Selected and edited by Sally and Robert Fitzgerald. New York: Farrar, Straus and Giroux, 1969.

The Presence of Grace and Other Book Reviews. Compiled by Leo J. Zuber. Edited with an Introduction by Carter W. Martin. Athens: University of Georgia Press, 1983.

The Violent Bear It Away. New York: Farrar, Straus and Cudahy, 1960. New York: Noonday Press edition, Farrar, Straus and Giroux, 1980.

Wise Blood. 2nd edition. With an Introduction by the author. New York: Farrar, Straus and Cudahy, 1962. New York: Noonday Press edition, Farrar, Straus and Giroux, 1974.

In discussing the two collections of stories, *A Good Man Is Hard to Find* and *Everything That Rises Must Converge,* I make a point of the ways in which the stories speak to one another to comprise an ensemble design; it is appropriate, then, to underscore the patterns by citing editions that preserve the volumes as O'Connor organized them.

Introduction

The creator of our nature has also imparted to us the character of love.... If love is absent, all the elements of the image are deformed.
Gregory of Nyssa

The strongest impression left by Francis Marion Tarwater on readers of *The Violent Bear It Away* is a sense of horror. Repulsion is inescapable, for there is much about Flannery O'Connor's exemplary protagonist to dread. At the age of fourteen, her backcountry hero is already a murderer and a pyromaniac, a destroyer of nature and a desecrator of the dead. Though he is raised to obey God's law, when the time comes for him to act upon the demands of justice, Tarwater carries out the bidding of the devil; and he does so with all the might that his rigorous upbringing has instilled in him for the mission of truth.

Tarwater's acts appall us. Possessed by bootleg whiskey, he tries to cremate his great-uncle's corpse, which he has strict orders to bury properly in consecrated ground; then, five days later when he is more tightly in the devil's thrall, the brazen delinquent drowns his young idiot cousin whom he is charged to baptize; and, as a crowning defilement, the shameless killer sets his homestead on fire to obliterate any reminder of the moral duty that he has violated, so that God will make no further claim on his fate. The attempt to be autonomous from God exacts a steep price. Tarwater must and does consent to be a servant of wrath in order to be lord of himself.

1

Yet Tarwater is not wholly vicious. Beneath his inclination to destroy lies a tenderness that is the basis of his remarkable spiritual formation. The evidence of compassion passes swiftly, but it calls all the more attention to itself for turning suddenly into vehemence. When Tarwater at the age of eleven or twelve comes into town for the first time with his great-uncle, the country boy wants to stop and shake hands with each person he meets on the street to introduce himself. At fourteen, when the novel takes up his life, he is more wary in public but still capable of kindness when caught off guard. His gentleness breaks out at a lakeside lodge the day before the murder. The insolent teenager, who loathes his dim-witted cousin, pauses to tie the afflicted child's shoelaces when the trustful idiot sits down to put his feet in front of Tarwater. Tarwater's submissive delicacy astonishes the watchful receptionist, who detects Tarwater's meanness at a glance and perceives the little natural as a holy child.

The reader is likely to be more amazed to learn just how much Tarwater has it within himself to feel for others. At the end of *The Violent Bear It Away* his inchoate vulnerability opens fully as he submits to the judgment of the divine word that he has evaded. He says Yes to the life of prophecy. In doing so, he accepts the physical misery that his great-uncle warned would fall on God's spokesperson, and he lets the will of God be done in him. This incursion on his autonomy proves excruciating, especially after a week of love-evading rebellion. He stands utterly and fatally drawn into his newly augmented consciousness of the divine. Only a personal love could account for Tarwater's self-emptying, and that surrender sets Tarwater's evil acts in the larger perspective of the saving word of God's love that Tarwater sets out to deliver to the people asleep in the dark city. The abuser of the world wills to be a man for others. Tarwater's incipient compassion at the novel's end is the sign of God's presence in his heart.

That love is also at the very core of Flannery O'Connor's fiction. The affection shrouded in Tarwater's personality seems still more inaccessible in the sensibility of his author, whose work has aroused even greater consternation than that stirred by the teenage murderer. Most readers come to terms with the perplexity surrounding O'Connor through familiar categories set forth by the grotesque or the romance or the allegory; some enthusiasts rely on regional and doctrinal explanations for violence in the writing of an orthodox Christian; and a few commentators take psychoanalytical approaches to the eccentricities of her characters. O'Connor's art warrants such varied tacks to clarify her startling dramas, and benefits from lively argument among her critics.

If such discussion has been necessary so far to sort out O'Connor's themes, and successful in establishing her reputation, the findings also have been hesitant and quite limited. A further constraint on the discussion arises from the uniformity of attitude that cramps debate. The initial assumption is that O'Connor depicts primarily the moral ruin that attends modern apostasy. That observation is so compelling that it doubles as the final comment on her art. The debate has taken as its central issue the ways in which O'Connor defines the peculiar notion of evil that brings about the spiritual waste she contemplates.

The focus of this controversy misses the Flannery O'Connor who wants to stop and greet each reader and who stands troubled, sometimes hurt, by the hostile response to her open hand. The ardor that readers find permeating her letters flows as well through her fiction. To recover this warmth of spirit we need a new perspective on her stories and novels. The question that cleaves to the bone is not the one constantly posed: What is the source of sin in her characters? It is exactly the opposite: How do sinners atone for sin? The result of sin is to destroy human nature by degrading the image of God that is the human person's glory, whereas the result of grace and retribution is to restore human nature to loving fullness. Read by the light of salvific possibilities, O'Connor's fiction can be seen as not only clarifying the idea of God for the unbelieving modern mind, but also as modifying our image of the human person.

There is no reason to contest the fact that human dereliction sets O'Connor's narratives in motion and directs their course and outcome. What we need to look for is the gift of grace, the exultant salute to the eternal that she avows in her lectures and correspondence and that brings her anguished conflicts to a higher resolution. "It is a sign of maturity not to be scandalized and to try to find explanations in charity" (*Letters* 346). O'Connor candidly challenges us to take a charitable view of her work, and scarcely anyone has met that challenge.

A shift in the locus of inquiry will bring about a change in our perception of O'Connor. We will see that harshness of event hides O'Connor's great tenderness of spirit. She will emerge as more than an astute recorder of casual disasters. A quiet, patient smile of controlled abandonment to love shines forth through all of her fictional violence. And an unexpected contour will emerge from her art. First in the individual stories, and then in O'Connor's full artistic development writ large, there will unfold a movement from *derelictio,* a being lost and abandoned, to *delectatio,* the joy that will never cease.

I emphasize the joyous aspect of O'Connor's fiction not to justify the appearance of yet another book on her. Rather, I judge Flannery O'Connor's writing to be a work of intimacy and ennobled humanity. The love shaping her stories is not set high above the earth like a firmament of stars, just as the charity that she stimulates us to find is not an abstract theological virtue; love is something personal, precisely defined, intensely alive; and love confronts every horrifying situation as it arises anew in the physical assaults and the emotional batterings that punctuate her stories. The impact of love comes through the small fidelities—the tying of shoelaces, the extending of a hand—performed in service to the mystery of the Word.

Love carries special meaning here. For O'Connor, the basic sentiment underlying acts of love is compunction. But the quality of remorse in her work is diffused with humility. In peak moments of the action true sorrow never disquiets or agitates, and therefore may be drowned out by raucous disturbances. Compunction brings a quiet and a gentleness that console. The writings of the Desert Fathers, which O'Connor admired, frequently urge that we pray for the gift of compunction, the gift of tears. When the soul is softened by inner weeping, God gives the experience of light. With the Desert Fathers, O'Connor believes that the shadow of grief holds the joy of illumination. The moment at his great-uncle's grave, when remorse fills Tarwater with an awareness of his past wrongs, is marked by a red-gold tree of fire that ascends "as if it would consume the darkness in one tremendous burst of flame" (242). Only in the stillness of sorrow can Tarwater grasp "THE TERRIBLE SPEED OF MERCY." And nowhere is compunction more poignantly dramatized than in "The Lame Shall Enter First." When a father's heart feels the mortal effect of his rejection of his son, then a transfusion of life rushes over him with the agonizing love he feels for the child he forsook.

This book examines the empowering of love in Flannery O'Connor's two novels and two volumes of short fiction. The exploration begins where it must, with the preponderant malevolence in the texts, and proceeds through a consideration of the guilt that such evil actions incur. The book looks closely at O'Connor's treatment of human culpability. To the undiscerning or the psychologically oriented, O'Connor's unrelenting exposure of human fault might seem like obsession or preacherly harangue; for O'Connor, however, the sight of inner wretchedness precedes the experience of love. The dynamics of guilt, with its need to repent and repay for sin, describe the problem of love in negative terms. The guilt and punishment that her characters bring upon themselves have no independent reality of their own, but are the dark shadows of the grace and life that O'Connor finds in existence. In the O'Connor universe, guilt understood as an obligation to the absolute—experienced as a debt each person owes to the divine imperative to love—is a prompting toward transcendence. By seeing the abysmal loneliness felt by those who try to find happiness outside of God, the character receives the opportunity of being spared the devil's fate. Guilt in O'Connor's writing is an intuition of repentance that bears upon ultimate reality.

Because guilt and love gain depth and subtlety from O'Connor's rich use of the Bible, this study takes time to examine numerous scriptural allusions in order to show the biblical cast of her technique. The genuine issues of O'Connor's writing are, I believe, related to her knowledge of scripture, and our understanding is impeded if we do not see that her theology derives from this interest. My exegetical lingering to provide biblical information accounts for the length of some of my commentaries.

Finally, however, my interest in the theology of O'Connor's fiction remains subordinate to my interest in the poetry of her ideas. Accordingly, I regard the biblical material from the point of view of a literary critic, and respond to the character of O'Connor's theological position as mediated through her fiction. With the theological context fleshed out, I try to re-create in the reader's mind the transforming power of guilt and love in each work. This goal entails taking each work as an artistic entity, just as O'Connor herself grapples with the unique requirements of form inherent in each story that she writes.

O'Connor also thinks in larger unities when the time comes for her to collect her stories. She does not complete each story in order to compile a book of her stories, but she does give careful attention to making a book of completed stories. As she reviews the accumulation of published stories, O'Connor seems to discover a fuller design, a continuity, among the pieces. Her arrangement orchestrates new affinities. Splendid as the stories are by themselves, the interlaced structure makes them doubly splendid and meaningful. With the stories, then, I try to show the contribution of each to the ensemble design that O'Connor fashions of her collections.

We need to reflect on these composite patterns, for they tell the story behind all of O'Connor's stories and novels. By following the chronological development through which her aesthetic objectives evolve, we can discover the largest unity of all, which is the story not only of how love gives form to her particular fictions, but also of how form gives life to the love that generates O'Connor's art. She praises on many occasions the theologian Romano Guardini for addressing the ageless problem of belief with special sensitivity to the modern person "in whom faith is often no more than a possibility." Guardini has a genius for addressing the sensibility behind issues; to O'Connor's thinking, it is "the realization of the modern condition that makes all of Monsignor Guardini's work so vital" (*Presence of Grace* 53).

O'Connor's art has the power that she admires in Guardini. She speaks to the hope born out of lostness, unveils the light hiding in the darkness that is the contemporary world. Her motive for creating is love. All of O'Connor's adventures chart her amazing movement from being a fictionist of dramatic immediacy in decrying our loveless world to being a poet finding within guilt and sorrow the love that does not end. Her strange choices for heroes—nihilists, petty tyrants, and killers— turn out to be wanderers in love. Their encounter with the mystery of their existence, the adventurer of love whom O'Connor calls God, brings the quest to a close. All the endings take both protagonist and reader by surprise. O'Connor believes, and in powerful action shows, unfathomable reality to suggest the overwhelming boldness of divine love invading human life. Her fundamental understanding of this mysterious incursion is that love is not a human right or a mental deduction but a divine revelation, a gift of plenitude found within the human heart. "I believe love to be efficacious in the loooong run" (*Letters* 97), she writes to a friend. O'Connor's fiction enacts her belief.

The Price of Guilt

Wise Blood

I dream of a new St. Francis . . . who will offer us the new type of
Christian life . . . that we need.
Pierre Teilhard de Chardin to Auguste Valensin, 21 June 1921

At a Saturday night revival meeting, an evangelist of the Free
Church of Christ intends to gain followers by showing his special
relationship with God to over two hundred people. He plans to blind
himself. A headline announces the event. The time is eight o'clock in
the evening on the fourth of October. The gospeller, Asa Hawks, is eager
to impress the jaded crowd. He preaches for an hour on the blindness of
Paul to rouse in himself the vision of his being struck by a divine flash
of lightning. Emboldened by the inner sight, Hawks thrusts his hands
into a ready bucket of wet lime to streak his face. Though he generates
enough fervor to fulfill his plan, Hawks at the last minute does score his
face but fails to let any of the caustic solution touch his eyes. This loss of
nerve shames the preacher. He fancies that Jesus beckons him to flee the
tent; so swept on his pretense, Hawks disappears into an alley.

O'Connor calls attention to Hawks's deception by setting it on
October 4, the only precise date given for an event in all her fiction.
October 4 is the Feast of St. Francis of Assisi, the anniversary of his
death on Sunday, October 4, 1226. In the historical background, then,

we have a legend of the gentle medieval fantasist who preaches to wolves and tames them with blessings; in the fictional foreground, we see a con artist maiming himself to titillate a mob of cynics who cannot be aroused even by gore. The contrast is pointed. Where Francis gives up great wealth to live by the will of God, Hawks tries to tell God what to do by imitating Paul for personal profit. Providence, however, obeys a will of its own. Francis gains the richness of God's favor, whereas Hawks, whose facial scars will outlast Paul's three-day blindness, deepens his poverty and pain. Hawks becomes what he worships. In trying to make God a commodity, he ends up a spleenful beggar.

The October 4 spectacle dramatizes with comic absurdity the subject of *Wise Blood* (1952): the position of the human person before God. The story arises from the possible turns in that relation. "It seems to me," O'Connor writes to a friend, "that all good stories are about conversion, about a character's changing" (*Letters* 275). Hawks exemplifies a negative transformation. On the day honoring the saint who achieved supernatural joy through obedience to God's will, the impostor attains the wrathful state of self-mutilation by heeding the demands of his pride.

The disparity between the spiritual ideal of entrusting oneself to God and His gracious guidance and the inept human groping toward the apotheosis of self depicts more than the twisting of reality that we have come to call the grotesque in O'Connor's art. This contrast conveys the theology underlying her first novel. The Paul who inspires Hawks on October 4 also engages the mind of Hawks's creator. In fact, O'Connor's attraction to negations and failures recalls Paul's practice of explaining the reign of Christ Jesus by showing the mortal condition of life without the gospel.

In *Wise Blood*, O'Connor presents the case of a character's changing through the man of our time who believes in nothing and sets out to prove his belief. This man, the hero of *Wise Blood*, is Hazel Motes. The fascination of his temperament lies not in his positive acceptance of grace but in his inability to live out the nothing he avows. By falling short of his doctrine, Hazel becomes, in O'Connor's words, "a Christian *malgré lui*." The hero does not want to follow Christ, but he cannot help himself. Such deficiency of will opens the possibility of dramatic inquiry for his author. O'Connor asks in her note to the second edition of the novel: "Does one's integrity ever lie in what he is not able to do?" (5). *Wise Blood* shows that one can be driven to virtue by what one is not, by a power that is not one's own. In technique as well as in theme, O'Connor's first novel draws upon the first Christian *malgré lui,* Paul, to portray a contemporary Paul *manqué,* Hazel Motes.

Two forces shape Hazel's destiny: his desire to avoid Jesus and Jesus' unwillingness to let him succeed in that aim. Since that time in childhood when his grandfather, a circuit preacher, singled Hazel out as "that mean sinful unthinking boy" (22) for whom Jesus died ten million deaths, Hazel has struggled to evade Jesus by avoiding sin. Hazel is understandably afraid of the suffering that goes with the cross. Such terror limits to unruly opposition his response to any claim that Jesus might make on him to share in His passion. By the age of twenty-two, Hazel's obsession has hardened into a set of reverse responses. He is confident that blasphemy will lead him to truth and that denial will safeguard him from pain. Jesus for Hazel becomes "too foul a notion for a sane person to carry in his head" (206). Like his namesake Hazael, the king of Damascus in 1 and 2 Kings, Hazel Motes in *Wise Blood* battles against God and God's people. But that foul notion, Jesus, takes the form of a "wild ragged figure" that beckons Hazel from the back of his mind to give up the fight, "to turn around and come off into the dark where he was not sure of his footing" (22). This scraggly figure has more power over Hazel than Hazel realizes, though Hazel's name proclaims that control. *Hazel* in Hebrew means *God sees,* and this solicitous God will not let Hazel out of His sight.

Fighting God, seeing God, and being seen by God stand in significant relationship to one another in *Wise Blood,* generating the hero's acute inner conflict and astonishing destiny. Fear, rebellion, injured pride: all these inducements to oppose God have a tight grip on Hazel. At the same time, a vision of Jesus on the cross, which Hazel cannot dispel, and the attentive eye in the crucified figure draw Hazel to God. These powers collide when the car that Hazel places his faith in is demolished. In the wreckage he sees the nothing that he believes in. He surrenders to the vision of the cross when the idea of nothing becomes a felt experience of emptiness. The satanic hold of disobedience loosens, and the cold defiance which deprives Hazel of his warm humanity reverses its direction to lead Hazel Godward. In the end, the would-be nihilist Hazel Motes becomes a saint for our unbelieving age.

The word *saint* as applied to Hazel requires explanation. My usage, as befits O'Connor, is scriptural rather than medieval. The saints of the Middle Ages, whose statues adorn houses of prayer, tend to yield legends that provide incentives. The moral direction they offer, however, invariably comes with the feeling that these holy perfections are inaccessibly far above us. Biblical sanctity is more down-to-earth. Paul gives the essence of such sanctity in Romans 8:19–39. In early Christianity the saint is a person who believes, who loves and obeys, who shares in Jesus' power, and who, with divine help, repeats what Jesus accomplished. The saint struggles to withstand Satan. In doing so, the saint makes actual within her or his individual sphere the kingdom of God.

Hazel Motes numbers among those persons whom God calls decisively to follow Him. Hazel himself always asks about God. For Hazel, the question of God merges with the grave question concerning the agony and the cross. O'Connor stresses the wonder of Hazel's involvement with God by setting his story against that of Paul. The evolution of a Pharisee into an apostle affords illuminating help in the exploration of the equally implausible conversion of a modern nihilist. In Paul's story, O'Connor has at her disposal the typology of a man with notorious fury making his way to divine tranquility, and it is love that consumes Paul's former anger. Hazel Motes needs to find precisely that peace, must pass through just that fire of love. During such a trial, dogma lends no support; faith is all. O'Connor can draw upon Paul's conflict and the felt belief that his struggle yields. She does not hold up Paul as a specimen of vulgarized holiness or as a man settled in the truth. Rather, she takes the apostle as he takes himself. In his irascible letters, Paul sees himself as seeking but not having attained the full measure of the stature of Christ. The vehement search born of his contentious personality is what interests O'Connor. As I plan to show, it is through Francis that O'Connor brings Paul together with Hazel Motes in the city of Taulkinham, Tennessee.

II

Wise Blood spans the last months of Hazel's life. He is only twenty-two. Two days before the novel begins he is discharged from the army after a four-year hitch. Duffel bag on his shoulder, and free at last from the government with its war and other tricks "to lead him into temptation" (23), the ex-soldier goes home to Eastrod, Tennessee. Home now is but a "skeleton of a house" (26) in which he spends one night before taking a train south. At six the next evening, he arrives in Taulkinham. The city is the end for him. He dies in Taulkinham some months later. Hazel dies as he lived, convinced "that the way to avoid Jesus was to avoid sin" (22); but a shift in the direction of his renunciatory practice makes all the difference for his fate.

Time, too, is Pauline in *Wise Blood.* O'Connor measures Hazel's change by decisive moments of his soul's journey. For all the turmoil within him, the fourteen chapters constituting his story follow a simple pattern. Chapter 1 is a preface giving the biographical details from Hazel's past that drove him to flee from Jesus. With Chapter 2 he begins to learn about the sin from which he dissociates himself. The lesson comes in two stages. Chapters 2 through 7 show Hazel willfully immersing himself in the life of sin, as though he can impugn Jesus by making sin a function of his will rather than an act against God's authority. The second stage runs from Chapters 8 through 13, in which a way opens for Hazel to see the untruth of his denial of sin. As he sees the falseness in others who serve themselves in the name of serving God, the stunned nihilist comes to see his portion of evil in the world, and he confesses the truth about his existence. Resistance gives way to repentance. Amends commensurate with the harshness of his obstinacy follow. As Chapter 1 prepares for Hazel's conversion, Chapter 14, the last, contemplates the effects of it.

Roughly outlined, Hazel's relationship to sin and to Jesus, Who paid for it, composes a movement of denial and flight that leads to perception and self-judgment that in turn prompt contrition and deliverance. "As sin came into the world through one man and . . . death spread to all" (Romans 5:12), so in *Wise Blood* another man makes the reverse passage back through the world to sin, and then through personal guilt to a new life. We appreciate the extent of his journey by noting O'Connor's arrangement of fourteen chapters to suggest that the nihilist who closes himself off to God's absolute summons to come close to Him repeats in a way appropriate to his negations the fourteen stations of the cross. Without fastening *Wise Blood* to the exact details in the devotional narrative, we can see that each crucial moment along Hazel's final way is a milestone of obedience and self-deprivation. The quest of the alienated modern person for home (Feeley 61) and the fusion of comic and serious modes (Walters 43) that provide the basis for most serious discussions of *Wise Blood* bear less on Hazel's essential drama than does his paradoxical course of forward search to shun Jesus and backward research (in the Proustian sense of the reliving of lost time) into the fullness of self through the passion.

The hero's ambivalence emerges in the first sentence of *Wise Blood:* "Hazel Motes sat at a forward angle on the green plush train seat, looking one minute at the window as if he might want to jump out of it, and the next down the aisle at the other end of the car." The tension behind his brow strains his cranium into a death's head. "The outline of a skull" is plain to see (10). O'Connor draws upon Job to fashion her *memento mori.* "My bones cleave to my skin and to my flesh," complains the tormented Job to Bildad, "and I have escaped by the skin of my teeth" (Job 19:20). Like Job, Hazel Motes contends with God, from Whom each narrow escape leads to spiritual exhaustion. Hazel may be only twenty-two, but he is old and worn in the grief that results from dodging the soul-hungry Jesus.

Hazel's battle begins in reaction to his righteous family. They raise the young Hazel to cower before a ruthless God Who is the image and likeness of their own pitilessness and yet Who extends approval to their weaknesses. At ten, Hazel sneaks into a forbidden carnival tent, where he discovers his father writhing in voyeuristic delight before a fat woman squirming in a black coffin. This arrant eroticism confounds the boy's trust in his father's moral strictness. Trained to abjection, the guiltless but shamed Hazel internalizes his distrust by taking on the guilt of his shameless father. When he arrives home, his mother, draped in her usual long black dress, displaces Hazel's adolescent sexual anxiety onto a vindictive Jesus. Without knowing that her son saw the accursed woman, she beats Hazel with a stick across his legs. Jesus is the benediction for her cruelty, the punisher of transgressions. " 'Jesus died to redeem you,' " she drones (63). As his mother victimizes Hazel to alleviate her own festering prudery, his grandfather uses young Hazel to harangue against a world he despises. The old traveling preacher wants each stony soul in the three counties that he covers in his Ford-pulpit to know that Jesus "had His arms and legs stretched on the cross and nailed ten million times" (22) to save them and even the undeserving abomination of a boy with clenching fists standing among them. That "sinful unthinking" and unclean object is young Hazel. He is the breathing offense for which Jesus was executed.

His family's rectitude cripples Hazel. Since this God is without mercy, the boy can only recoil in terror. His legs retain the pang of his mother's stick, and the pattern of guilt and pain that they establish persists until he dies. He tries to avoid the image of his personal wickedness not by seeking virtue or love but by getting rid of the Jesus

Who atones for the evil that is his nature. After his mother beats him, Hazel tries to satisfy "the nameless unplaced guilt" (63) through self-mortification. Only ten, Hazel fills his sabbath shoes with stones to grind away his hurt as he hobbles a mile into the woods. O'Connor portrays the boy in the deepest loneliness. His family teaches him about God without showing him how to make contact with others, or to share their conflict or suffering. Each step in his life hereafter is haunted by his inherited belief that his personal evil is the only thing that matters. Every human encounter becomes an obstacle to his escape from that belief. Everyone will come to be his enemy or an instrument in his battle. Like Saul of Tarsus, who had always striven to be "blameless" (Philippians 3:6) under the law, Hazel will persecute those who he thinks disobey the law.

The army brings out the resemblance Hazel has with Saul as he becomes Paul. Hazel feels bound to a government willing "to have his soul damned" (23). They send him from one desert "to another desert" (24). The ordeal extends the warfare he began in Tennessee against sin. "Put on the whole armor of God," Paul exhorts the embattled converts in Ephesus, "that you may be able to stand against the wiles of the devil" (Ephesians 6:11). Hazel both carries the shield of dread to protect himself from the devil and stands up against the principalities and powers of "this present darkness" (Ephesians 6:12). He has a scar as well, shrapnel in his chest. Even after the army surgeon removes the pieces of metal, Hazel feels a fragment rusting away, "poisoning" his insides (24). The residual shred of ammunition is the thorn in the flesh (2 Corinthians 12:7). Medicine cannot reach this wasting away, and we can tell from the pressure of Hazel's skull that this ache is no phantom pain. The shrapnel is Hazel's Pauline affliction. The Tennessean sustains a blow from a messenger of the devil. No medal or monthly check from the Veterans Administration can compensate for the sting of this adversary. Yet there is a benefit. Paul explains the way to make amends. The apostle understands his chronic debility as denoting a possible spiritual turning. The thorn could be remedial in that those "delivered to Satan," the author of physical ills, "may learn not to blaspheme" (1 Timothy 1:20). Under the power of Satan's wound, the sufferer may be moved to repentance.

These facts about the hero's past come to the reader as the good soldier Hazel Motes, injured and limping inwardly after the government dragooned him into its war, resumes his search for a place safe from sin and Jesus. This leg of his flight is by train going south. The passengers in their everyday manners concretize for the reader and the hero O'Connor's unswerving belief that "if you live today you breathe in nihilism" (*Letters* 97). Mrs. Wally Bee Hitchcock, prim in pink collars and cuffs, rides along with the comfortable knowledge that "life was an inspiration" (14); and when Hazel asks Mrs. Hitchcock if she thinks that she is redeemed, the godlessness beneath her decorum shows. She scrutinizes others from the judgment seat and acts like a good woman, but her notion of goodness is shallow. It is bad taste to speak of God; redemption is an inappropriate topic for discussion. Then, in the dining car, a "poisonous Eastern voice" (16) stings his ear with the venom implied in Mrs. Hitchcock's sweetness. Three women at Hazel's table size him up as a bonehead and descend to the occasion of his presence to belittle him. With a "bold game-hen expression," one of the women imperiously blows cigarette smoke in Hazel's face. Since all action for him manifests a relationship with God, he responds to such high-and-mighty conduct by dissociating himself from the women's claimed virtue: " 'If you've been redeemed . . . I wouldn't want to be.' " To one of the three table companions who laughs, he asks, " 'Do you think I believe in Jesus?' " The question, however, taxes the mind of the lady, whose attention to nail polish leaves no time for trifles. " 'Who said you had to?' " she pipes (16). The atmosphere is the essence of nihilist swank.

The cartoonist in O'Connor catches the evil hidden in finery in one graphic exaggeration. The diners are "three youngish women dressed like parrots" (15). As with the magpie, Mrs. Hitchcock, unbelief puts on fancy dress to strike a self-esteem which its vacuity denies. These birds are the ladies vain. Their twittering selves go forth with a haughty air that obscures their ferocity. When the smoke clears away, however, we see them ready for the kill. "Their hands were resting on the table, red-speared at the tips" (15–16). Respectable clawing draws blood.

Later, as Hazel tries to sleep, other deadly voices haunt him, echoing back from his stint in the army. Some soldiers once asked Hazel to join them at a whorehouse. He hears in the offer an inducement of the powers tampering with his soul. His battle against evil makes no sense to soldiers who fight with mechanical arms against a physical enemy. The very idea of soul, still less its being worth fighting over, escapes them. They react with stout defiance to Hazel's fear. "They told him he didn't have any soul and left for their brothel" (24). These males are of the same feather as that of the taloned ladies. All are in flight from the transcendent. Their flamboyant hauteur, so lopsided next to their spiritual abjection, bespeaks a worldliness that never even understands the world. They rely on a few selfish gestures and cynical maxims that are not true.

For Paul, *world* means not only general humanity (Romans 3:19) but also the total situation in which one lives one's life (1 Corinthians 7:31), and upon which one places confidence and wisdom. Transient and lost, cruel and dangerous, it is the realm of Satan, "the present evil age" (Galatians 1:4). To expose the powers of sin, Paul regards himself as set apart from the thinking of his time.

O'Connor shares Paul's view of the world and his reaction against it. "Right now," she says to a friend, "the whole world seems to be going through a dark night of the soul" (*Letters* 100). The scribes and wise men of Corinth who "did not know God" (1 Corinthians 1:21) through their learning reappear as O'Connor's proper people who are at home in a godless situation. O'Connor responds to the present darkness with Pauline vehemence. Her lectures and correspondence warn repeatedly of "the necessity of fighting it" (*Letters* 97), this ruling toxemia, this doctrine that finds life so pointless as to make extinction desirable— "it's the gas you breathe" (*Letters* 97).

The author of *Wise Blood*, like the apostle, believes that to belong to the world means to be a sinner, a participant in sin and a recipient of its judgment. The world and sin coincide. Sin cannot be understood as an individual act, as Hazel Motes tries to make it, but as the condition in which one shares. O'Connor pronounces our time satanic and through her art is determined "to give the devil his due" (*Letters* 103), the fear he commands and the retribution he deserves. Hazel's mission follows from O'Connor's perception of the world's satanic activity as hostile to God; yet while Hazel's habit of battling temptation and sin is salutary, it is not sufficient. His seeking to avoid sin in order to avoid Jesus is really a refusal to subject himself to God. He must learn that his greater task is to confess his part in the opposition and pay for it. Hazel sins by denying that he is a sinner.

Before Hazel can turn around to follow the bedraggled Jesus into the precarious unknown of faith, he must first pass through the cozy dark of the nihilism that he professes. The place devoid of light is Taulkinham. Taulkinham is any city, anywhere, which is to say that its everyday life covers the gamut of corruptions through which Paul explains the essence and effect of sin. Body, flesh, soul, heart, and mind: each provides a different perspective on the rule that sin has over this modern Corinth. O'Connor conducts Hazel through its lowlife by following Paul's distinction between our outer and inner nature (2 Corinthians 4:16); and so Hazel begins with the carnal and works his way down into the mental.

Upon arrival, Hazel obeys the graffito in the men's toilet of the train station that sends newcomers to "The friendliest bed in town" (30) where Leora Watts receives clients. The welcome of this glistening icon of grease is a warning. Mrs. Watts's mindless repose while cutting her toenails with a large scissors guarantees that those who enter Taulkinham will form no responsible or lasting relationship through human contact. "For those who live according to the flesh set their minds on the things of the flesh" (Romans 8:5). *Flesh* for Paul denotes the domination by earthly desires, not simply those of sex. Mrs. Watts incarnates total submission to the physical. Her boudoir is the world. Hazel, for his part, comes to her to prove that " 'I don't believe in anything' " (32); and the sultana of unfeeling administers the right anesthetic to the man who believes in nothingness.

Just outside Mrs. Watts's house Hazel finds his cherished belief institutionalized on the city streets, where everything is for sale. Chapter 3 begins with the hero walking along by the town's stores, which are open late on Thursday night. Hazel's nighttime excursion reads like a modern documentation of Paul's sketch of heathenism in Romans (1:18–32). As Paul introduces his reminder of God's wrath with a reassurance that God has shown His invisible nature in the created cosmos, O'Connor prefaces her exposure of Taulkinham with a description of the seen things that manifest the divine character of the world: "The black sky was underpinned with long silver streaks that looked like scaffolding and depth on depth behind it were thousands of stars that all seemed to be moving very slowly as if they were about some vast construction work that involved the whole order of the universe and would take all time to complete" (37). Here is the first of many revelations of sacred history in *Wise Blood,* the eternal scale against which our age is measured and toward which Hazel turns in the end. The design is plain and alive. Pristine stars compose a catalytic beauty as they ply through darkness according to no will other than the desire of the source of being. To heed the astral framework in motion is to feel the pull of divine building in the cosmos. All one has to do is to lift one's eyes to observe the plan that sustains and controls the sum of things. Though redemptive activity shines on high this Thursday night in Taulkinham, "No one was paying any attention to the sky" (37).

These moments of descriptive purity that fill O'Connor's fiction are not mere decorative touches; they constitute a poetry that is her theology. Some of the flashes emanate divine glory, while others yield full theophanies; but all give a perspective of judgment on the dramatic situation. In this instance, the shoppers and pleasure-seekers stand culpable of missing a free magnificent presence. While the silver streaks guide the eye toward a spacious composition, a man demonstrating a potato peeler rivets the crowd's attention. The man stands before his "altar" (38). "The glory of the immortal God," as Paul calls creation, has been exchanged "for images" (Romans 1:23), here the silliest mechanism. The implications of this substitution are far-reaching, for the loveless-ness and violence in *Wise Blood* follow from the fact that humanity ignores God.

Here among the other wares, Hazel finds for sale the Jesus he wants to avoid. A cadaverous man with dark glasses, scarred face, white cane, tin cup, and a female assistant with tracts headlined "Jesus Calls You" (41) appears to work the crowd for a few nickels. This specter is the fraudulent Asa Hawks. " 'Help a blind preacher. If you won't repent, give up a nickel,' " he mutters to the crowd (40). Hawks is the pardoner for our time. His spiritual role is assigned by providence, which suffers pardoners in each age for a greater use. While the gogglers watch the man with the potato peeler argue with Hawks over business rights to the crowd, Hazel stares at the blind man's scars and the girl's tracts. Hazel takes seriously the fake blind man's testimony for Jesus. Hazel's visible and audible severity, on the other hand, attracts Hawks, who can engage the people through this challenger. Hawks charges Hazel with fornication, blasphemy, and corruption, and he dares Hazel to repent. Each accusation contains an accidental truth that Hazel must deny in order to preserve the image he has of himself as clean and therefore not in debt to Jesus, his real summoner.

The street exchange dissolves into theological ranting. Though Hawks bears witness only to the money he begs, his message, like his fake blindness, contains a truth. He confronts Hazel with his sinfulness, announces Jesus' love, and foretells that Hazel will " 'have to see some time' " (54), though now he has eyes and sees not. The old judgment of his grandfather swells inside Hazel to press on the shrapnel, the pain of which is assuaged only by a declaration of universal blamelessness. " 'Every one of you people are clean,' " he announces; and he offers a church to go with his doctrine, " 'a new church—the church of truth without Jesus Christ Crucified' " (55). The passersby who already live as though the crucifixion was not for them merely glance at Hazel and move on.

If the city-dwellers are too spiritually depleted to need principles to justify their idolatry, Hazel has too rich and deep a soul to live by an unsanctioned nihilism. His proclamation serves to enshrine negation. All his personal stumbling blocks—the incarnation, the solidarity of sin, the crucifixion—are surmounted by assertion. Guilt disappears. Belief costs nothing. What remains, nevertheless, is the torment that compels Hazel to posit his cleanness in the first place. This rankling need to be blameless shows his theology to be not so much a contradiction as a self-punishment. Hazel can only do himself in because vehemence without emancipation from the insistence on getting one's own way by one's brains and fists leads to the subjugation Paul describes as the "hard and impenitent heart . . . storing up wrath" for itself (Romans 2:5). The need forcing Hazel's accumulation of anger is his claim to autonomy. He refuses to subject himself to Jesus. He wants to command himself. His argument is airtight. " 'What do I need with Jesus? I got Leora Watts' " (56).

The boast underscores Hazel's self-entrapment. " 'Do you not know that he who joins himself to a prostitute becomes one body with her?' " warns Paul (1 Corinthians 6:16). The issue for Paul is not sexual, as it never is for O'Connor. The evil consists in replacing the relationship one should have to God with the relationship one sets up with the body. Whereas the Christian is exalted by cleaving to the Lord, the fornicator is degraded by the soiled flesh of the partner. In *Wise Blood,* Leora Watts is culpable not for who she is but for Whom she replaces. When Hazel is with her he has no need of Jesus; therein lies his judgment.

Enoch Emery is Leora Watts's male counterpart. As Leora embodies flesh without spirit, Enoch is mind without spirit. The isolation foretold by Mrs. Watts and the despair in Hawks's ministry come together in Enoch, who roams the world in a state of terminal loneliness. He has spent his entire life looking for a human connection that is never made, and two months in Taulkinham do not improve his luck. " 'This is one more hard place to make friends in,' " he confides to Hazel (48). His life story bespeaks a helpless innocence misshapen by sin but without the facility of reason to be responsible for sin. His estrangement also indicts the hard-hearted society that formed him. A welfare woman " 'traded me from my daddy' " (46), after which he was remanded to the Rodemill Boys' Bible Academy, where they had the papers on him and kept him in line with threats of the penitentiary. Daily living, however, seems penance enough for this forsaken, runaway bondman. His life is a cycle of incarceration and escape, broken only by his giving his latest captor a heart attack.

O'Connor calls Enoch a "moron" (*Mystery and Manners* 116), and in doing so aligns herself with Paul, who associates bondage with want of mental wholeness. Paul characterizes "doing evil deeds" as being "estranged and hostile in mind" (Colossians 1:21). Neither Paul nor O'Connor is deriding mental subnormality. Rather, they are considering the total state of human sin from the aspect of mental deficiency to point out how much more than mental competence humanness involves. Human life sold into sin is moronic in that it is life without spirit. The mind darkened in understanding is the mind of Taulkinham. Caught in their feeblemindedness, the consumers and moviegoers fail to grasp the vast airy construction work that gives purpose to the human share in the order of the universe. Moronism is the human mind locked into its own unacknowledged limitations and therefore cut off from the magnificent silver streaks in the sky that make us wholly human.

The moronism of Enoch Emery serves as a warning to Taulkinham and to Hazel. Enoch knows " 'a whole heap about Jesus' " (51) yet has no faith. As the meaning of Jesus cannot penetrate Enoch's mind, the townspeople will not let Jesus affect theirs. They run the risk of becoming Enoch. Given the ignorance that is claimed as wisdom in Taulkinham, Enoch speaks a certain truth when he boasts that he "had wise blood like his daddy" (79). Wisdom by this scrambled definition consists in keeping the Spirit from integrating Enoch's nature. Success in avoiding the Spirit in Taulkinham wears the guise of sophistication. Leora Watts provides a good example: "It was plain that she was so well-adjusted that she didn't have to think any more" (60). As it turns out, the body as well as the mind feels impaired by Leora's spiritual destitution. Hazel's foray into the bed of Mrs. Watts stultifies him. His throat gets dry and "his heart began to grip him like a little ape clutching the bars of its cage" (60). Hazel feels what it will be like to fall captive to the life without spirit. Enoch only works at the zoo; Hazel must take care that his heart does not end up living there.

This image of the heart as a terrified, puny ape gripping its cage is noteworthy. It caps a sequence depicting intellectual refusal (to see the stars, to repent, to confess God, to care for another person), deceit (Hawks), and mental insufficiency (Enoch, the city-dwellers). The dramatic action defines *heart* not as the faculty of sentiment and affect but as the power of understanding what can be known about God through the surrounding world and people. Heart in O'Connor's first novel is mind plus the emotional response to intelligent recognition. *Wise Blood* makes vivid the crimes and the anguish of the heart. Paul extends the meaning of heart (*kardia*) when he writes that the heart of the person *wills* (Galatians 4:9; 1 Corinthians 4:21). In this novel O'Connor examines the human heart that wills not to accept. She refers to such mulishness as the condition of *wise blood.* That dark state is the outcome of one of the "many wills conflicting in one man" to which O'Connor refers in her 1962 note to the novel's second edition. Multiplicity within human choice makes human will at once free and mysterious. The unfolding of Hazel's conflict lies in his discovery that there are ways to respond to Jesus other than the mechanical reaction of childhood flight.

Before Hazel can see his moronic wisdom of self-willed obstinacy, he must get himself a car. His grandfather had a Ford for a pulpit, and fifty dollars buys Hazel an Essex.[1] The jalopy makes him an official preacher. His mission to Taulkinham begins as he zigzags the mechanical ark out of the used-car lot. Ensconced in his temple, Hazel can keep going forward while "thinking nothing" (74). His wise blood fuels his aimless momentum. So that the reader does not miss the Pauline thrust of Hazel's conscience as a push against the shackles of the Law, O'Connor has Hazel drive his automobile around Taulkinham without a license. Along the route of his test ride, a painted boulder asks passing blasphemers and whoremongers, "WILL HELL SWALLOW YOU UP?" to which is added, in smaller letters, the assurance "Jesus Saves" (75). Though the admonition is from a society that glories in its possession of the law but does not observe it, the sign obviously points toward the woe at the end of Hazel's rebellious trip. We can take a shortcut through his swervings and go directly to the museum, where an encased shrunken mummy is on display for all to see the death-in-life that results from the pursuit of nothingness. The shriveled corpse depicts what sin does: it produces death (2 Corinthians 7–10). Death sucks the body dry of spirit; where death rules, humanity exists in arid captivity. Before Hazel preaches his new church, O'Connor shows in the museum what the Church Without Christ promises. Moreover, it is out of this dustbin that Enoch, playing aide-de-camp in the war against God, will disinter the New Jesus to go with Hazel's new dispensation.

If the mummy foretells Hazel's possible fate, it also recalls his moral adventure up to the present. He too has been shrinking, recoiling from Jesus, Whose misery calls Hazel from the hanging ragged figure in the trees of Hazel's mind. The heart that gripped Hazel at Leora Watts's—that confronted him with the ape's doleful plea for release—will shrink into a beastly hardness unless Hazel changes his course. He will prove himself to be the stone soul that his grandfather accused him of being. The mummy is the destiny of life outside Christ. Paul refers to "the sinful body" (Romans 6:6) also as "this body of death" (Romans 7:24), from which one is to be delivered. Sin corrupts our true humanity by devolving us back into animality. Hazel's retreat carries him in this direction.

The ramshackle car gives new impetus to Hazel's spiritual regression. Righteous before his own law of negation and standing on the nose of his holy car, he announces his ministry. " 'I'm going to preach there was no Fall because there was nothing to fall from and no Redemption because there was no Fall and no Judgment because there wasn't the first two. Nothing matters but that Jesus was a liar' " (105). With logic that a Pharisee would appreciate, Hazel transforms salvation back into its opposite. The means of freeing humanity becomes a curse, for the death of Jesus creates our sin in order to account for His spilled blood. The stumbling block that Hazel sidesteps is Jesus' cross—the trees in his mind from which the ragged figure pursues him. Hazel tries to remove the cross from his consciousness by means of condemnation, or reverse justification. Since the cross issues a verdict of guilty rather than innocent, Hazel can feel sinless if he can invert Jesus' expiatory sacrifice. The doctrine of justification—that God forgives sins on the basis of Jesus' death—is Paul's special way of expressing the effects of Christ's redeeming action. For Paul, Jesus "was put to death for our trespasses and raised for our justification" (Romans 4:25). But Hazel has his Essex, and " 'Nobody with a good car needs to be justified' " (113).

Bragging masks Hazel's fear of suffering and also lays bare his bankruptcy, just as the confidence of the Jewish nation in their prerogatives as God's people (Romans 2:17) reveals their failure to live by the Law they avow. Boasting may be humanly understandable, but in Paul's theological economy, it is fatal. What is at stake for Paul, and for Hazel in *Wise Blood,* is that in which one places trust. Hazel prides himself on his car and on his rhetorical boldness, but neither a created machine nor a creaturely word can sustain Hazel. Like all boasting before God (1 Corinthians 1:29), Hazel's effort to establish trust in things of this world will prove unfounded.

Our awareness of Hazel's regression comes in stages. In keeping with her tenet "that moral judgment has to be implicit in the act of vision" (*Letters* 147), O'Connor patterns Chapter 7 so that the reader sees both with and beyond the tunnel vision of the protagonist. After visiting Hawks, Hazel takes his car to have the leaks and horn fixed by a mechanic who, looking under the hood, finds the car beyond repair. Hazel of course appraises the Essex by his emotions, and the next afternoon we see him on the open road testing how well his " 'good car' " runs (115). O'Connor begins the sequence by casting the reader's eye upward to observe the daytime variations of the night sky that glimmered over the city. The sky is bright blue "with only one cloud in it, a large blinding white one with curls and a beard" (117). The billowy haze of a man's face enhances the blueness, but Hazel stares straight ahead, ignoring the sky. Nor does he see Sabbath Lily Hawks, the fake blind preacher's daughter, hidden in the back seat. She and her bastardy interest Hazel only as a logical contradiction of her father's being justified before God. Sabbath tries to seduce Hazel, but he is already won over by his lust for a new kind of Jesus. During their slapstick lovemaking, the blinding white cloud moves ahead of them, then floats to the left until it hovers before them when they stop on a clay road. Sabbath's erotic gambit cannot rival the appeal of the Essex, with which Hazel has his most intimate relationship. He runs to the car to get away from the girl; the car, however, fails to start.

A nameless man appears out of the woods to help the stranded pair. This man acts, gives freely, while remaining taciturn, unboastful, anonymous. He listens without comment to Hazel's impassioned description of his Church Without Christ. This unflappable man can lend an ear to Hazel's tirade but he cannot do anything with the car. The machine is beyond his ability to fix it. All he can do is restart the Essex with a push and give Hazel some gas. The stranger speaks only to refuse payment for his help or gas. Hazel manages a grudging " 'I thank you.' " When out of the man's earshot, though, he repays the man's freely given aid with a boast and an insult. His good Essex was not built " 'by a bunch of foreigners or niggers or one-arm men' " (126–27). The stranger, whose liquid slate-blue eyes duplicate the sky, has one arm. Head up high, Hazel peers onward, unaware of the attentive white cloud above, now transfigured into a bird dissolving in the opposite direction on fine extended wings. The tin lizzie jiggles down the road trailing clouds, clouds of glory.

The sequence shows Hazel's vision progressively falling short of things as they are. His not noticing Sabbath's importunity is comic. Mocking the one-armed stranger, however, is truculent and serious. The man's inexplicable appearance out of the woods recalls Jesus' mysterious drawing near two of His followers and vanishing on the road to Emmaus (Luke 24:13). Whereas this postresurrection episode brings out the distinction between the perception and recognition of the risen Jesus by the travelers, the encounter along the road to Taulkinham exposes Hazel's blindness to everyday acts of love. "Every opportunity for performing any kind of charity is something to be snatched at," O'Connor believes (*Letters* 214). The man volunteers to bear with and help Hazel. This suffering servant endures Hazel's ingratitude just as he suffers the loss of an arm. Hazel's pride blinds him to what another does and suffers for him. Since apostolic times it has been difficult for humankind to accept the suffering servant Who made the ultimate sacrifice for all. Hazel Motes makes recognizing love more difficult for himself by trying to stand beyond the cross.

From that self-exalted place, Hazel cannot see the most primitive reflection of divinity, the cloud. The cloud in the light blue sky makes known the luminous quality of the glory of God. It is large and blinding and white, yet Hazel still cannot see it. His failure to feel the kindness of the one-armed man with azure eyes, whose suffering shares in the invisible glory of God, is part of Hazel's blindness to the cloud, God's share in the glory of the earth. Paul understands humanity's "beholding the glory of the Lord" (2 Corinthians 3:18) as a progression from recognizing the likeness of God in persons to perceiving the divine likeness in the cosmos. We train ourselves to see reality by degrees. But Hazel drives on away from the cloud into deeper zones of unseeing, from the ludicrous to the blasphemous. No matter; the cloud cleaves to him even as he denies the Spirit. The cloud-bird hovers patiently. When Hazel's eye is ready to catch sight of it, the radiance will be there in saving visibility.

In O'Connor's art, love always takes plain and "practical forms"

(*Letters* 102); consequently, the joyous aspect is implicit. So much of her warmth and intelligence comes through her poetry here that we do well to reflect on how splendor frames the seventh chapter of *Wise Blood*. The theophany first appears as it does in Exodus (34:30). The large white cloud with curls and a beard suggests Moses, through whose face God's glory first shone forth to Israel. This image concludes the chapter in the shape of the dove from the Gospels. From Old through New Covenant to the present, the radiance of God remains undiminished for Flannery O'Connor. The shining mirror was too strong for Israel, so Moses had to veil his face. The hardened mind that obscures truth has not softened. The same veil that Moses used to hide the glory of God coats the mind of Hazel Motes, who knows that the Essex and not Jesus will save him. Splendor has no significance for Hazel; it is a disappearing quirk of nature.

Splendor in the exact center of *Wise Blood* limns the vast perspective of sacred history from which the entire action is to be viewed. Appearing as it does at the end of Chapter 7 (the perfect number), the cloud-bird manifests the total perfection in which creation participates and against which Hazel wages war. The cloud sails in one direction: the way of holiness and true blamelessness. Hazel races in another direction: the way of denial and increasing wrath. Sacred history assimilates all ways. After Hazel passes through his own negations, he will have gone all the way around to meet the imperishable hazy cloud that links his life to the glorious coming.

Chapter 7, in sum, concludes the first part of Hazel's quest with an admonition and a promise reified in one figure. The cloud-bird gathers together the assorted references to crows, parrots, game-hens, eagles, owls, shrikes, and hawks that precede it. All these winged beings suggest the ways in which the characters seek to aggrandize or spiritualize themselves. All except the ethereal bird, however, are harbingers of debasement. The swarm is an emblem of vanity, predacity, and greed. The delicate sky-bird alone points the way to genuine transcendence. But the more Hazel relies on his willfulness to drive his high rat-colored Essex, the farther away he flies from the peace he seeks. Here on the road to Taulkinham, as on the road to Emmaus, presence is a promise of another day of the Lord when a divine visitation will intervene in Hazel's search. Though God's glory seems to be vanishing, it merely withdraws to rendezvous with the traveler. When they meet again in *Wise Blood*, the bird, a formidable foe of the serpent of self-adoration, will guide Hazel home and to the stars.

III

The second phase of Hazel's attempt to prove that there is nothing to believe in or to be guilty about shows what life is like along the road he chose at the cloud crossing. In Chapters 8 through 13 the comic grimness of daily existence in Taulkinham erupts into monstrous moral and physical violence. We see a Tennessee version of the folly of humankind swapping "the glory of the immortal God for images resembling mortal man or birds or animals or reptiles" (Romans 1:23). This section traces a descent from glory played out through the theological carnival that O'Connor stages so well.

Enoch Emery leads the spectacle. When he hears Hazel call for a new Jesus " 'that's all man, without blood to waste' " (140), Enoch decides to steal the mummy and hide it until Hazel and his listeners are prepared to receive their god. The seed Hazel sows in Enoch's moronic imagination gestates in the arms of Sabbath, who cradles the dwarfed corpse. The bearer of the new eon delivers one more message to the city before he fulfills his mission and disappears. After being insulted by the ape-star Gonga at a film publicity promotion that he joins to make friends, Enoch relieves his humiliation by mugging the man wearing the gorilla suit and putting the suit on in a nearby pine grove. The last reference to Enoch reduces him to the beast he wants to be. "It sat down on the rock . . . and stared over the valley at the uneven skyline of the city" (198). Enoch's bestiality serves as O'Connor's totem for the city that has forsaken its savior.

Gonga against the sky depicts the failure to face the enemy within. Anguished and torn inside, Enoch cannot locate the true cause of his pain and so he attaches it to whatever or whoever is at hand—an ape, a moose, an owl, a waitress, Jesus. When he steals the mummy, he darkens his face and hands with brown shoe polish to put the blame for the theft on a black person. His strategy is to insure that he feels no guilt. Though he does succeed in stamping out remorse, Enoch cannot shake off humiliation, the feeling of being dragged down at every encounter into something subhuman by the constant pain of ridicule and rejection. He has only his moronic wise blood to guide him, and that impulse sharpens his sense of exclusion. Instinct without spirit, action without responsibility, is brute creation. The Enoch of Genesis may have been translated to heaven (Genesis 5:18–24), but the gorilla on the rock is humanity shorn of glory. Some critics have found it useful to call this condition O'Connor's "grotesque."

Enter Hoover Shoats—or Onnie Jay Holy, as he is called in the Jesus business. Holy is the evangelist in motley who duncifies the Spirit to accommodate the public. For three years he ran Soulease, a fifteen-minute radio program of Mood, Melody, and Mentality; and he knows a good show when he sees it. When he hears Hazel preach on the hood of the Essex, Holy comes up with the right scenario to promote the act. He concocts a testimony about being converted two months ago by the loving kindness of the preacher on the car. Hazel becomes in this script the prophet who saved Onnie Jay from suicide by bringing out his " 'natural sweetness' " (150). To be sure that the crowd understands that the prophet's Church Without Christ offers salvation without the crucifixion, Holy amplifies the name to the Holy Church of Christ Without Christ. The inhabitants of Taulkinham take such muddled impromptu reformations in stride, because Holy proposes a do-it-yourself salvation that sanctifies the self-absorbed life without Jesus that the citizenry has been leading all along.

Holy's sweetness ends in pain for himself and death for another. Hazel has no tolerance for the lies Holy cynically mouths to get money. The truth is what Hazel seeks; blasphemy, not sweet talk winning friends and collecting dimes, is the way to truth for Hazel. Though denounced as a " 'liar' " (153), Holy persists until Hazel retaliates physically, slamming the car door on the pest's thumb. "A howl arose that would have rended almost any heart" (159). But not Hazel's heart. His hardness prompts Holy to hire Solace Layfield, Hazel's look-alike, to take advantage of their resemblance. After Layfield's second night of imitation, Hazel pursues him. First, one rat-colored car ditches another rat-colored car on a lonesome road. Then the Essex, Hazel's means of salvation, becomes the instrument of retribution: Hazel strips Layfield, runs him down, and backs over him. Hazel's uprightness before the law he obeys brings him to arrogantly identify himself with that law.

Several judgments arise from this brutal scene. The first falls on Hoover Shoats. Though he did not run Layfield down, he did set him up. Shoats's doctrine of inborn sweetness effects a chain of events that ends in a bitter death. His flattery blinds him to his lies and to the harm he brings to others. As with Milton's Lucifer, the absentee originator behind all indirect complicity, Hoover's coaxing is made more venomous by its deceptive, pleasing taste.

The full blame for murder belongs to Hazel. He equates killing Layfield with restoring truth. " 'You ain't true,' " he decrees (203). The verdict displaces the onus of punishment onto the victim. The refrain makes absolute Hazel's subjective notion of truth, arrogating and becoming the lawful judgment. Hazel is a judicial murderer.

Again Paul helps us through the turn of O'Connor's thought. More than any other apostle, Paul had to come to terms with the law and its potential contradictions. The law of Judaism sanctioned Paul's persecution of Christians, and yet that same law in its inadequacy prepared for Paul's conversion to the Christ Who brought an end to law. The law that was meant to convert Israel to the will of God led to the opposite condition of confidence in Israel's own merit apart from God. Paul's warning about these deceptions (Romans 2:1–20) illuminates the powerful tensions in Hazel's conscience. Hazel uses others for the rigid law of his personal nihilism, and he uses the law to excuse his evil. Paul warns of just such an abuse of the law. The law "which promised life proved to be death to me" (Romans 7:10). The full impact of Paul's thought on *Wise Blood* comes from his exposing the habit of mind that leads to self-adoring legalism. Over and over, because the prompting is so human, Paul denounces the pursuit of righteousness separate from God and His mercy.

Self-centered obstinacy creates the lovelessness and alienation that *Wise Blood* dramatizes. It blinds one to glory; it cripples the young; it impedes an understanding of the gospel; and it kills. O'Connor sees the uprightness that the law promotes as the source of Hazel's cold-blooded execution of the false prophet Layfield. The moral training of Hazel's family to obey without love comes full circle. At ten, returning from the carnival, Hazel was blameless yet felt massive guilt; at twenty-two, after killing Solace Layfield, he is guilty and feels no blame. Hazel cannot afford to express the anger he carries from youth without causing harm to others and to his own soul. The more guilty Hazel is, the less guilt he feels.

Hazel reacts to bloodguilt[3] by planning to escape to a new city. Since guilt is torment, the sinner wishes to flee from it. But the Essex does not totter five miles before Hazel gets back the contempt that he gave out. The boomerang comes as Paul says it does for the righteous: through the law. "All who have sinned under the law will be judged by the law" (Romans 2:12). A black police car stops the leaky Essex. With a suavity that only ruthlessness would use, the policeman gets Hazel to drive his car to the top of a hill, from which the officer pushes the car down thirty feet. Like the new Jesus, like the false prophet, the Essex is demolished. The policeman dusts off his hands as tidily as Hazel wiped away the bloodstains from his car after killing Layfield. These shattered forms serve an important purpose. They are the "earthen vessels" Paul writes of, which show in their defectiveness "that the transcendent power belongs to God and not to us" (2 Corinthians 4:7).

On the road to Damascus, Paul is jolted out of his rigid Pharisaism; on the road out of Taulkinham, the car is ditched from Hazel. Both blows affect vision. First, Hazel's knees buckle, as though struck once again by his mother's stick; then Hazel sits on the edge of an embankment looking at his broken parts: "His face seemed to reflect the entire distance across the clearing and on beyond, the entire distance that extended from his eyes to the blank gray sky, that went on, depth after depth, into space" (209).[4] The magnificent work of art that is the sky subsumes Hazel's power of seeing.

The reader must infer what Hazel sees reflected through depth after depth by what Hazel does. By instinct he resumes the penitential walk of his childhood. For three hours he treads back to Taulkinham, pausing to buy quicklime and a tin bucket. When he arrives at the boarding house where he lives, he mixes the lime with water and blinds himself. The act is pure Hazel Motes—willful and bloodcurdling to the end, for the end. O'Connor is unambiguous about the love Hazel expresses in the blinding that her readers regard as self-destructive. The year that *Wise Blood* was published, O'Connor denied the charge of impiety and lovelessness in Hazel's self-gouging. "It seems to me the form of love in it is penance," she writes to Sally and Robert Fitzgerald, "as good a form as any other under Mr. Motes circumstances" (*Letters* 40). O'Connor did come to see weaknesses in the novel (*Letters* 117), but Hazel's blinding took on spiritual value. "All H. Motes had to sacrifice was his sight but then . . . he was a mystic and he did it" (*Letters* 116), O'Connor says in 1955, three years later.

Even a modern reader schooled in penitential literature may find it hard to see mystical accomplishment in Hazel's self-mortification. We can only speculate on the rabbinical turn of mind that brings him to burn out his eyes. Since he had eyes yet did not see the car for the wreck it was, his legalism might run, he ought not see at all. Killing his sight would make the word *blind* true to the spiritual darkness that he lives in. The idea to use lime, of course, comes from Hawks, who tried to use Paul's psychosomatic blindness as proof of his own election. Hazel the positivist outdoes Hawks and Paul. Oedipus the king may help us see how Hazel the nihilist is awakened to life by exacting justice on himself (Walters 45), but Attic grandeur will not lead us to the depth after depth extended in the gray sky. Nor will the assertion that "Hazel Motes receives no revelation" in this novel "of many nightmares but no visions" (Asals 53) help us comprehend the " 'more' " (222) that the hero's agony opens up before his bottomless eyes.

We need a view of suffering to go with Hazel's change of heart about the cross. Suffering is inimical to the modern sense of life; it is to be obliterated or removed from view. Hazel wears the blinders of our age at the beginning of the novel when he flees from the ragged figure chasing him from the trees of his conscience. That flight from suffering belongs to the false wisdom that lies demolished with the Essex in the ditch. Counterpuncher that he always will be, Hazel takes up his struggle against his old belief with inveterate vigor and new heart. The quicklime pouring over his eyes is the opposite affection of submission breaking over him; it bestows new life through repentance. Hazel's *metanoia,* or change of mind, is based on a change of attitude that demands practical expressions of his decision. O'Connor does not have in mind for Hazel certain mechanical or legalistic prayers that would hardly counteract the present-day notion of sin as unreal or separate from the whole of life. Rather, she has in store the concrete biblical acts of confessing, fasting, vigils, and almsgiving, all of which Hazel performs, and all of which administer "a baptism of repentance" (Mark 1:4) that Jesus makes the heart of His good news.

We can appreciate the nature of Hazel's *metanoia* if we remember that his first act of contrition, his blinding, goes back to the day when Hawks pretends to be Paul—October 4, the feast of St. Francis, a scandal of a man if there ever was one. Francis's life was every bit as "ugly" and "morbid" (211) as the respectable landlady, Mrs. Flood, finds Hazel's life. Certain facts about Francis would interest the author of Hazel Motes. Francis was a soldier who suffered from a long-standing and severe disease of the eye. Blurred in physical sight, he was haunted his entire life by a keen inner vision of Jesus suffering His passion on the cross. The grim sight made Francis flee. But like Paul, Francis experienced a sudden conversion. When he submitted at last to the hand of God, Francis forsook the world to embark upon a life of self-denial. He sought to live the life of Jesus, especially that of His passion. Before he died, Francis was cauterized from ear to eyebrow. Painfully blinded, he accepted this and all anguish with the gratitude with which he received his gift of faith (*Omnibus* 5–9).

O'Connor does not replicate Francis's life in *Wise Blood* to give her stark tale of a Protestant saint a hagiographic aura. By temperament, Hazel is a far cry from the gentle Italian lover of birds who preached community while welcoming solitude and who cared for lepers while refusing aid for his own ills. By faith, Hazel cannot choose to walk in the footsteps of Christ through which Francis leads his followers. Hazel Motes of Eastrod knows nothing and cares not at all about the Little Poor Man of Assisi. Francis would be to the Tennessean just another one of those foreigners.

That contrast points up O'Connor's handling of Christian materials in her art. In his difference from Francis, as in his difference from Paul, Hazel lives out the truth of atonement that shaped both saints' lives. For O'Connor and for Francis, following Christ is not something purely external. To be a Christian for O'Connor means to take up the cross and accept scorn, *imitatio Christi*. This acceptance involves more than enduring the trials that beset all women and men; the prerequisite to faith is to be found only in the passion a person voluntarily takes upon herself or himself. The outcome of faith is an interior transformation.

St. Paul, St. Francis, and Hazel Motes meet on the ground of chosen suffering. The works of all three men lead to their climax in the voluntary sacrifice of their individual lives. The positive witness of Paul and Francis leaves no doubt about the value of their sacrifice. But a sanctity that comes into being through protest involves an exaggeration and a one-sidedness that call Hazel's holiness into question. When the car is taken out from under him, the world becomes devoid of meaning. This experience, which many readers interpret as atheism, is in fact for O'Connor a genuine experience of the most profound existence. Hazel's atheism and self-indictment acquire redemptive import as his self-mortification leads him to an act of total surrender. Through affliction Hazel finds a place in a lonesome world. Sorrow opens a way into the space on which Hazel "concentrated" (210) after losing his car. It is a new country without borders of time and place, a milieu unchanged from apostolic and medieval times. Paul stormed into it. Francis embraced it. And in the last chapter of *Wise Blood*, Hazel inches his way into the silent order of the stars. The common *centrum* toward which all three gather is the indestructible source of life.

IV

If we line up the introductory word or words of all the chapters, we can see that the first word of Chapter 14 notifies the reader of a radical turn of events in *Wise Blood:*

1 Hazel Motes
2 He
3 His
4 He
5 That morning Enoch Emery
6 That evening Haze
7 The next afternoon when he
8 Enoch Emery
9 Hawks
10 The next night, Haze
11 The next morning
12 In spite of himself, Enoch
13 On his second night out . . . Hoover Shoats
14 But she

Reinforced by grammatical parallelism, the substantives first decline the hero's conscious preoccupation with himself, then subordinate that concern to his entanglements with others, until a conjunction reverses the reference away from him. The overarching outline traces a shift of the center of gravity, with the chapter beginnings roughing out Hazel's conversion as an abrupt release from himself. When the car disintegrates, Hazel sinks into a hollow abyss of dashed hopes that becomes God's opportunity. *But* marks Hazel's passage into a new relation with God, and the burden of Chapter 14 is to put all thirteen preceding chapters into the moral equilibrium struck by his encounter with God.

The reader could use help through the puzzling conclusion to *Wise Blood.* We know from the author's note that the hero is a Christian *malgré lui* but he also seems to be a Christian despite his author. O'Connor portrays a convert who does not directly attest to God or to Jesus during or after his change of heart. When he ceases to shout war cries, Hazel has little to say. His taciturnity and O'Connor's withholding of an explanation seal Hazel's *metanoia* behind his brows in a mystery secured from rational analysis and heightened by a blindness that sharpens the hero's new vision.

If Hazel's turning toward God is subliminal, the habits he develops in this dazzling darkness are clear, startlingly so. Money goes only for his few physical needs; the rest he throws away. Influenza does not hold him down. While his body wastes away, his spirit quickens. He spends half his day walking, taking what numbing ease comes from wandering within four or five blocks of his boarding house. He does not eat much. Out of the truculence that is his nature, Hazel derives a practice that shows his humility and hope. Though there is in his discarding of money neither the justice nor the charity that would make his gesture a joyous almsgiving, Hazel does live by an economy that makes him poor so as to enrich him by a higher poverty. In his abstention from food, Hazel shows his sorrow and repentance. These privations give new meaning to his old vigilance. Now he is on guard against his own carelessness, and stays alert so that he can live in darkness without being a part of that darkness. This watchfulness enables the hero to reach his desired goal.

One day while snooping through Hazel's belongings, the landlady, Mrs. Flood, sees that an extra pair of shoes are lined with gravel, broken glass, and bits of stone. Mrs. Flood has heard about strange practices in European monasteries and wants to be sure that such conduct does not violate the decorum of her orderly house. Even for Taulkinham, where eccentricity is a way of life, Hazel is regarded as going too far. Mrs. Flood needs to know just what her guest is up to. "'Mr. Motes,'" she asks while he is eating his dinner, "'what do you walk on rocks for?'" Mr. Motes responds, with his customary harshness, "'To pay'" (222).

These two words define his penitential world. He has a debt to pay. Debt is a synonym for guilt.[5] In using the infinitive *to pay*, Hazel suggests that his debt demands endless payment. The rationale behind this economics escapes Mrs. Flood. "'Pay for what?'" she asks. Hazel's words are sparse. "'It don't make any difference for what,' he said. 'I'm paying'" (222). Repentance becomes his life, as his life is his theology in practice. Hazel claims only to be a sinner. When Mrs. Flood asks for an explanation, Hazel can only bear witness against himself by acknowledging an unspecified and universal debt. Along with fasting and watching and becoming poor, paying is repenting. Hazel's use of the progressive tense, *I'm paying*, predicates his ongoing contrition for the guilt that is his here and now as a result of his individual action. The magnitude of his guilt gives mystical value to his blindness. " 'If there's no bottom in your eyes,' " he says to the curious Mrs. Flood, " 'they hold more' " (222). Instead of striving after sight and truth, as if they were the highest goals, Hazel puts self-denial and obedience in the place of understanding. Not-seeing means pure affirmation without definite limits. Like the walled eyes of ancient Greek statues, Hazel's lime-seared sockets seem fixed on eternity.

The mystery of not-seeing also manifests itself in Hazel's relations with others. Seeing himself a sinner, he no longer looks for evil in another. " 'I'm as good, Mr. Motes,' " claims the landlady, " 'not believing in Jesus as a many a one that does.' " Since Hazel now knows that belief in Jesus effects a humility that gives the believer both guilt and spirit at the same time, he feels united with Mrs. Flood's need to appear virtuous. " 'You're better,' he said, leaning forward suddenly. 'If you believed in Jesus, you wouldn't be so good' " (221). Mrs. Flood's boasting is no different from that of the other good people of Taulkinham, but the response of Hazel has changed. The persecutory Hazel is gone. Though it would be helpful, in establishing a Christian scheme for his conversion, to propose that Hazel is forgiving, the text belies such a claim. O'Connor is after a harder virtue and a more daunting love. Conversion for Hazel shows in his ceasing to strive toward righteousness, which, as his comment to Mrs. Flood implies, belongs to God alone, and in his taking up the struggle to pay for the sins that are very much his own.

Though Mrs. Flood is a witness to Hazel's final effort, his struggle, like the passion from which it derives meaning, takes place in solitude. Human solitude holds the possibility of being either totally closed or totally open to God. Hazel's solitude comprehends both as his stance shifts from turning his back on God to facing only God. Hazel's realm of solitude takes on another dimension through cleansing. As Hazel willed that his body be soiled to prove that there was no such thing as sin, now he must purify his body to bring it in line with the filth he finds in himself. Defiled flesh is no metaphor. To scour his body, Hazel ties three barbed wire strands around his chest. The fine metal thorns will also scrub his soul. He feeds his spirit with rocks.

The sight of Hazel in bed with blood on his nightshirt from the wire's cutting into his chest so scandalizes Mrs. Flood that she becomes an inadvertent instrument of his agony. At first she is irate, then admonitory about his toilet, before turning solicitous and vindictive. She experiences the same fright before Hazel's tattered body that Hazel feels before the ragged figure in the tree. And at the end of the novel, O'Connor does nothing to soften the blunt impression made by the approaching nearness of God in the novel's beginning. On the contrary, she sharpens the effect by presenting Hazel's obedient love of the ragged figure as an exciting horror. Once again suffering causes senseless flight. As a last-ditch effort to deny the anguish before her eyes, Mrs. Flood retreats into self-sorrow and rants in "the voice of High Sarcasm" about her boarder's debts to her. *Sarcasm* comes from the Greek *sarkazein*, "to tear flesh," and that is what the landlady brings about. The more she complains of what is her due, the more she feels cheated and the quicker she loses her source of income. Her verbal tearing drives Hazel out into the wind slashing "at the house from every angle, making a sound like sharp knives swirling in the air" (225).

The storm serves Hazel like the cleansing water in Ezekiel (36:23–28) by means of which the Lord converts "the heart of stone" into "a heart of flesh." One of the "coldest days of the year" (226) followed by a night of "driving icy rain" (228) is the climate of Hazel's soul and the right condition for his death. Mrs. Flood adds a legal wave to the torrent by calling the police with the pretext that Hazel owes her rent. The law is freshly invigorated. Two fat officers with yellow hair and sideburns, cockily appointed in "tall new boots and new policemen's clothes" (230), find Hazel lying in a drainage ditch not far from an abandoned construction site. Here Hazel lives out yet another meaning of *repent,* namely, "creeping, prostrate"; but the law sees him only through myopic technicalities. While the law is under orders to take Hazel back to pay his rent to Mrs. Flood, Hazel is obeying the beckoning hand that calls him all the way back to pay his portion in the house of Adam.

The last pages of *Wise Blood* contrast the clarity of Hazel's submission against the insensitivity of legal domination, the language of mystery against the language of the seen, the economy of contrition against the economics of greed, and the sentimental brutality of the law against the fine endurance of self-surrender.

> "I want to go on where I'm going," the blind man said.
> "You got to pay your rent first," the policeman said. "Ever' bit of it!"
> The other, perceiving that he was conscious, hit him over the head with his new billy. "We don't want to have no trouble with him," he said. "You take his feet" [230–31].

The legal hirelings do what they always do. The law, warns Paul, kills. The blind man dies in the squad car, unnoticed as dead, voided utterly by the righteousness that justified him when he drove his car, and hauled away in another terrible mechanism of mockery.

Inseparable from this public scorn is the extraordinary surge in the mystery of not-seeing. After the policemen deliver the corpse to Mrs. Flood, she installs the dead Hazel on her bed, locks the door, and watches over him. The landlady has her tenant for keeps. This ghoulish final scene leaves a double impression. On the surface, Mrs. Flood's vigil is the last of several tableaux depicting a mummy in a case. Hazel ends by replacing the woman in the carnival coffin, the shriveled man in the museum, and the puny ape of the heart clutching the bar of its cage. But there is also in this eeriness the hint that for Hazel and Mrs. Flood another outcome is in the making. Hazel's face is "stern and tranquil." In fact, the landlady "had never observed his face more composed" (231). The last impression of the hero's head duplicates and enlarges the first impression he makes. "The outline of a skull was plain under his skin and the deep burned eye sockets seemed to lead into the dark tunnel where he had disappeared" (231).

The face of the dead hero joins agony with peace. The time Hazel passed in hostile pursuit of his negative truth is seen now as a preparation for a time of contemplation, and the time of his not-seeing has prepared for the supreme moment of deliverance. His renunciation of material things and his deeper giving up of ownership of himself lead to the "quiet and peaceable life" (1 Timothy 2:2) given to those who have fought the good fight. The peculiar character of Hazel's ordeal derives from the value that O'Connor attributes to affliction. With Paul, she affirms that "suffering produces endurance" (Romans 5:3). Suffering in her first novel betokens the victory toward which all of her subsequent work moves. The sign is present from the beginning of *Wise Blood* in the figure moving from tree to tree in the hero's consciousness. And after all of his dodges, self-mortification leads the hero back in the footsteps of the God Who has been nearer to Hazel than Hazel has been to himself.

Hazel's integrity lies deeper than his aspect. The face that Mrs. Flood contemplates is a composite. The underlying lineaments are the rebellious and suffering lines of Job. The burned eye sockets belong to Francis. In the *Major Life of St. Francis*, Bonaventure says that the friars attending Francis at death saw him as "a second Job" (*Omnibus* 738).

Francis's protracted agony "eventually reduced him to a state where he had no flesh left and his skin clung to his bones" (*Omnibus* 737). Hazel is a third Job. The modern counterpart has similiar facial details, but his expression carries particular meaning for his age. Since O'Connor is writing modern hagiography for "people who think God is dead" (*Letters* 92), she surrounds her protesting saint's head with shadow instead of a halo. Her technique is clearer if we recall the representation of Bonaventure, who pictures Francis at death "hung, body and soul, upon the Cross with Christ," burning with "love for God" and thirsting "for the salvation of the greatest possible number of human beings" (*Omnibus* 737). Against the Franciscan ideal of self-donation O'Connor sets the life of the renegade Hazel Motes, whose compulsive rush down the blind alley of nihilism plunges him into the tunnel of self-extinction. The modern searcher for the absolute, unlike Francis, has no denominational program, no communal attention, not even a cosmological excitement to support his undertaking. Malaise and rage and nausea stimulate a pursuit conducted among enemies and strangers. The venture at times may not even have a religious emphasis. What engagement there is with the absolute comes in the void and happens in a flash, forcing the searcher to her or his knees. In the exemplary case of Hazel, his gory end appalls more than it uplifts.

And yet O'Connor does not abandon the reader to terror. Hazel's venture counts precisely because it is hidden in a profane world. There is that "pin point of light" (218) that Mrs. Flood imagines at the end of the tunnel through which Hazel travels. She must shut her eyes to see this light that is the beacon of the mystery of not-seeing. By an inner light, she fancies it as some kind of star, "like the star on Christmas cards" (219). The star image sharpens and expands as it moves from the Taulkinham sky to the interior of Mrs. Flood's imagination. At the end, Hazel becomes that starlight for Mrs. Flood, and O'Connor leaves the reader with that epitomized figure in the last words of the novel: "he was the pin point of light."

The star image flickers in several scriptural and symbolic directions. The most important radiance points toward the strange saint from Assisi. The main accounts of Francis's life all transform him into a star. "Francis shone forth like a brilliant star in the *obscurity of the night* and *like the morning spread upon the* darkness," writes Thomas of Celano, his earliest biographer (*Omnibus* 259). Bonaventure polishes the halo a bit. As Francis falls asleep in God, one of the friars "saw his soul being borne on a white cloud over many waters to heaven, under the appearance of a radiant star" (*Omnibus* 740).

The star signifies glory. It marks the home of light and peace. In Thomas of Celano's account, the star celebrates glory as applied to Francis's fame; fame is the ancient concept of glory out of which Christian ideas of glory developed. Francis's light shattered the darkness of sin and disobedience, and aroused others from "their old and deeply rooted sins" by speaking "the truth boldly" (*Omnibus* 259). The light and star extol the conversion of many to God through the longing "to attain love and reverence" (*Omnibus* 259) of the Creator. The same brightness appears in O'Connor's admired Dante. Each of the three parts of *The Divine Comedy* ends with the word *stelle*, "stars." At each crucial moment the stars summon the wayfarer to gaze upward, the direction in which the mind and heart will find God, "the Love which moves the sun and the other stars" (*Paradiso* XXXIII 145).

Hazel Motes numbers among those who obey the injunction to turn their sight toward the long silver streaks that move "depth on depth" amid "thousands of stars" (37). Hazel's change of heart does not take place on the grand scale of Paul's intellectual and missionary odyssey or of Francis's massive self-sacrifice and political reform. Hazel's desire for justice remains personal. His solipsism closes him off from everyone around him; his nihilism blinds him to God's glory. His connection to the physical world is only empirical. At the end, he has only Mrs. Flood, whose use of *Mr.* in her tender appeal measures estrangement as much as it does southern courtesy. When the hero is out in the icy rain, she wants to rescue him and say: "Mr. Motes, Mr. Motes, you can stay here forever . . . " (229). Solitary community is all that the seeker of the absolute can hope for in a friendless world. Still, Hazel has his zeal, and his zeal sustains him.

The conversion of O'Connor's nihilist follows the limited way available in our time. Hazel fights the good fight not as the mighty soldier Paul summoned and not as "the most valiant knight" (*Omnibus* 258) that Francis became, but as a drafted resister in motley. Neither Damascus nor Assisi, but the city of Taulkinham, where God is forgotten, is the place for Hazel. Paul's theology of conversion provides a perspective, and Francis's spirituality the aegis, for O'Connor's Taulkinham story. With both in mind, we can pick up certain clues in the name of her imagined locale. *Tau* is Greek for "cross." The Greek *tau* is what Francis used to sign his name after his famous letter to Brother Leo (*Omnibus* 118–19). *Kin* is a diminutive suffix. *Ham* means "home," "place." By going backward, as we should in matters concerning Hazel, we can read *Taulkinham* as the "home of the small cross," the lesser path that O'Connor's protesting saint follows. He is, so to speak, snared in order to be dragged as a captive from foreign land to alien city for bizarre, unknown, and yet mysterious, well-planned service.

St. Paul, St. Francis, and Hazel Motes make up an odd fellowship, but within the conditions of their respective times all join the communion of saints by taking up the passion. Those who suffer for the world are one. They are, as O'Connor says, "Christ continuing in time" (*Letters* 337). Through the unity of witness they meet in the Taulkinham of the spirit. In that Taulkinham, there is always work to do, the positive side of which prompts these saints to take on their harsh suffering. In Jeremiah we hear the call that attends surrender: "to build and to plant" (1:4–10). The call that Francis answered was from a painted image of Christ crucified, moving His lips to say, "repair my house, which, as you see, is falling completely to ruin" (*Omnibus* 370). Francis went around collecting stones by hand to rebuild the physical church, and he ended his labor with a vast vision of church as mystical body. Taulkinham is nothing less than a spiritual disaster area in need of any helping hand it can get for restoration. It is an urgency carefully built into the center of *Wise Blood*. The scaffolding in the sky (Chapter 3) and the forsaken construction site on the town's outskirts, where the civil authorities find Hazel after the storm (Chapter 14), link the contribution of building anew on earth with the vast construction work in the sky that will take all time to complete. Hazel construes his job also as gathering stones, stones for punishment; these remnants erect an inner edifice. The stones of mortification raise Hazel's spirit beyond the bounds of sinful servitude that would ultimately destroy Hazel's whole inner nature and undermine the cosmic construction work as well.

Hazel's asceticism is powerful enough to impress the woman who does not believe in Jesus. By Babylon's sad waters, Mrs. Flood, a mourning exile in a lonesome place, is brought to the shores of guilt and compassion by the weird Mr. Motes. She starts to see the dark around her as " 'a empty place' " (227); she turns to ease her and her boarder's shared loneliness; and she confesses in the "last part" (229) of her life the decision " 'to wait on' " (231) the dying man and to follow him wherever he is going. She no longer regards him as a source of money.

He has become one in need of mercy. When she thinks of the blind man out alone in the terrible icy rain, she weeps. Tears, like quicklime, pour forth the recognition that she too is a debtor, not a proprietress. Jolted out of her complacency, she feels vulnerable enough to plan marriage to the unresponsive blind man, whom she will nurse in her last years. The vow of service attends her determination "to penetrate the darkness behind" his face (225). In Mrs. Flood's confusion over the respectable sense of herself that she has lost, we can see that God is also closer to her than she is to herself. Bewilderment and excitement about the absolute open a way for Mrs. Flood to turn toward God. In staring at the pinpoint of light with her eyes shut, she is another Christian despite herself; for in the O'Connor world, this is precisely what Christianity is, this finding when we think we have not found it. In the end, Mrs. Flood is waiting for the Spirit as she watches over Hazel.

The final scene of the novel returns the perspective to the first scene, in which Hazel sits at a forward angle on a train seat with edgy watchfulness. Mrs. Flood's death vigil thus recapitulates the mystery of guilt and love in *Wise Blood*. We feel guilty because we are guilty. Struggle and sorrow are the debts one person owes to another. Guilt in this economy is negative in word only, and then only because our modern dread makes us think that a life without remorse is desirable. *Wise Blood* dramatizes culpability as both personal and collective. At a time when humanity seeks ways to deny and remove guilt, Flannery O'Connor redirects the reader to see the value of guilt. For O'Connor, it is the salutary burden out of which humanity recovers the humanness lost in sin. Contentment blinds O'Connor's characters to the wonder that sorrow seeks out. Guilt reveals to Hazel the abyss of his insufficiency, which serves as God's opportunity to draw Hazel closer. Guilt exposes Mrs. Flood to the empty place she inhabits. This emptiness must be uncovered before the divine can fill it. Guilt, then, prepares a way to God.

O'Connor's treatment of conversion through guilt to love puts into theological perspective all the anguish and escape that fill her first novel. Her view is angular, at odds with how we are trained to seek out integrity. It culminates in Mrs. Flood's inner vision of the dead Hazel "going backwards to Bethlehem" (219). We need Franciscan sight to take in this picture. Francis, too, looked at spiritual progress in a reverse way. He was unable to separate the passion and death of Jesus from His nativity. Francis made the first crib (in Greccio, 1223), legend has it, to show the faithful how the hardship suffered by the infant was responsible for raising a temple out of a manger (*Omnibus* 299–302). Thomas Merton reiterates the association in a more personal way when he says that the "soul of the monk is a Bethlehem where Christ comes to be born . . . where His likeness is reformed by grace" (*Seven Storey* 372).

O'Connor, too, fuses suffering with birth. But her Christmas message is not a greeting that modern readers welcome. *Wise Blood* moves from Calvary to Bethlehem to argue that Hazel must discover and accept guilt and then pay his debt in order to be awakened to new life. These paradoxical demands confound his will to the point at which he cannot help himself from becoming a Christian. Hazel announces his public mission by calling for a new Jesus who is " 'all man and ain't got any God in him' " (121), and he dies fulfilling the condition of the divine incarnation. His way to Christianity lies not in dogma but through the felt need to go beyond himself. Hazel's theology was first derived from the nature of man. Now this one man's nature is derived from God.

If Hazel's heart matched his head, Hazel might have been a St. Francis. Still, in his own cerebral way, Hazel is a martyr in the original sense of the word as "giving testimony to the truth," sealed in his own passion and unwise blood. "Faith," writes Hans Urs von Balthasar, "is the surrender of the finite person in his entirety to the infinite Person" (8). Hazel's surrender is not a majestic rise to the cross; he crawls and digs his way down the tunnel of not-seeing. After a brief life, which encompasses a cruel lonely childhood, a truncated ministry, and a fiercely obedient death, Hazel finds his birthplace east of the rood. There, affliction fulfills the promise held in his name *Hazel.* For one seen by God, the night of Bethlehem becomes the light of Calvary. In that hour Taulkinham is the new Bethlehem.

NOTES

1. Part of the charm now of Hazel's choice of the Essex comes from the critical comment it has yielded. Asals notes that "the broken-down machine embodies his apostasy" (48). Anything one says about the car applies also to Hazel; for example, the car's distorting yellow windows and its habit of shooting in reverse describe Hazel's jaundiced vision and his counterpunching approach to life.

2. Holy's strategy of foisting coarse materialism as spirituality onto people fascinates O'Connor. In her letters she delights in commenting on the purveyors of palliatives for human fallenness. Her "favorite Protestant theologian" is Dr. Frank Crane, whose daily columns in the Atlanta *Constitution* appear next to the funnies and offer readers "salvation by the compliment club" (*Letters* 81). "Blessed are the smilers," O'Connor writes on another occasion; "their teeth shall show" (*Letters* 114). She recommended that a study be made of Dr. Crane's face, and took her own advice in her portrait of Holy. His teeth do show, but so too does the "great strain" (154) exerted to keep the smile from falling off his face.

3. Hazel slays a man who did not deserve to die. Where there is innocent blood, there is always bloodguilt (Exodus 22:2–3). Bloodguilt defiles, and incurs punishment by the ultimate avenger, God.

4. Critical comment on Hazel's new vision goes to extremes. Asals insists that "unlike a number of her later protagonists, Hazel Motes receives no revelation" (53). Anne-Marie Mallon, on the other hand, finds that "Hazel's gaze now takes in all that is immanent and Real" (79). Both views are tenable. The point of the passage is that we cannot know, but we must watch Hazel to see what he does.

5. *Schuld* in German means both "debt" and "guilt." *Schuldig* ("guilty") means also "owing a debt or duty." See Helen Merrell Lynd, *On Shame and the Search for Identity* (New York: Harcourt, 1958), pp. 17–26.

2

Looking for a Good Man

I never found man that knew how to love himself.
Iago, *Othello* (I, iii)

It is here, in this bad, that we reach
The last purity of the knowledge of good.
Wallace Stevens, "No Possum, No Sop, No Taters"

An incident in the life of St. Francis of Assisi captures the enigmatic diligence that lends his spirituality so readily to the austere fiction of Flannery O'Connor. The episode occurred during the last months of the man's many illnesses. A physician named John Buono, a close friend, visited Francis while he was lying in great pain; and though Francis was prepared either for union with God or for more suffering, he nevertheless wanted to know the extent of his disease, especially whether the intense pain would continue or death was imminent. Afflicted as he was, Francis was nonetheless as much concerned with the way in which he posed his question as he was eager to have his friend's medical opinion. *Buono* means "good," of course, and as legend hands down the event, Francis would not use his friend's proper name because "he never addressed anyone who was called Good by their name out of reverence for the Lord, Who said, *God is Good, and He only*" (*Omnibus* 1262).

This remembrance from *Mirror of Perfection* reflects Mark 10:18, a passage that could well have been read back into Francis's life in order to square his sanctity with the gospel Master he emulated. In Mark, Jesus says to a starchy questioner who calls Him "Good Teacher," " 'Why do you call me good? No one is good but God alone.' " Jesus' disclaimer gathers force when Paul, with similar language, examines his own desire to be good through the limitations inherent in human nature: "For I know that nothing good dwells within me, that is, in my flesh." Paul's recognition of innate human weakness brings him to stress the power of sin over his inmost self. "For I do not do the good I want, but the evil I do not want is what I do" (Romans 7:18–19).

Jesus' disavowal, as recalled in Francis's linguistic finickiness and amplified in Paul's anguished sense of how far actual performance falls short of moral aspiration, opens a way into the subject and strategy of O'Connor's first collection, *A Good Man Is Hard to Find and Other Stories*. The title playfully borrows from a popular song to echo the sober biblical precedent of measuring human nature against the preeminent form of virtue. The implied distinction in O'Connor's title between human defect and divine perfection, when seen by the light of the stories, has less to do with asserting the essence of God than with reminding us of the tragic truth that humankind can only learn good by doing evil, by violating God's commandments.

If most readers have not had the full context of the title in mind when commenting on the collection, they have nevertheless responded to its implication that sin reigns over the human condition in all ten of the stories. Since publication of *A Good Man Is Hard to Find* in 1955, general sentiment holds that O'Connor does not find a good man. She seems no more able to discover goodness in her characters than Francis was willing to call his friend *Buono* or than Paul could discern goodness in himself. In 1956 an undergraduate, Shirley Abbott, who took the matter directly to O'Connor, anticipated mature critics when she equated her inability to find a good man in the book with O'Connor's assumption that, in the student's words, " 'it is probably impossible to know how to be one (a good man)' " (*Letters* 147).

When O'Connor read the student's article, she respected the argument enough to contradict its conclusion. "Not at all," O'Connor flatly states. "It is possible to know how to be one. God became man partly in order to teach us, but it is impossible to be one without the help of grace" (*Letters* 147). Though intended as helpful, this explanation seems to beg the question. While asserting the possibility of knowing how to be good, the response leaves unaddressed the difficulty, announced in the collection's title, of finding a good man in the stories. Does the reader require grace to read the stories? O'Connor's citing the incarnation as the guide to virtue, moreover, increases bewilderment. For one thing, God's taking human form is an awesome teaching to comprehend and, if grasped, is very difficult to live out. Suffering and execution follow the birth of Jesus as night follows day. Taken in full seriousness, the lesson of God's becoming human is so onerous that O'Connor's protesting saint in *Wise Blood,* Hazel Motes, pleads for " 'a new kind of jesus' " who is " 'all man and ain't got any God in him' " (121). Hazel shows us that the cost of discipleship is mortification. No wonder a good person is hard to find—anywhere. The teaching is one that only a Francis would embrace or a Paul would preach—or a Hazel Motes would stumble upon. Alien as the precept is to modern ideas of wholeness, which measure humanity against itself, O'Connor proposes that moral perfection imitates God's perfection; and the fallen readers among us who value her writing will require aid to follow her search for the good person.

O'Connor believes that she indicates the requisite guidance in adducing grace as the special condition for understanding; but since grace for her readers and characters alike is sometimes unrecognizable as a gift, and is always unpredictable and upheaving, O'Connor's understanding of grace stands in need of clarification. To enter her thinking on the subject, we do well to stay with the Marcan story (10:17–31) that points to the ultimate goal of life by pointing out the barriers to attaining it. Here is a good man, albeit pompous about his integrity; to him Jesus spells out the lesson He was sent to impart (and to which O'Connor's stories allude). Jesus recites the commandments as guides to eternal life, and the good man has fulfilled them. Then Jesus looks at the kneeling man and says, " 'You lack one thing; go, sell what you have, and give to the poor, and you will have treasure in heaven; and come, follow me' " (10:21). The good man who has obeyed the law since youth suddenly finds his virtue inadequate. The way to eternal life lies not in flattering titles, such as Good Teacher, but in doing the will of the Father. Jesus here capsizes everything. First He shocks His disciples, who share the honored Jewish belief that wealth signifies God's favor. Then He sets absolute renunciation as a condition for goodness. This demand meets resistance, as the worthy man's countenance falls and he goes off in sorrow.

O'Connor's readers know that downcast expression well. Grimaces of aversion leer throughout *A Good Man Is Hard to Find,* as each successive story portrays the tortured aspect of recoiling from challenges that reiterate Jesus' charge. In the same way that Jesus disappoints the good Jew by piercing his bubble of effusive loyalty to the law, grace distresses O'Connor's upstanding southerners by exposing their pretense to virtue. Since false appearances do not vanish easily, the disclosure of grace will alarm, even seem insupportable. In fairness to those perplexed by O'Connor's work, what comes across in the encounters with God in *A Good Man Is Hard to Find* is less the efficacy of grace than the impossibility of accepting it, and therefore readers respond more to the difficulty of seeking the good person than to the finding of one.

To find the image of the good person that O'Connor insists her stories offer, the reader will need to consider a range of experience beyond the emotional change in the character. True goodness for O'Connor is not so much a psychological state as a new reality. It is a condition of spirit transformed by love after false claims dissolve and after masks fall.

From her earliest work, O'Connor involves the reader in a quest for goodness through her characters' engagement with evil. *Wise Blood* (1952), which her early prospectus terms "a search for God through sin" (Getz 21), outlines the negative way, as we saw. *A Good Man Is Hard to Find* maps a sequel to Hazel Motes's dark adventure; however, instead of resuming the pursuit where *Wise Blood* leaves off—with Hazel Motes putting sole trust in a pinpoint of miraculous light—O'Connor's first collection of stories retraces with new searchers particular stages along Hazel's purifying journey. The gospel route to goodness marked by Jesus' footprints seems too daunting and mysterious for O'Connor to take in at once, and her fables never minimize the full difficulty of modern following of the ancient path. She knows that to be a good person one will have to become, in some sense, the person imitated, Who, in this case, imposes bitter demands. It is as though O'Connor must send the righteous inquirer of Mark 10 back again and again to be saved from the bane of self-satisfaction. Only when he learns that mere blamelessness is not enough can the aspirant to goodness heed Jesus' momentous command to give up everything and follow Him.

Repetition is a method that allows O'Connor to refine meaning. She makes a conscious point of the usefulness of returning to a crucial incident to plumb the invisible lines of motion that interest her. "A slight shift in emphasis," she says to a Georgia audience while discussing her favorite topic of regional writing, "may produce an entirely different version, without endangering the truth of the previous one" (*Mystery and Manners* 52). When it comes to writing stories, a revised focus can deepen the truth she explores, as it does in *A Good Man Is Hard to Find*. Each of the ten stories in this collection gives a fresh perspective on O'Connor's inexhaustible story of the response to the terrifying experience of guilt.

O'Connor devoted five years to working out the paradigm in *Wise Blood*, an unwavering commitment that may account for her describing the short stories written after that novel as "all relatively painless" (*Letters* 81). Ten stories, however, can, and in this instance do, offer the reader a testimony that even a rapidly eventful single novel such as *Wise Blood* cannot provide. Grouping these early tales "about original sin" (*Letters* 74), as O'Connor boldly presents them in a dedicatory gesture to Sally Fitzgerald, enables O'Connor to emphasize the rhythm of divine providence, whereby each satanic attempt to make her vulnerable Georgians and Tennesseans disobey and destroy is followed by a still more wonderful display of God's creative love.

II

The title story, "A Good Man Is Hard to Find," begins the volume's exploration of God's transforming love by confronting the reader with a condition of true goodness amid the stark brutality of serial murder. One ordinary summer morning at 8:45, a Georgia family sets out on a motor vacation to Florida; after a barbecue lunch they are shot in some backwoods off a dirt road. Aware that any clement influence mitigating such carnage might be too soft to divert attention from the horror, O'Connor forewarns readers to "be on the lookout for such things as the action of grace in the Grandmother's soul, and not for the dead bodies" (*Mystery and Manners* 113).

O'Connor's advice, however, is hard to follow. A heap of corpses rivets even the callous modern mind, and the grandmother has demanded so much attention from those around her that readers instinctively pass over her subtle spiritual change in favor of fixing on her the blame she deserves for causing the catastrophe. Even at the end of the story, when she reels in heartbreaking grief, the action of grace can go unnoticed because the woman seems so full of herself that there would be no room for grace to squeeze into her swollen soul. Whatever divine activity is at work in the old lady's soul remains either hidden or uninteresting to critics. The more sympathetic take O'Connor at her word and allow that the grandmother "achieves a redemption of a traditional sort" (Gentry 35) while adding a reservation about the "high price" (Walters 72) paid for salvation or qualifying the transcendence gained by stressing the ambivalence of "a beatific corpse in a puddle of blood" (Asals 152). What fascinates readers more than the activity of grace is the psychopathology of the killer, who obliges our Freudian interest by setting out to kill his parent.

The old lady is just too scatterbrained and bossy—too much Everygrandmother—for the critical mind to accept as worthy of the moral focus O'Connor places on her. The woman is smug enough to do our analytical work for us. She has looked into herself and found the good woman. Practiced in the art of immodesty, she does not mind letting the world know how pleased she is with the discovery. When preparing for the car ride, she puts on a navy blue dress printed with small dots and trimmed with collars and cuffs of white organdy and lace. Her daughter-in-law might throw on slacks and tie a green kerchief around her head, but the widow dons a blue sailor hat sprouting white violets. Since one never goes abroad without white gloves and a purse, she carries white gloves and a purse.

The grandmother obviously works out her life on surfaces, a trait worsened by a sentimental moralism that disposes her to the critical animosity she has received. But trifles, particularly the innocent ones by which we define ourselves, elicit more tender care from O'Connor. With the grandmother, delicate accessories add finishing touches to her garments, garments for the end which will vouchsafe God's favorable last judgment. The grace activity in "A Good Man Is Hard to Find" turns precisely on the way in which the events deepen into felt love the evident shallowness of the grandmother's moral claims.

Before we can know the grandmother in her fineness, as she believes God knows her, we must see her as others do, which amounts to feeling the aggression in her exhausting grandmotherly solicitude. The family experiences the old lady's propriety as a weapon. She wants her own way and schemes to get it. Florida, on this occasion, does not appeal to the grandmother because she has in mind going east to Tennessee. Tennessee is a whim that takes on any value that will convince Bailey, her son, to make a detour. First she tries terror. Without believing a word she utters, the old lady worries aloud that The Misfit, loose from the Federal Pen, is also heading toward Florida. When cajoling fails, she tries edification. Tennessee would broaden the children's minds. When Tennessee is out of the question, she will settle for a side trip to an old plantation in nearby Toomsboro; she gets the children to pester their father into seeing the place by regaling them with a picture of an old house with a secret panel.

Throughout her contriving, the grandmother couches self-interest in a language of morals that shifts responsibility onto others. Bailey *ought* to do this and that or else he fails as a father and a son. Conscience may tell her what others should do, but it does not dictate her own actions. Pride short-circuits the message enjoining goodness. When the old lady realizes that the plantation she has in mind is not in Georgia but in Tennessee, she cannot admit the mistake. Though being wrong embarrasses her, physical injury does not. Gravity would be worthy of her. She causes the car to turn over as she upsets the cat, Pitty Sing, which she has hidden in a basket and which sends the car out of control as it jumps on Bailey, the driver. To mask her blunder, the grandmother feigns injury so that others will pity her.

The old lady meets her match in a gulch off the dirt road. Shirtless and sockless, accoutered with black hat and gun, impressive with scholarly spectacles and distinguished by graying hair, The Misfit steps out of a hearselike car. The lady astray has a rendezvous with the gentleman eccentric. He flaunts the very deviation and evil that the grandmother conceals beneath prim hat and gloves. With systematic formality he and his two accomplices, Bobby Lee and Hiram, terrorize the family. When Bailey rebukes the lady to tears for stupidly blurting out The Misfit's identity, The Misfit intensifies his courtesy. Tears embarrass the decorous convict, who has tried to deaden feeling. True to her belief that fine feeling wins out, the grandmother relies on decorum to save her: " 'You wouldn't shoot a lady, would you?' " Flattery polishes the petition: " 'I know you're a good man' " (22). While she indulges in the numbing ease of adjusting her hat, he finesses a tidy massacre, commanding Bobby Lee and Hiram to kill the family by twos in the adjacent woods. The Misfit comes calling to show a deadly version of the appearance and disorder that constitute the old lady's nature.

A peculiar light-darkness sets in to make this kinship visible: "There was not a cloud in the sky nor any sun" (27). It is as though the obscurities of the daily world and conventional human relations must disappear for this resemblance to emerge. One by one the characters step off center stage until the hunted killer and lady victim are alone. Then deceptions fail, defenses collapse. Pistol reports from the woods slice the air to mark the ripping away of things to a stark grandeur of annihilation.

The grandmother tries to cope with exposure through the banalities that have served her all her life, but this time she cannot pull a fast one. The Misfit responds with a biographical account of agony that lies beyond conventional pleasantries. The shirt she offers to cover his bare chest cannot swathe his radical shame of being alive. Though he cannot remember ever being a bad boy, " 'somewheres along the line I done something wrong and got sent to the penitentiary' " (25). The death-in-life of which Hazel Motes dreams in his nightmares is the reality of The Misfit. Boxed within walls and ceiling and floor, The Misfit tries to figure out the crime that accounts for his punishment. He cannot. The penitentiary brings this penitent not to atonement but to panic. Whereas the grandmother feels blameless, The Misfit feels only guilt: " 'You can do one thing or you can do another, kill a man or take a tire off his car, because sooner or later you're going to forget what it was you done and just be punished for it' " (26–27). In this confession, the absence of moral discrimination, which reduces all transgressions to a state of terminal futility, betokens the sinner who has surrendered to his own evil impulses.

It is essential to the very notions of morality and goodness to affirm that in all sin there is personal assent. The Misfit's granting that one's nature can be so corrupt that one's will is powerless to obey God's commands illustrates the disastrous submission to Manicheanism that O'Connor sees ruling our age. Guilt without responsibility and suffering without meaning define The Misfit's despair. As a result, he can only build up wrath for himself.

Though the grandmother never stops trying to save her life with words of sweet reasonableness, The Misfit's tormented life cuts through her self-interest to touch the best part of her, just as Hazel's alarming mortification at the end of *Wise Blood* affects Mrs. Flood. In this story, though, O'Connor goes deeper into the spirit of the affected woman. The grandmother feels for a vicious murderer, and she experiences that sympathy as the victim before her assailant. When she notices The Misfit's thin shoulder blades, the stunned woman forgets her need and turns to his. " 'Do you ever pray?' " she anxiously inquires (25). The more he insists upon the hopelessness of being released from entrapment, the more the grandmother urges him to pray, until she cuts to the core of his vanity by citing the benefit of prayer: " 'If you would pray,' the old lady said, 'Jesus would help you.' " He clings to his self-sufficiency, however: " 'I don't want no hep,' he said. 'I'm doing all right by myself' " (26).

The killer's boast of self-sufficiency contains the crux of the psychological tensions that catalyze the theological shocks at the end of the story. Is there an authority for action beyond oneself? Not for The Misfit. He feels unrelated to the ultimate authority of Jesus that he himself admits alters life. Such misadaptation of the spirit causes deeper ruptures. The Misfit knows that Jesus " 'thown everything off balance' " by raising the dead, and he owns that, if one accepts Jesus once and for all as the norm of truth, " 'it's nothing for you to do but thow away everything and follow Him' " (28). We are back in Mark 10, with The Misfit giving answers he does not have the humility to apply. The Misfit excuses himself on historical grounds; he feels mistimed. He was not among the small company who conversed with Jesus, and he believes that it " 'ain't right I wasn't there because if I had of been there I would of known' " (29).

The Misfit's need for certitude is a modern misreading of faith. Those who were there with Jesus conducted themselves as clumsily as we. They misunderstood Him. They also deserted Him. Only after the resurrection did the disciples understand the Word they listened to. The Misfit may already be more privileged because the inner meaning of the Word he hears comes invisibly. Those are blessed who believe without seeing. And the comfort of love, a small Pentecost, is imminent, but The Misfit clings to his autonomy. And so he is miscast " 'like I am now' " (29), recognizing that he shares " 'the same case with Him' " (27) and yet being separated from the sacrificial event that would have spared him a life of pain. " 'No pleasure but meanness' " (28), he concludes, almost snarling. His torture shakes the grandmother into covering his exposed humanness with a maternal embrace: " 'Why you're one of my babies. You're one of my own children!' " (29). The trembling woman reaches out to touch the feeble shoulder blade she saw earlier.

Tenderness misfires when aimed at The Misfit, because a person who cannot feel pleasure abhors human contact. The Misfit's dread of human intimacy keeps open the emotional wounds of his past. The grandmother's kindness calls to the frightened softling buried deep within the hardened criminal, but he will do anything to avoid facing the vulnerable part of his nature. What he does most readily is kill. The Misfit shoots the grandmother three times through the chest. In doing so, he destroys the love that would give him coherence and would explain that in his inexorable pain, as in the grandmother's sorrow, lies the opportunity to repay the spiritual debt one person owes another.

Like Hazel Motes, The Misfit is deeply involved with God. Both know the cost and way of goodness and are haunted by Jesus' order to " 'thow away everything and follow Him.' " The Misfit, however, unlike Hazel, refuses to pay. Nihilism justifies his rejection, and murder gives him the illusion of power and freedom. Though he kills to hide his true character from himself, his real conflict is with God, Who will not leave him alone. In attempting to be sufficient unto himself, The Misfit turns away from the truth of life. The ending of the story shows The Misfit falling away from God, as bitterness sinks the murderer into senselessness and anger hurls him into the spiritual ditch where he discarded his victims. The power to be complete, or merely to be content in his choice, does not lie in him. The Misfit does nothing except what pleases his will, and the result is a joylessness that scars his soul into a mass of hard, dry tissue. When an accomplice takes delight in the grandmother's twisted corpse, The Misfit becomes enraged: " 'Shut up, Bobby Lee,' The Misfit said. 'It's no real pleasure in life.' "

These, the last words of "A Good Man Is Hard to Find," do more than highlight the private tragedy of an escaped killer stalking the byways of Georgia. The story of The Misfit provides a spectacular example of a spiritual disposition that medical science now discounts as emotional disturbance and that our literature deems authentically heroic, but that theology once respected as a root sin. For Evagrius, a fourth-century Desert Father, dejection or lack of pleasure numbers among the eight principal sins (Chadwick 181). O'Connor draws upon this early Christian understanding of sin to explore the "unhistorical, solitary, and guilty" (*Letters* 90) dimension of the modern consciousness. Her interest in dejection is not to point a vengeful finger at the age; nor would she disparage the natural feelings of jeopardy and impotence that attend the deepest responses to life. Rather, O'Connor recovers a venerable idea of sin to rescue us from the peculiar, unnoticed tenor of self-hatred that oppresses our time. Lack of pleasure, the first story of the volume shows, is not the result of alienation but the cause of it. The Misfit freely wills dejection. He wants to make himself impassible and succeeds in deadening emotion. The decision to numb feeling makes

The Misfit a misfit by impairing his mind. At the moment of triumph, the shrewd convict utterly and fatally misjudges the reality of love in the situation. Dejection precipitates and extends his brutal irresponsibility to God and others.

The story, however, goes beyond its achieved horror into the distant reality missed by the killer. The challenge to the reader is to find the secret action that fits the butchering of The Misfit into the scheme of grace. The Misfit points the way: " 'She would of been a good woman,' The Misfit said, 'if it had been somebody there to shoot her every minute of her life' " (29). Vicious even when complimentary, the gunman speaks the truth. Execution tears away the old lady's old definition of herself. With a nice hat or hatless, she cannot now rely on herself. Her trite pieties are as much an evasion of her real self as is The Misfit's cruelty. In the grandmother's case, readers are amazed to learn, bird-brained truisms conceal a loving woman. Her effort to adopt a killer whom society condemns wins a victory. Humility and bare truth invoke a standard for action that brings her assailant to a standstill. The norm is Jesus, Whose name she mutters, and it turns out that the widow pays the ultimate price Jesus paid for love. She, unlike the morose killer, finds a way to pleasure by becoming a child of love. O'Connor's controversial image of the dying grandmother explains the paradox. The grandmother squats in blood "with her legs crossed under her like a child's and her face smiling up at the cloudless sky" (29). Though her cheerful expression before ignominious death scandalizes sullen readers, we do well to recognize in the first story of *A Good Man Is Hard to Find* O'Connor's strategy of combating sorrow with exuberance, because a sense of humor is an important ingredient of her faith. In the grandmother's bearing of The Misfit's burdens, her weakness strengthens her to endure her executioner's scorn with joyful compassion. With her share in the world to come open above her, the lady can beam a smile.

If the trial the grandmother passes through in the secluded ditch leads to goodness, then we ought to pay as little attention as possible to her foibles and none at all to her physical loss. Goodness has a gain of its own. The grandmother achieves the liberty to choose a response beyond the anger and revenge that violence induces in its victim. She chooses to love, and her tenderness crushes the gunslinger's might. After he shoots her, and just before he orders her carcass tossed with the others, "he put his gun down on the ground" (29). A victory of the heart commemorates the moment of grace in the action. The grandmother's gesture, in fact, carries so much spiritual momentum that O'Connor envisions a continuation. The seed planted by the old lady's kindness, O'Connor muses, will become "a great crow-filled tree" that will swell The Misfit's heart with enough pain "to turn him into the prophet he was meant to become" (*Mystery and Manners* 113).

The charity in O'Connor's remark deserves a momentary digression. It recalls the attitude of Abbot Anthony, another Desert Father, who believed that the devil had some good in him because God could not create evil (Merton, *Desert* 21). At the same time, the comment alerts us to the most extraordinary aspect of divine creativity revealed in O'Connor's final collection, *Everything That Rises Must Converge* — namely, that its repeated surges toward the ultimate express a universal salvation accomplished through the merciful love of God. But the crucial point to be made now about the first story of the first collection is that its message is love. Love is more than the grandmother's curling June Star's hair or seeing to it that Pitty Sing is not left alone or being nice to Red Sammy Butts and other strangers. "A Good Man Is Hard to Find" demonstrates love as spiritual identification. Interior resemblance, in turn, locates the good woman. In the end, the grandmother takes The Misfit as she takes herself, and loves him with the humility that allows access to another's subjectivity.

III

The ending of "A Good Man Is Hard to Find" shows how evil, to O'Connor's comic temperament, becomes a means of propitiation both for the grandmother in her hour of death and, as one critic argues (Gentry 35–38), for the implied narrator through extensions of the point of view. The power of comic reversal and technical dexterity is grace. O'Connor explains the alliance in her famous letter to John Hawkes. The devil "can always be a subject for my kind of comedy," she says, "because he is always accomplishing ends other than his own." The intensity of evil circumstances prepares for the devil's becoming a messenger of good *malgré lui*. Then there flashes "the indication of Grace, the moment when you know that Grace has been offered and accepted—such as the moment when the Grandmother realizes the Misfit is one of her own children" (*Letters* 367). This occurrence holds the greatest interest for O'Connor and arouses the sharpest debate among her readers. For the fiction writer, who O'Connor insists must never ıbstitute attitude for action" (Cheney/O'Connor 46), the urgency is to ınsform grace as a timeless attribute of God into a process of divine ...tervention in human affairs. O'Connor may believe that her immortal comedies end well because grace makes them well, but for fiction to be convincing, the force of God's presence must come not from dogma but through felt life. No reader of O'Connor's fiction misses the impact of evil in her stories. Redeeming action enters into the life of her characters through a consciousness of guilt, an understanding that as a sinner one participates in God's mercy.

Grace, in O'Connor's art, constitutes an event. In *A Good Man Is Hard to Find,* the main characters pass through the timely encounter with love by going either the grandmother's way of acceptance or The Misfit's way of refusal. The sign of grace accepted is a soft openness of feeling, a compunction, that leads the character into a gracious disposition of generosity toward self and others. The sign of grace refused is either a denial of guilt or a submersion in punishment without end or cause; both kinds of refusals flow from dejection.

Three of the ten stories in the collection end with a turning away from the Spirit's message: "The Life You Save May Be Your Own," "A Stroke of Good Fortune," and "Good Country People." The trio constitutes a courtship-marriage group in which the appeal to share in God's life comes through the opportunity of a healing bond of intimacy with another person. Each story recounts a despairing involvement. One character meets another, uses her or him, goes about daily business, gets angry, flees. And, in a final unadmitted despair, the character tries to suppress any question of the meaning it all has by dismissing the encounter as meaningless. As we might expect after observing the dismal woe of the denier of grace in the title story, pleasurelessness pervades the moral atmosphere of this group of stories.

Tom T. Shiftlet, from Tarwater, Tennessee, is the prospective bridegroom in "The Life You Save May Be Your Own." At sunset he ambles up to a "desolate spot" (53) where Lucynell Crater lives with her daughter, Lucynell Crater, a thirty-year-old idiot. A ready man, Mr. Shiftlet sports a black town suit and brown felt hat, and carries a tin tool box which holds implements to fix anything. Haggard and missing half of his left arm, Mr. Shiftlet may not be the perfect image of a country beau, but Mrs. Crater, looking from the depths of desperation, sees in him the right mate for Lucynell. And when they are married, the old lady will have a handyman around to get the place into profitable shape. The fixer, in turn, cases the place and aims his "pale sharp glance" (55) on a rusted car that has not been used since Mr. Crater died fifteen years ago.

Mr. Shiftlet and Mrs. Crater are a fine match. They meet like foxes, sly, guarded, poised for the kill. They are also as brazen as foxes. Mr. Shiftlet's arrival is more like his paying a call on the cosmos than a sudden appearance at a strange place. He turns to the sunset with his arm-and-a-half swinging like "a crooked cross" (54) that stakes out his personal claim on the whole expanse of the sky. Mrs. Crater rises to the occasion of his arrival as she watches "with her arms folded across her chest as if she were the owner of the sun" (54). Lord of the sky and mistress of the sun soon communicate with gallant indirection over lesser things. He praises the sunset while preparing to nick the car; she speaks of her jewel of a daughter, whom she would not give up " 'for nothing on earth' " (58), while trying to snare a husband for the girl and cheap labor for herself. Beneath the country charm of their joust lies a moral horror. Both displace their base motives onto the other as though willing to grant the other a favor, and Lucynell serves as commodity for the trade.

Mrs. Crater's self-interest is so plain, her machinations as would-be mother-of-the-bride so shameless, that her conduct verges on slapstick. Mr. Shiftlet's deception is more grave. What is most shifty about him is not his floating among odd jobs in various places but the way in which he deflects his intentions through language. He tells of a surgeon in Atlanta who cut out the human heart for study but " 'don't know no more about it than you or me' " (55). This grisly exemplum from a man whose wrathful face has the look "of composed dissatisfaction as if he understood life thoroughly" (54) lays claim to a sense of mystery. Then he asks, with rehearsed solemnity, " 'what is a man?' " (57). Later, he waxes philosophical when bargaining a marriage deal: " 'Lady, a man is divided into two parts, body and spirit' " (62). Scaling further Pauline heights, he spits out, with apostolic contempt, " 'It's the law that don't satisfy me' " (64). For Mr. Shiftlet, Christian liberty means, as it does for Hazel Motes, an automobile. " 'I got to follow where my spirit says to go' " (63) translates into a demand for money for the honeymoon. These are words that have never passed through anyone's heart; or, if they did, they flit through on the speed of demonic wings brushing nothing of the human condition in passing. Mr. Shiftlet's language partakes of the aphoristic mode cherished by O'Connor's fallen angels. His maxims give the air of sagacity while allowing him to ignore his moral debts and his pain. We know from his half arm and his wandering and his corrosive bitterness that he suffers, but cynical pet phrases block him from finding the courage to alleviate that suffering. Obsession with sentimentalities, the cynic's pretense to feeling, is what Mr. Shiftlet has instead of moral intelligence. " 'Nothing is like it used to be, lady,' " he laments (55).

Again, his wisdom proves false. Lucynell Crater the younger, for one, is as she used to be and as she always will be. Though she is nearly thirty, her innocence makes guessing her age impossible. Mrs. Crater tries to pass her off as fifteen or sixteen. Large, mute, dressed in a short blue organdy dress, Lucynell strikes a timeless presence. Her pink-gold hair and "eyes as blue as a peacock's neck" (54) evoke the angelic image that marks her importance at the ending. *Angel* (Greek *angelos*) means "messenger," and Lucynell embodies the call to love in her vulnerability. Like her shimmering eyes and hair, her presence sheds light in the darkness of her mother's and Mr. Shiftlet's selfishness; and, like her idiocy, her message of love will seem like folly to the world. There is, however, nothing sentimental about O'Connor's idiot angel. (Her angels, we will see, can be stalwart.) Lucynell implies a system of values that inverts the economy of the world, just as "the wisdom of this world is folly with God" (1 Corinthians 3:19). God calls to Mr. Shiftlet through Lucynell's dumbness.

We can judge Mr. Shiftlet by how he responds to the angel of light. After a quick marriage at the courthouse, he drives one hundred miles to The Hot Spot, where he abandons Lucynell. A warning sounds when the golden-haired Lucynell moves the counterboy to say to Mr. Shiftlet, " 'She looks like an angel of Gawd' " (66). He is correct. The Spirit's natural invitation to compassion comes by way of the idiot girl asleep at the counter. Something seminal—happening in this world but from another—is offered Mr. Shiftlet, but he turns his back on the gift with a dismissive shrug: " 'Hitch-hiker.' " Accepting Lucynell would not have been easy, but it would have been fair, given the bargain. Ingratitude makes Mr. Shiftlet's life worse than it was, and it has been without pleasure all along. The car for which he married and betrayed fails him. The dejection out of which he acts seizes him. Loneliness sets in, but the answer to his depression is left with his humanness at The Hot Spot. O'Connor's meteorological sensibility has the atmosphere dramatize the villain's inner commotion. Sky anger signals a menacing storm.

The ending of "The Life You Save May Be Your Own" goes beyond hints of heavy weather to gauge the inner turmoil of dejection. We see that each rejection of grace deepens the pleasurelessness it was meant to dispel. Out of loneliness, Mr. Shiftlet picks up a boy standing at the road's edge. The boy does not have his thumb raised, but Mr. Shiftlet, with his usual distortion of the situation, says, " 'I see you want a ride' " (66). He tries to banish his sadness by feigning joy and camaraderie. The dejected traitor has just ditched a helpless idiot one hundred miles from home, and the best he can permit himself to feel is the sham sentiment of a cliché: " 'Son,' he said after a minute, 'I got the best old mother in the world so I reckon you only got the second best' " (67). Mr. Shiftlet's eyes become misty as he recalls this maudlin figure of maternal perfection. He weeps crocodile tears. Grief over an imagined slight to his angelic mother gives the drifter the illusion of atoning for his desertion of the real angel in his life.

At the base of Mr. Shiftlet's dejection is a trick that language itself plays on him: he misreads a lie, taking it literally. The runaway, on the other hand, knows better than to share blandishments about motherhood, a painful reminder of which is the suitcase on his lap. The boy hits Mr. Shiftlet with the truth and jumps out of the car: " 'My old woman is a flea bag and yours is a stinking pole cat!' " (67). His invective, however, bounces off the preoccupied driver. Weepy conceit has Mr. Shiftlet around the heart so that he keeps up the charade of moralist even when he is alone. He who spurned the Lord's messenger now calls upon divine wrath by invoking the commission of Cyrus (Isaiah 45:1–8) to restore righteousness: " 'Oh Lord!' he prayed. 'Break forth and wash the slime from this earth!' " (67).

Sure enough, thunder cracks. Heaven sends down "fantastic raindrops, like tin-can tops" (68), but celestial depth-charges do not yet strike the cavernous bottom of Mr. Shiftlet's spirit. This crashing rain can no more catch him than human obligations have snared him or than simple pleasures of the heart have arrested him in the past. He steps on the gas and beats it to Mobile and adjacent migratory places of the mind. He must stay on the move to avoid responsibility and feeling; in doing so he becomes a comic ally of evil because, in O'Connor's words to Hawkes, "nothing in him resists the Devil" (*Letters* 367). For now, acquiescence has the momentum of the freshly painted square automobile that got him away from the burdensome Lucynell, but he cannot speed past all the envoys of good. The fantastic raindrops, the Lord's largesse, will keep pounding him from above.

"A Stroke of Good Fortune" presents a female analogue to Mr.

Shiftlet's evasion and gloom. Concomitant with the prophet's warning that the life one saves through a loving response may be one's own comes the prophet's assurance that each such demand is a stroke of good fortune. The lucky event in this story is a baby. Ruby is pregnant. As Mr. Shiftlet rejects the sacramental grace given in marriage, Ruby refuses the actual grace that flows from marital union. Once again, dejection lies at the root of her denial. During childhood in the back-woods of Pitman, Ruby saw how each of her mother's eight children made the woman "deader" (72), and Ruby ever since then has been determined not to be destroyed by childbirth. She wants comfort. Her entire life is devoted to attaining it. A woman of gumption, Ruby lifted herself up out of Pitman by marrying Bill Hill, with whom she has been climbing in life ever since. They live in town now, but Ruby casts her eyes still higher to Meadowcrest Heights, a subdivision "where you had your drugstores and grocery and a picture show right in your own neighborhood" (71). No hick life of collard greens for Ruby.

Ruby's fear of slipping back into the Pitman trap determines the countersacramental pattern of "A Stroke of Good Fortune." The action follows Ruby as she climbs the stairs to her fourth-floor apartment. Four or five months pregnant and still denying her condition, Ruby has trouble making each step. Her body tells her the truth that her mind denies. She is breathless and has swollen ankles and is struck by pain and is getting heavier. Everybody but Ruby knows. Madam Zoleeda on Highway 87 reads Ruby's palms and, with a discretion fitting her client's desire, warns Ruby to expect " 'a stroke of good fortune' " (71). Bill Hill, after five years of precautions, seems to have taken a turn toward happiness now that he is a prospective father. Laverne Watts on the third floor, a chiropodist's secretary who is not given to humoring people, has known for quite a while. Her diagnosis: " 'MOTHER!' " (81). Though Ruby can rationalize away anything people say, her body refuses to be forsaken. Each step up the stairs registers the physical fact that sinks her into a lifelong depression over maternal responsibility. Where joy would heal Ruby's anxiety over labor pains, despondency oppresses her mind with bizarre pathological longings. Heart trouble or cancer would be welcome alternatives to pregnancy. She feels " 'insulted' " (82) by Laverne's confronting her with the eventuality of giving birth, because to Ruby, a baby will drag her down and is an affront to her freedom and well-being. About her imprisonment Ruby is right, but it is melancholy, not the baby, that weighs her down. Freedom lies in being able to respond beyond conditioned negativity, and her grim mood deprives her of feeling her way to the possibility that delivering the baby might uplift her.

Physical ascent and spiritual descent in "A Stroke of Good Fortune" bring out the dynamics of humiliation and exaltation in the life of grace. Edward Schillebeeckx's *Christ the Sacrament of the Encounter with God* (1963) accounts for this action with keen perceptivity; though O'Connor did not know this important book, its examination of theological ideas through the mystery of Jesus and through the felt life with which faith concerns itself is in keeping with her thinking. Grace for Schillebeeckx flows from the actions of Jesus, Who, from the moment His spirit was displaced from the Father into the womb of His mother, was "always the humiliated 'Servant of God'" (19). His life of obedience and sacrificial death manifests the love to which the Father responds with redeeming grace. In His humiliation as Servant of God, Jesus remains the Son of Man Who is the grace-giving revelation of God.

The downward movement of grace begins with the incarnation and continues as the redeeming mercy of God comes to humankind through the human heart of the man Jesus. He infuses humankind with divinity by bestowing and teaching love. The upward movement flows up from the human heart of Jesus to the Father. It finds completion in Jesus' death and resurrection. For O'Connor, as for Schillebeeckx, Jesus lived out the total human situation. If the "way to despair" in O'Connor's psychology is "to refuse to have any kind of experience" (*Mystery and Manners* 78), then Jesus is unalloyed hope in His embrace of whatever life entails. In addition to making the Father's love visible to the world, Jesus is the supreme realization of the human response to the Father's offer. He shows us how to love. Again, as The Misfit says, His example "'thown everything off balance.'" Laying down His life before a sinful humanity touches a mystery of unfathomable depth.

The obligations imposed by this downward movement may not be a sacrifice of blood, but at the very least involve acknowledgment of God's existence through obedience and service and enjoyment of creation. We began this chapter by citing O'Connor's statement that it is possible to know how to be good by recognizing that God showed the way by becoming a man. After considering several protagonists in O'Connor's stories who shackle themselves by refusing to live freely, we can add that her fundamental tenet holds that if one does not know Jesus, one does not know the human person.

Ruby Hill's share in this vast design of grace lies in the necessity of the moment. The child she bears requires her to submit to a will greater than hers. She need not look beyond the duty of the moment to grasp that will. Freedom comes not from rising to a duplex bungalow with yellow awnings in Meadowcrest Heights, but from saying Yes to her body. To be passively loyal and accept what she cannot avoid would ease her weariness and disgust. Then she could rise through love and pleasure. Despair, however, holds her back. The restraints she puts on her liberty appear at the end of the story. We see Ruby looking through the banister poles, sitting on a step, sullen, "clutching the banister spoke" while her eyes "gazed down into the dark hole" (84). Her glare travels beyond the place at the bottom of the steps to the time when she started to climb out of the horror she felt in Pitman. The tableau sums up the effects of dejection on Ruby's spirit. She has caged her heart in terror.

O'Connor uses the cage image several times in her fiction. In *Wise Blood* she describes how Hazel Motes feels his heart beginning "to grip him like a little ape clutching the bars of its cage" (60), and she gives another version of a protagonist caught on a stairway in "Judgement Day," the last story in *Everything That Rises Must Converge.* From start to finish, the figure behind bars is the human heart, the inmost center of human life, both trapped in its disobedient willfulness and stopped by its encounter with God. This encounter is the moment when, as with Ruby, the character "opened" her or his eyes into the abyss hollowed out by dread. The moment also provides an indication of grace. With Ruby, grace is content to wait out her resistance. The final words of the story remark an inexplicable sensation in her body—rising "as if it were out of nowhere in nothing, out nowhere, resting and waiting, with plenty of time" (84).

"A Stroke of Good Fortune" has not had a favorable critical reception. O'Connor intended it as part of *Wise Blood* (*Letters* 100–101), to which Ruby's sadness would add another illustration of the reign of dejection in the city of Taulkinham. O'Connor's publisher urged her to include it in *A Good Man Is Hard to Find,* and her agreeing to do so has brought a retraction whenever "A Stroke of Good Fortune" is mentioned. "It don't appeal to me either," she admitted to Sally and Robert Fitzgerald. "It is, in its way, Catholic, being about the rejection of life at the source, but too much of a farce to bear the weight . . . " (*Letters* 85). O'Connor's judgment is fair. "A Stroke of Good Fortune" does carry a polemic; yet, if

the argument strains the action, broad humor brings into plain s:
the dynamic of grace that informs O'Connor's most realized fiction.

The story of a woman fighting against grace that did please
O'Connor is "Good Country People." The plan was to replace "A Stroke
of Good Fortune" with it because, she assured Robert Giroux, her
publisher, "Good Country People" is "really a story that would set the
whole collection on its feet" (*Letters* 75). The discovery in the story by a
Ph.D. philosopher "that she ain't so smart" (*Letters* 170) gratified O'Connor
no end. A "very hot story" (*Letters* 76) that converts a salesman's dirty
gag into a modern exemplum, "Good Country People" stoked O'Connor's
fieriness to take on "pious atheists" after having dealt with "irate
Catholics" (*Letters* 86) for so long.

O'Connor's approach to unbelief is through the effects of shame.
We have seen how guilt can prepare for grace; now in "Good Country
People" O'Connor shows the way in which fear of exposure can block
the incursions of grace. From the outset, aspects of shame lurk behind
the physical deformities, madcap vanity, pride, violence, escape, and
disillusionment that make up the O'Connor world. All of her central
figures have pasts so excruciating that they resort to extreme measures
to hide from rather than face that suffering. With Hazel Motes and The
Misfit, two notable cases in point, public accusations and indignation
allow them to hide a sense of humiliation from themselves. Being *The
Misfit* is preferable to acknowledging a need for the grandmother's love
and the duty to obey Jesus. The Misfit can justify murder, but he cannot
fit the grandmother's kindness into his emotional scheme without
exposing himself to both the grandmother and himself. By killing
Solace Layfield, Hazel Motes can wipe away the black dirt that his
preacher grandfather pointed out to him as a boy before staring spectators.
For both heroes, murder conceals self-degradation.

The essence of shame is exposure. (The grandmother, we might
recall, is devastated by the prospect of being found dead without her
proper attire.) Whereas guilt signifies debt, shame indicates uncovering,
divesting, and wounding. Both shame and guilt imply an awareness of
self, and each kind of awareness partakes of the other; however, guilt
denotes a law broken, a legal failure to pay a debt, whereas shame
conveys a loss of esteem from falling short of one's idea of oneself. Given
all the anatomical deformities and moral contortions driving the characters into pronounced cover-ups, O'Connor's fiction would seem committed to probe shame. Country courtship heightened by sexual wackiness

offers O'Connor the social context through which to expose the distrust and the fear of contempt secreted beneath guilt.

Within the misery of shame, however, lies revelation; "Good Country People" shows it. The opening scene fleshes out the ambivalent meaning of "good" in the title. Good country people are plain-spoken, and so we find the brazen Mrs. Freeman standing in Mrs. Hopewell's kitchen giving blunt details of her two daughters' intimate lives. Mrs. Freeman passes over the amorous exploits of the eighteen-year-old redhead Glynese in favor of the vomitings of Carramae, the fifteen-year-old blonde, who is married and pregnant. Good country people are also unflappable, and nothing makes Mrs. Freeman blush. Such audacity comes from clear moral understanding. Mrs. Freeman knows human nature down to its last sordid detail. Confidence allows her frankness; shrewdness frees her from caution. Mrs. Hopewell, her employer, excuses the Freemans' crassitude as the earthiness that makes for good country people, a class just above white trash and markedly beneath her. Concessions to workers distinguish the large-mindedness a virtuous landowner should adopt toward employees. We find, in sum, another good woman in Mrs. Hopewell. Since she has "no bad qualities of her own" (171), the proprietress can handle any situation with detached assurance. Moreover, Mrs. Hopewell knows well that she harbors no ignominy that could, by exposure to others, bring chagrin. On the contrary, others bask in her sunniness because she has a good word for all. Glynese and Carramae are "two of the finest girls she knew," and Mrs. Freeman is "a *lady*" whom one is "never ashamed to take . . . anywhere or introduce . . . to anybody" (170). Whatever disturbance arises, sprightly sayings preserve the world for Mrs. Hopewell in sanguine acceptability. "Nothing is perfect," she is given to remark; "well, other people have their opinions too," she knows; and, after all, "that is life!" (171).

Such cheer fools no one. Mrs. Freeman recognizes Mrs. Hopewell's charm and toleration of her family as ways to keep the industrious Mr. Freeman farming the place. Joy, Mrs. Hopewell's learned daughter, scorns her mother's persuasion of mind as a fatuity that dilutes goodness to a thin veneer of politeness spread over Mrs. Freeman's suggestive indecencies or over anything that does not fit into her mother's emotional plan. Joy is a living reaction to this twaddle. She shoulders a "constant outrage" (171) over her mother's unseeing conviviality. What little delight Joy feels comes from unmasking the weaknesses her mother and others try to camouflage. In her etiquette, making people squirm is a social accomplishment. Now thirty-two, Joy has developed a mode of cutting frankness into her identity.

Joy first feels the need to defend herself at ten, when one leg is shot off in a hunting accident. The gun also shatters the image of her body as whole. Her mother's shame over the girl's loss, reinforced by pitying niceties, produces in Joy a similar sense of shame at her failure to be the girl she is supposed to be. Since Joy "never danced a step or had any *normal* good times" (173), Mrs. Hopewell considers her a child. Such an image of incompleteness is the seed of shame. At twenty-one Joy leaves home to get a Ph.D. in philosophy in order to negate her maimed body by living in her mind, where she can prove herself a full person. Ideas alone, however, do not integrate desire. Instead of showing that her missing limb does not curtail maturity, graduate study exposes how systematic thinking can be a form of infantilism. Joy uses learning for revenge. She espouses the nihilism of our time because it puts issues on a level of derision congenial to her defensive anger.

At majority she also changes her name to Hulga to make permanent the incoherence she felt in childhood about her name, her mother, and the world. *Hulga* brings into the open the unacknowledged shame both mother and daughter feel. The reality of rebuke which the philosopher Hulga constructs permits the crippled woman to feel whole because she and her mind set the ideal. Not only does intellect sustain the illusion of piecing together what her body keeps disjoined, a nihilistic stance gives Hulga's raging fury controlled utterance. " 'Malebranche was right,' " she blurts out during a meal, " 'we are not our own light' " (176). Her disdain finds comfort in grand pronouncements. " 'If science is right, then one thing stands firm,' " she marks with blue pencil in a text, " 'science wishes to know nothing of nothing' " (176). Hulga spends years legitimatizing her reproach of a world that she feels rejects her.

Manley Pointer puts Hulga's highfalutin nay-saying to the test. He is a nineteen-year-old Bible salesman with seventy-seven books sold in only four months. Manley falls just short of the twenty-some years it takes Hulga to refine her philosophical position, but he, a fast learner, has a riper, more impelling nihilism. The salesman knows firsthand that in a desperately threatened world, the way to succeed is to hold yourself just below the image others have of themselves. One gains power by allowing others superiority. " 'I'm just a country boy,' " Manley assures Mrs. Hopewell, who descends to the occasion of his entreaty: " 'Why, I think there aren't enough good country people in the world!' "

(179). To gain the trust of the Hopewells, Manley abases himself further. He reveals that a heart condition has softened his ambition into a life of " 'Chrustian service' " (180). He is too weak to do anything but bear the word of God.

The apple offered Eve could not have been sweeter than the delight twinkling from Manley's voice. Hulga takes the bait. The woman of ideas fantasizes about seducing the visitor through dialogues that reach "depths that no Bible salesman would be aware of" (184). Their discourse is truly one for the books. Diotima tries to enlighten Caligula. Hulga's scientific method, she believes, can accommodate any question Manley puts to her; but Manley has the advantage of a bizarre audacity. " 'You ever ate a chicken that was two days old?' " he asks (185). " 'Yes,' " she replies, with an unconvincing sublimity that construes obscene fooling to be his mental handicap. By humoring the yokel, Hulga thinks that she can convert his stupidity into a power that sees the meaninglessness of things. In her imagination she takes "all his shame away" and turns it into "something useful" (186).

The reverse happens. Something useful and human, Hulga's femininity, becomes shameful by virtue of a weird combination of bravado and impotence that underlies Manley Pointer's sexual humor: disembodied flirtations, concentrated with exquisite sensitivity on anatomical parts. Uppity women with a physical impairment appeal to Manley—all the better if they too believe in nothing. At the trysting place he hides behind a bush to savor Hulga's limp, which arouses him to stand erect and "very tall" (187) to escort her. While Hulga lumbers toward the barn, he warms to speculations about where the wooden leg joins her torso. In a flush of excitement he kisses her; the kiss, Hulga's first, charges her brain with the idea of control over the boy. The throes of kissing in the haystack do not check the neurological power Hulga has accumulated over twenty years of pulling emotion into her head. She expatiates on how he is damned for peddling the word of God and she is saved by not believing in God. The eager pupil becomes the complaisant lover. He, whom she takes to be a naive sentimentalist, beseeches words of endearment. She, the cool scientist, casts pearls of wisdom: " 'I don't have illusions. I'm one of those people who see *through* to nothing' " (191). Such detachment coincides with the opportunist's screwball longing to see how Hulga's prosthesis joins flesh. Hulga can handle obscenity in the abstract, but the request for proof of her affection in the form of showing her peg leg shocks her. The jolt, however, does not go deep enough. As a child she had been "subject to feelings of shame," but education, like successful surgery, removed any trace of self-consciousness; and "she would no more have felt it over what he was asking than she would have believed in his Bible" (192).

Had Hulga believed in something beyond herself, she might have resolved her shame, but she trusts only in her mental skill to disguise her damaged psyche. By cloaking childhood shame in the adult garb of philosophy, she makes that shame more pronounced. Intellectual gambits not only keep the old wound of ten open, they render her unprepared at thirty-two to deal with life. By flaunting her injury, Hulga tries to preempt the inescapable exposure to others, but the unexpectedness of Manley's erotic attraction to her leg razes her philosophic composure. The artificial leg becomes her soul, the recognition of which tortures her. She submits to Manley's goading rather than have her own weakness exposed to herself. Thrilled by Hulga's demonstration of how the leg comes off and goes on at the knee, Manley himself tries the mechanism and fondles the limb with his eyes as he unsheathes it with his hands. His artfully slow dismantling reduces Hulga's entire person to a mere gadget, and we feel from her puny cry of alarm and his cocky rapture that he who was so alluring turns out to be injurious.

The philosopher-temptress reaches the end of the speculative road. At ten she was a physical cripple; now she is a moral invalid. Prostrate anew, fully clothed yet spiritually stripped, Hulga deep down is superficial. More than twenty years of couching shame in abstraction has trained her to tolerate Manley's systematic assault on her dignity as her confrontation "with real innocence" (192). So much for the life of the mind. Hulga begins by thinking away God and ends up blind to the devil. When Manley hisses that the fake leg makes her " 'different,' " she sees his remarks as insightful. At this level of headwork, Doctor Hulga Hopewell is moronic, which accounts for the echoes of Enoch Emery in *Wise Blood* running through her rationalizations. Like Enoch, Hulga is carried away by mindlessness. She remains stiff-necked before the God Who knows her weakness, and wills to bow before her god of negation. Removing her leg to please Manley is "losing her own life and finding it again, miraculously, in his" (192).

It is a good thing that she finds new life in the caller, because she will never again get that wooden leg. The salt of the earth stashes it in his black valise with his other sexual toys. Manley swings down the hole in the barn loft with the alacrity of a morality-play devil slipping out a trap door. While exiting, he brandishes the contempt that his admiring leer no longer need conceal: " 'Hulga,' " he taunts, " 'you ain't so smart. I been believing in nothing ever since I was born!' " (195). The dissembler's punch line locates the cause of Hulga's delusion and heartache in her search for identity through negation. At best, her indifference to others and rejection of pleasure can foster a sense of her own importance; at worst, her effort leads to solipsism and dispiritedness as the only significant experiences.

We can now appreciate more fully the gravity of dejection, observed earlier by a Father of the Desert as a root sin, and endured as a choice by The Misfit prowling dirt roads, by Ruby Hill sulking down the stairwell, and by the Doctor of Philosophy stomping the countryside. The change of the philosopher's name from Joy to Hulga issues a new warning about the perils of dejection. *Hulga* worships the sadness that *Joy* could overcome. Hulga's ideal is not to belong to or enjoy the world but to discredit it. Such recrimination takes her in two contradictory directions. First, Hulga mocks herself by exaggerating her physical unattractiveness. In this way she need not admit her fear of being held in contempt. At the same time, she enjoys piercing the poses that others strike, and disvaluing any satisfaction that others find. This stripping bare is how the devil operates; this uncovering is what Manley Pointer is all about. In the haystack Hulga meets that satanic aspect of herself.

In O'Connor's fiction, the encounter with the underside of one's nature is always two-edged. If weakness is exposed and the character reaches beyond her or his vulnerability, as with the grandmother in "A Good Man Is Hard to Find," then the shame that is healed can integrate a person; but shame opened raw, as in "Good Country People," can annihilate a person. Hulga caves in. O'Connor uses the language of mystical surrender in the scene to point out the radical disintegration of Hulga's personality. Erudite Hulga, the personification of "an age which doubts both fact and value" (*Mystery and Manners* 117), ends without a leg to stand on. The heroine's downfall, O'Connor assured her publisher when proposing to include the story in the book, would send up the entire collection; and so it does. "Good Country People" sets *A Good Man Is Hard to Find* on its feet by dramatizing the subject of grace in a negative action showing what God's favor does *not* do: grace does not disjoin, it integrates.

The contrast between the sentimental evocations of the epithet *good country people* and the appalling abandonment of Hulga is so striking that we might be tempted to end our consideration of the story with the comic disparity. That, however, would be a mistake. There is more to learn from "Good Country People" about the use of shame to depict the state of disgrace. Throughout the volume God's communication with the protagonists brings them to their knees; some rest contritely on the eternal ground of being to which they are brought, but not Hulga. Shame removes her encounter with Manley Pointer from the world of adult passion that can lead to awareness, and reduces his evil to the modality of infancy, where Hulga remains prostrate in demoralized helplessness. Her paralysis points up the difference between the action of God and the action of His adversary. With grace, the exposure of sin invites the character to turn to virtue. Disgrace, on the other hand, excludes the possibility of accepting God's invitation by leaving the character questioning the reality of any significance. Whereas a sense of sin, guilt, or purgation affirms significance because each condition leads to expiation, shame leaves the character feeling the lack of meaning in life. Hulga's bereftness comes to the reader through an image of perception. At the end, sitting on straw in dusty sunlight, the desperate woman turns her face toward the open hatch and sees Manley's "blue figure struggling successfully over the green speckled lake" (195). Pointer, one critic observes, is walking on water (Asals 71). True, the villain seems to be, but not by virtue of his supernatural power to awaken faith. O'Connor is subtle but not so crafty as to transform Pointer into a herald of the kingdom. Rather than defining the villain, the water image brings us back to Hulga and closer to her inner nature than we have been. We see the vanishing adversary through her eyes as he treads off on the tears of devastation left in his wake.

The concluding two paragraphs of the story amplify the way that shame blocks the Spirit's message. O'Connor shifts the angle of vision from Hulga's weeping eyes to the "squinting" eyes of Mrs. Hopewell and the driving gaze of Mrs. Freeman. They see Pointer from the back pasture, where they are pulling up "evil-smelling" (196) onion shoots. Mrs. Hopewell still perceives him as " 'that nice dull young man' " (195) whose simplicity attests to good country ways, while Mrs. Freeman frowns on his plainness. The hired woman may be more outspoken than the landlady, but she is not keener. Both women share a need to protect themselves from belittlement that requires them to look down on the Bible salesman. That disregard works to Manley's advantage, for the satanic ploy is to encourage the illusion of superiority in those making fools of themselves. Mrs. Hopewell needs to be thought of by others as good-natured, and Mrs. Freeman needs to be taken as bold-minded and independent; yet their shared destiny, like that of Hulga, whom they pity, is to be tricked. They are mistakers of shadow for substance. The two women have to dupe each other into believing that they can turn up their noses at Manley, as they do from the malodorous onions; but their labors of self-inflation result in a morbid resentment that others do not give them the respect they deserve. Critics have noted the resemblance between Hulga and Manley (Shloss 45; Feeley 23–24). The view at the story's end enlarges that similarity to include Mrs. Hopewell and Mrs. Freeman. All four, agent and bystanders and victim alike, share in a partnership of shame.

The strangest paradox about these rural antics is that all is not lost. In the characters' names and aspirations lie hints that direct the search for goodness in country people. There is the liberty that Mrs. Freeman would like to have in her responses to others and to her own predicament; there are the cherished desires of Mrs. Hopewell that all be well; and, most reassuring of all, there are tears in Hulga's eyes that release her interior sorrow, a sorrow that calls for interior comfort, itself a true joy.

Always it is like this with Flannery O'Connor: the reader cannot consider her trials of shame and guilt to any serious degree without seeing that she transforms them into a fresh key restating anguish and duty in terms of grace and joy. Even the guilt of a mass murderer on the side of a dirt road is recorded as a sign of grace denied. The defection from duty at a remote eating place by a confidence man comes to us as a fulfillment missed. And a pregnant woman's need to forswear motherhood marks a love rejected.

O'Connor's fullest account of the sorrowful mystery of dejection, "Good Country People," reminds us that the experience basic to life and goodness lies recoverable in the discarded name of the story's heroine, Joy. The Misfit, Mr. Shiftlet, Ruby Hill, and Hulga do not set out to do themselves in with their denials, but their long-faced remorse breeds despondency, depresses the spirit. Grimness makes them live at a distance from themselves in that concrete part of their lives and the world around them that can be manipulated and controlled. Such is the daily excuse, the unadmitted dejection, that passes for ordinary existence but is an evasion of transcendence. The characters' duty is to enjoy. It is the most useful thing they could do, for it points the way out of self-destruction toward goodness.

Finding the Good Man

"Yet even now," says the Lord, "return to me with all your heart, with
fasting, with weeping, and with mourning; and rend your hearts and
not your garments."
Joel 2:12

Then it becomes clear as daylight that God's word is always right, and
that it is edifying always to be in the wrong before God.
Hans Urs von Balthasar, *Prayer*

The ending of "A Good Man Is Hard to Find" is starkly simple
in atmosphere and action. Sun heats the afternoon. The sky remains
clear. In a ditch an escaped convict, The Misfit, unbosoms the needs
of his soul to an unknown grandmother whom he holds hostage. He feels
torn, the old lady learns, between the impulse to follow Jesus and the
dread of doing so, but all he can do is suppress Jesus' call by killing
and burning and destroying. The woman's heart goes out to her captor.
When she sees up close her tormentor's twisted face about to break
into tears, she reaches out to touch him; her irrepressible consolation,
however, agitates the criminal's lifelong terror. To relieve his fear,
The Misfit shoots the grandmother. The old woman lies soaked in blood,
smiling up at the cloudless sky.

The facial expressions of murderer and victim embody the themes
unifying the ten stories of *A Good Man Is Hard to Find.* No sooner does
his gun go off than The Misfit scowls with a displeasure indistinguish-
able from self-loathing. He departs oppressed by his own wrath but

blames Jesus for living two thousand years too early, while missing Jesus' presence in the grandmother's love. Despondency reappears on the protagonists' faces in three subsequent stories (which accounts of grace discarded were considered in the previous chapter). By contrast, the grandmother, battered but not diminished by gunfire, bears the look of contentment. The upward curve of her smile extends into the remaining six stories of the collection. These histories of grace accepted are the subject of this chapter. They take us deeper into the source of the grandmother's smile, the blue expanse of God's gracious dealings with His remnant people in Tennessee and Georgia.

O'Connor cannot avoid associating the condition of pain with that of contact with God. Holiness, she says on many occasions, costs. Though both groups of stories in *A Good Man Is Hard to Find* involve wounding, O'Connor distinguishes between kinds of suffering. One is sorrow produced by recalcitrance, which surfaces in varying aspects of The Misfit's sullenness and self-lacerating anger. This grief causes spiritual death. As with The Misfit's dourness, heavy dejection on the face of the sinner overshadows the likeness of God in the character. The other kind of sorrow results from grace that works contrition. This sorrow is a form of love. Like the grandmother's happy gesture, this sacrificial tenderness gives life by widening the horizon of transcendental possibility. The grandmother's joyous face unseals the inner divine likeness that is the good woman.

O'Connor's good person presents no single countenance of delight. Those accepting the invitation to enter God's own joy as creator and savior comprehend the mysterious horizon in different ways. The gift of divine love may precede knowledge of God. In fact, the need for love may be the cause of seeking and the goal toward which grace takes the seeker. Understanding may not inform the experience at all. With little Harry Ashfield in "The River," love is all the knowledge of God that he gains and all that he needs. Though clothed, housed, and fed by his mother and father, Harry feels hungry and bereft. During the course of wandering through the ashes of parental neglect, Harry stuffs himself with party leftovers and swallows the beguiling promise of a circuit preacher until he drowns himself to find the love he seeks. In the end, however, the orphan looking for a parent finds God.

The events of two days crystallize the lovelessness driving Harry to death and to God. At 6 A.M. Sunday morning, Mrs. Connin collects

Harry to mind him so that the Ashfields can nurse their weekly hangover. To please herself and to teach Harry things he should know, Mrs. Connin takes the child to hear Bevel Summers at a riverside faith healing. Summers uses Harry to show how an unbaptized child will " 'count' " (44). The bony-faced preacher dunks the boy's head into the river and holds him submerged until he has uttered the complete formula of cleansing. Harry is horrified beyond tears. Without any religious awareness to soften the shocking immersion, Harry learns from experience that counting hurts deeply. The next morning, alone again while his parents sleep off their sabbath indulgence, Harry decides to pay the price for counting; he returns to the river and drowns himself.

Though some readers agree with Miles Orvell that "the little boy has done little more than confuse a literal meaning with symbolic meaning" (35), O'Connor and most commentators call "The River" a story of baptism. Still, among those addressing the issue, there remains a lively dispute over how the child protagonist's death conveys "traditionally redemptive qualities" (Gentry 96–97). One early reading argues for a balance in the ending between the sacred and the profane (Feeley 132), while another sees a resolution that marks "a transcending leap of faith" (Muller 59). But anthropological categories distance us excessively from the child's raw need for love, and Kierkegaardian speculation hurls the four- or five-year-old far beyond his mental reach. Confusion and urgency are so built into little Harry's suicide that we do well to allow his contrary emotions and concrete desire to guide us to his fate.

O'Connor writes of Harry's shocking conversion from an understanding of baptism that is more basic than that of popular notions of the sacrament. Her approach is scriptural. One way into O'Connor's treatment is to consider "The River" as her response to Paul's question to the Romans: "Do you not know that all of us who have been baptized into Christ Jesus were baptized into his death?" (Romans 6:3). Since her faithless readers would not know that Jesus' death makes any difference, O'Connor shows how the tragic destruction of a child of our time participates in a death that bestows the newness of life.

The action prepares for Harry's paradoxical destiny through the immediate paradox of modern family life that amounts to the death of the child's human significance. Harry's parents live for themselves. Shadows of their unbelief darken the living room in which we find Harry. The scene is familiar. Abstract watercolor on the wall, phonograph, cigarette butts, ginger ale bottles, anchovy paste on crackers, shriveled vegetables, brown oranges, stale bread—sterile accouterments and unpalatable leavings from the perennial night before define Harry's world. Here nothing lives. The Ashfields' pleasure palace neither accommodates pleasure nor admits light. Self-absorption shuts out any hint of mystery. God does not exist; cash calculates prayer. The atmosphere tends to promote taking and using. A child's book on prayer, stolen by Harry from Mrs. Connin, interests visiting friends of the Ashfields as a collector's item; they in turn steal it from Harry. The rights and needs of others make no impression. Harry has not been baptized. If he has any parents, they are fear and indignity: "They joked a lot where he lived" (38). Four or five years in this gloom compile a legacy of rejection that erodes Harry's self-esteem and distorts his view of the world.

Harry may be too young to sin but he is old enough to know pain. The education of Harry Ashfield into suffering goes beyond the indifference of his parents. Mrs. Connin's boys school Harry in terror as well. Duped by one boy's playful nastiness, Harry pulls a board off a sty to see a pig. From his picture book he imagines the animal to be cute and friendly, but the real thing is an ugly, humpbacked, ear-bitten shoat that overwhelms the child with brute power. Harry screams for five minutes after the assault. Later, Harry's instruction seems to take an amicable turn when Bevel Summers teaches the child that he counts. Summers's fundamentalism puts the lesson of belonging in a concrete appeal to a child who makes no distinction between the physical and the unseen, the literal and the mysterious. Even Summers's rehearsed seriousness comforts Harry as a relief from his parents' vapidity: " 'If I Baptize you . . . you'll be able to go to the Kingdom of Christ. You'll be washed in the river of suffering, son, and you'll go by the deep river of life' " (44). The words are as old as the river, but they hold the news that the friendless child is eager to hear. The message speaks to him at last as son.

Each scene in the course of Harry's moral training has an image of swine to show the defilements attacking Harry. Animality externalizes the spiritual death hidden beneath pleasure. Harry goes from the family's pigsty to the Connins' hog to the healing where Mr. Paradise, who resembles the Connin pig, challenges the power of Summers to cure, pointing out the greed behind his talk of recovery from muddy water. At the end, Mr. Paradise's head bobs on the river's surface "like some ancient water monster" (52) pursuing Harry deeper into the flowing tide. In the Bible, Jesus drives the unclean spirit out of a man into a nearby herd of swine. Degraded as they are, the pigs reject the demon by rushing into the lake to drown the fiend. Death purifies the swine of alien evil. O'Connor depicts the herd as still on the run in Harry's pursuit. Like the Connin boys who shift blame to Harry for what they told him to do, all the adults in the story displace their selfishness and irresponsibility onto Harry; an inborn desire for integrity then prompts Harry to get rid of the evil laid on him.

Harry's feet show the way, guide his yearning. With the same unseen gravity as that in the rock- and glass-lined shoes which pulls Hazel Motes back to the light, Harry's shoes, still wet on Monday from his Sunday baptism, lead him back to the river that makes him count. The source of this mysterious influence surfaces at the story's conclusion: "the waiting current caught him like a long gentle hand." This hand snatches Harry out of the evil breaking over him. The watery hand, which takes other forms in the collection, manifests spiritual contact. In the opening story, the grandmother extends her hand to comfort The Misfit, whose hand pumps three rounds into her chest. "The River" returns the woman's gesture of kindness, as a saving hand retrieves the innocent child whom the iron fist of Bevel Summers held down. The grasp is tried and true. Jesus' saving hand extended to the sinking Peter (Mark 14:23–31). Now Harry floats in a flowing palm that sustains him until "all his fury and his fear" (52) leave. The child puts no hindrance in the tide of grace.

Abusive rejection by others and struggle within do not in themselves make Harry the good man who is hard to find; they are only valuable as urgent inducements to turn to the single place, the river, where he can find access to love. In the water, the power holding Harry requires merely the unthinking abandonment that a four- or five-year-old can make with his entire being. To give himself into this hand is to deliver himself from evil. Psalm 3 sings of the strong hand that safeguards one who trusts: "When I lie down to sleep, I wake again, / For the Lord holds me in His hands" (5). Psalmic sleep and waking in the Lord's protection correspond to Harry's sinking and rescue by the gentle hand; both are transports from death into life. Harry's final passage also conveys the idea of human wholeness underlying O'Connor's treatment of childhood. She does not present the numerous children in her writing as potential adults because time does not confer maturity. What completes Harry Ashfield, O'Connor's first child hero, is grace. More than patching up the hurt child, the long gentle hand lifts him into "a new creation" (2 Corinthians 5:17).

Harry's felt release is a gift of spirit, and communion with the Holy Spirit best defines baptism in "The River." Two colors vivify the way in which this sacramental exchange occurs in a child who must feel rather than reason his way to God. The old river is red, with flecks of gold shimmering on its surface; these same colors dress a "low red and gold grove of sassafras" and highlight red human faces caught in the bright sun. Bevel Summers explains redness when pointing to " 'the rich red river of Jesus' Blood' " (41), and his preaching is true to O'Connor's painterly rendering of her sacred material. Harry's baptism immerses him in Christ's life, an identification that invites us to see how even an unknowing youngster suffers a passion as a result of the wounds of others. Several details join to help us interpret the anguishing climax of Harry's life. The child must pass "purple weeds" that make him dusty and sweaty. Just as in Hazel Motes's mind Jesus moves from tree to tree assuming everyone's pain, Harry takes up his share of the burden wandering from "tree to tree" until he finds "a line worn in the pine needles" (51).

The path beset by stings is the way of the good man. It originates in the selfless obedience commanded by Jesus, and at the juncture where Harry discovers the route, it twists down to the red-yellow river. The pieces of "white sun scattered in the river" (44) flash Harry's becoming Christ's follower *malgré lui*. The sun signals the Son's glory. It shines forth God's promise of receiving Harry as His own. By seeking love, Harry gains experiential knowledge of the first mystery of faith: afloat in ignorance, weighted by loneliness, but buoyed by love, Harry, without understanding God's words, can trust His acts. The words transmitted to the child live in his flesh.

"The River" is the earliest story to make explicit the new relationship between God and the human person that lies at the root of O'Connor's stories of family ties, which is to say at the center of her fiction. Paul, extending the sonship of Jesus to all believers in God, calls this new relation the "adoption as sons" (Galatians 4:5). The sunlight and the mighty water-hand together build the abode where the adopted children dwell and count. Many scriptural passages use river imagery to describe the joy of the believer in drawing from the source of life. Psalm 36 (8–9) expresses the serenity concluding O'Connor's story: "thou givest them drink from the river of thy delights. / For with thee is the fountain of life...." Harry Ashfield in "The River" imbibes from the steady stream of God's love. For a split second he is "overcome with surprise" (52) and then sinks peacefully downstream. Taken unawares, as charity invades all the protagonists, Harry reaches his timeless identity in an instant of mystery lived.

"A Temple of the Holy Ghost" brings another young seeker to find God's immediate presence. As in "The River," the action progresses to the locale where divinity makes itself known in a way that allows the youngster to share in its life and favors. The destination, however, changes. From the sanctuary of water O'Connor shifts to the sanctuary of flesh—which Jesus, the good man *par excellence,* speaks of as the temple of the Spirit (John 2:21). O'Connor's personalizing the sacred place comes about from the different age and moral capacity of her protagonist. Whereas "The River" begins with a child's physical need for love and satisfies it with his felt intuition of love, "A Temple of the Holy Ghost" takes an adolescent's abstractions of love and fulfills them by working back to the physical fact embodying them.

The story concerns a girl of twelve. She is precocious enough to grasp the idea of God's dwelling in the human body but ingenuous enough to be stunned when a crucifix hanging on a nun's belt mashes her face with the actual hardship imposed by God's inhabiting flesh. The accidental crush hastens the girl's growth. Critics who call the girl's change a story of confirmation (Martin 109–112; Gentry 65–69) rightly point up O'Connor's sacramental molding of the girl's awareness. And with the intimateness of God's contact with Harry's drowning fresh in our mind, we are in a position to see O'Connor's cohesive rendering of baptism and confirmation. Though separated in the stories, as they are in time for the recipient, baptism and confirmation make a single rite of initiation and participation in the earthly life of Jesus. Confirmation for O'Connor perfects and confirms the character's immersion into the life of the good man, and marks the beginning of the fullness of life that baptism promises. "The River" and "A Temple of the Holy Ghost," needless to say, are more marked by physical suffering than these critical remarks imply. The stories plunge the protagonists unceremoniously into the sacramental foundation of their lives. Two youngsters strive to count; through their bodily encounters with how love operates and what suffering love entails, they come to know something of Jesus' death.

"A Temple of the Holy Ghost" evolves through O'Connor's favorite strategy of having visitors upset the order of the visited place. Two fourteen-year-old girls from Mount St. Scholastica come to spend the weekend with relatives. The girls, Susan and Joanne, who are second cousins to the heroine, welcome the break from convent restrictions. They get rid of their drab uniforms for sexier clothes, high heels, and lipstick. The hallway mirror reflects the attention they seek. To entertain Temple One and Temple Two, as they nickname each other between glances in the mirror, the hostess arranges for Wendell and Cory Wilkins, farm boys, to have supper with the young ladies before taking them to the fair. The next afternoon Susan and Joanne return to the nuns. For them the weekend is a relief from the dreary repression of convent school. For the unnamed twelve-year-old daughter of the hostess, however, the visit brings to life an idea of God she has carried around in her head for years but never fully comprehended. "A Temple of the Holy Ghost" is the unnamed girl's story. It is the story of sudden impact. The shock that the girl feels gauges for O'Connor the reception of the Spirit's messianic power. Confirmation, like baptism, upheaves.

The Mount St. Scholastica students bring a pubescent notion of spirit expressed in meaningless rote phrases. Like the girls' real wardrobe, spirit concerns boys. Spirit is sexual combat, with male attention as the prize confirming the fullness of life. The convent plays into their preoccupation by presenting the Spirit as a weapon in their sexual contest. Sister Perpetua arms the girls for skirmishes with young males in the back seat of a car. She gives them the defense: " 'Stop sir! I am a Temple of the Holy Ghost!' " (88). Susan and Joanne can only giggle at the notion of a power that furthers maturity and the exalted life within by demanding protection from the male attention that is the badge of womanhood. They call each other Temple One and Temple Two to shrug off the naiveté of the foolish nun's counsel. The confusion created by old Sister Perpetua's setting the spiritual in opposition to the sexual increases when the hostess rebukes the girls' silly mockery and asserts that they are indeed temples of the Holy Spirit.

Divine kinship in each person is a mystery to the young heroine. While the reader realizes that the invisible truth of this indwelling rests not on the nun's misleading presentation of a conflict between body and soul but on Jesus' distinction between the unredeemed person and the person redeemed by the Spirit, the girl must rely on her native intelligence. Common sense tells her that the Spirit is not the adversary of boys but of sin, against which she could use help. Moreover, the thought of dignity and intimacy in an exalted sphere delights her. Being a place in which God might abide makes her feel "as if somebody had given her a present" (88). She also detects stupidity in the glum rejection of a lofty presence, and thinks that Susan and Joanne must be "morons" (85) to pass up the privilege of welcoming a sacred guest into their body. For the girl, accommodating the Spirit involves joy and brains, not clothes and self-indulgence. The gift of presence deserves intelligent gratitude. On this score the heroine shines. Susan and Joanne may be older and know more about makeup and anatomy, but she is smarter. To defend herself against advantages of age and sexual development held by others, the twelve-year-old takes great pride in esteeming herself the brightest person around. The Wilkins boys are dumb oxes, too; she refuses to have dinner with those " 'stupid idiots' " (92), farm-bred boys and convent-finished girls alike.

From a distance, the heroine scrutinizes the ritual of double-dating. Harmonica and guitar in hand, but totally lost about how to be with girls, the rural worthies entertain the girls with a country song set to a religious lyric. The love-hymn sings of Jesus' friendship which protects and frees. The girls are too uncomfortable and snobbish to feel anything but disdain for the hillbilly music, and so to overcome their awkwardness they respond with a musical version of Sister Perpetua's command to men. They sing the *"Tantum Ergo,"* a devotional celebration of the Holy Spirit dwelling in the Eucharist. Though the Latin serves the girls' purpose of putting down the boys and their country music, the *"Tantum Ergo"* shares with the Church of God song an expression of thanksgiving (*eucharistia*) for God's intimate presence. (The song ends: "And I'll always have Him near!") Again, all of these implications float above the heads of the boys and girls. Their effect lies in the young girl observing from a distance. She turns her own discomfort into a sneer at the ungainly way the four express themselves, and she offers a thanksgiving of her own—this one in the high tone of contempt in which she thanks God that she is beyond the convent and above the crude Church of God.

Adolescent flirtation is not yet the young heroine's affair. She now can understand growth only through intelligence, her principal strength. Her need to defend her integrity takes the form of perceiving deficiencies in everyone around her. The price of such superiority is isolation and the risk of a terrible comeuppance. The black cook warns the girl: " 'God could strike you deaf dumb and blind' " (93). This warning, which foretells the ending, falls on deaf ears. The girl's desire to raise herself above the stupidity around her produces a grandiose conception of herself. Doctor or engineer falls short of the heroism she seeks. Saint is closer, but she lies and sasses and therefore feels disqualified for sainthood. Martyrdom, with its sudden retributive violence, will have to do. Her quick imagination provides the scenario for the high drama in which she stars. The script adapts Cecil B. De Mille's pageant of Christian massacres in the Roman Colosseum to the melodic calliope wail from the fair that the girls are enjoying without her. Between charging lions, intense flames, and consuming self-congratulations that she is smarter than others, the child has unexpected glimpses of Christ crushed three times under a hard cross on the way to Calvary. Jesus' anguish accepted in love, the real measure of maturity, deflates her fanciful flight to martyrdom.

Another mystery of affliction undermines the girl's romantic view of spiritual heroics. Just before midnight Susan and Joanne return from the carnival with accounts of the freaks they saw. One, a hermaphrodite, haunts them. They do not recall the performer's name but the words, in a country voice, linger. First to men and then to women, the man-woman says point-blank: " 'I'm going to show you this and if you laugh, God may strike you the same way.' " Admonition leads to wisdom: " 'I'm showing you because I got to make the best of it.' " The body of two sexes in one person is a living obedience to a higher law, baffling and inescapable: " 'God made me thisaway' " (97). At first the freak seems to be a trick mirror that gives back to a proud, leering audience their image in fearful ugliness; however, when we consider the accepting words in light of the story's subject, we can hear the hermaphrodite speaking for the vital endowment received from God. The convent girls equate prettiness with human wholeness, but the double-sexed performer reveals that no physical condition impedes the Spirit's entry. Abnormality, on the contrary, is the absence of spirit; that is the true grotesque. Danger lies in denying the Spirit's secret transforming power. Laughter at mutations in physical or mental shape desecrates the temple because scorn ridicules the Spirit's unitive love that makes creation one by inhabiting all its parts.

The young heroine learns more about the Spirit's activity while accompanying Joanne and Susan back to Mount St. Scholastica. To dissociate herself from the girls' prattle, the child looks up at the ivory sun set in the blue afternoon, eager to absorb the light on high. On the ground a moon-faced nun, the sun's cohort at the convent, greets the child with a rough handshake that cracks her knuckles, and then drags her and her mother to the chapel for benediction. Angered by the nun's bossiness, the girl arrives engrossed by habitual "ugly thoughts" as the priest raises the monstrance containing the eucharistic Host. To the singing of the *"Tantum Ergo,"* the piqued girl faces, against her will and in a private sanctuary, the presence that anoints and seals the universe. Her mood changes. A calm pours over her thoughts to press them forward to contrition. She expresses remorse by combining the hermaphrodite's testimony, her own admission of impudence, and the recollected glare from the blinding sun. In a transfigured state, these associations communicate with "the Host shining ivory-colored" (100) in the monstrance.

"A Temple of the Holy Ghost" reaches its climax when the gilded sunburst displayed before the heroine's mind takes irrevocable form in her flesh. The stout nun does the confirming and perfecting. As she hugs the child good-bye, she smashes the child's face with the crucifix on her belt. The embrace impresses on the heroine the second countenance of the trinitarian God, the visage of the sought-for good man. The mark results from love and moves toward love, which always cuts. O'Connor explains the imprint left by the affectionate farewell as "the ultimate all-inclusive symbol of love" (*Letters* 124). Before the devotional service, the child understood bearing the weight of the cross to be rhapsodic adventure; however, in recognizing the need to give up her arrogance, she has an inkling of a truer heroism of self-donation. Such surrender, O'Connor says in words echoing the freak's statements, involves "an acceptance of what God wills for us, an acceptance of our individual circumstances" (*Letters* 124).

While the girl returns to the comforts of home, the sun that has attended her trip vivifies the benediction liturgy and charts the way of acceptance that she must follow to preserve the gift she has received: "The sun was a huge red ball like an elevated Host drenched in blood and when it sank out of sight, it left a line in the sky like a red clay road hanging over the trees" (101). The bloodshot afterglow unlocks the horizon of confirmation, which the girl observes from a revealing silence that pride does not break. The sun maps her commission to share the visible activity of bestowing the Spirit. Maturity lies in fighting against the daily forms of her inner darkness. Her manner, while it rarely abases, frequently embarrasses, and there is a latently contemptuous tone that produces sneers out of her inward disdain. She must abandon visions of sleeping with lions in favor of correcting her disrespect at home. Mindful of her derision of others, she will see that physical condition does not distinguish the temple and that intelligence does not hold it together. Suffering houses the Spirit, and all suffer. Then, as a temple of the Holy Ghost, she will join the prolongation of the violated body of Jesus built anew in the sky out of the red clay. The *"Tantum Ergo"* heard at the convent intones the collective cheer felt on the heroine's new journey from the altar of Eucharist to the awaiting altar of reposition.

> Bond of love, in Godhead one!
> Blest be God by all creation
> Joyously while ages run! Amen.

It is the movement of love in the heroine's conversion that shines forth the third countenance of God, the invisible aspect of the good man. Psychological and physiological details are incidental to this countenance. In fact, individuality, which the gifted heroine treasures, is not the reward. Collective oneness is. The spiritual fruitfulness in store for the girl lies in her namelessness. O'Connor keeps the young protagonist anonymous because the task of increasing the temple assimilates all without distinction into the one identifying Spirit.

A blazing horizon confirms another twelve-year-old girl in *A Good Man Is Hard to Find.* In "A Circle of Fire," Sally Virginia Cope enters spiritual maturity. Her passage, too, comes about when visitors upset the serenity of her home. The outsiders in "A Circle of Fire" are not convent girls seeking diversion, however, but young Atlanta toughs eager to gratify their will. One late summer afternoon, a pickup truck drops off Powell, Garfield Smith, and W. T. Harper on Mrs. Cope's dairy farm. Powell is the son of one of Mrs. Cope's numerous former hired hands. While growing up on the Cope farm, Powell became attached to the open freedom of the countryside, and he regaled his city friends with details of " 'the best time of his entire life . . . on this here place' " (136). Horses are the strongest attraction. Powell's remembered pleasure over the years hardens into covetousness. He promises his friends rides on the horses and invites them for a vacation on the Cope property before school begins in the fall. Powell's insolence emboldens the other two, and against Mrs. Cope's orders, the three intruders ride roughshod around the place, taking particular delight in unbridled defiance. When the time comes for them to leave, they start a fire to destroy the place rather than be haunted by its being there without their enjoying it. Annihilation allows the young firebugs to allay their inordinate envy of the place. Readers familiar with Milton's Satan will recognize the logic. " 'If this place was not here any more,' " urges Powell with avaricious goading, " 'you would never have to think of it again' " (152). Its being theirs to burn makes it theirs to keep. Depriving others of the joy deprived him is the only way this young hood, like Lucifer, can relieve his bitterness. Sally Virginia enters the ring of sorrow as she helplessly watches the three young arsonists set their raging fire.

Mrs. Cope, emotional cousin to Mrs. Hopewell, copes by searching out the cheerful side of a situation. Her need to control every contingency molds her geniality into armor against expected menaces. Nut grass and weeds sprout "as if they were an evil sent directly by the devil to destroy the place" (131). Alone with a young daughter to raise, Mrs. Cope believes that she must reckon with more than the usual difficulties of making a comfortable life, and that by sheer vigilance she manages to make ends meet; but her grudging satisfaction comes across as vindicating rebuttal to a hidden plaintiff trying to reclaim her hard-won security. She will have the uninvited boys and everyone else know summarily that " 'this is my place' " (144) — " 'my woods' " (140), her pasture, her horses, her cows, her sky. The prayer of thanks she offers daily is more a clinging to than a counting of blessings. As she tells it, " 'we have everything' "; yet her defensiveness leaves her feeling deprived. She bears responsibility with fear: " 'Lord,' she said . . . and she looked around at her rich pastures and hills heavy with timber and shook her head as if it might all be a burden she was trying to shake off her back" (133). The widow Cope is on to a truth about our essential poverty and her stewardship, but she cannot summon the selflessness that makes detachment bearable. The woman's real opponent is herself. Her place weighs her down because she clutches it as something that gives her being and distinction. Any change in the weather, especially a wind shift that would fuel a fire, or rank growth of herbage, or hint of litigation weakens her tight hold on herself.

Mrs. Cope cannot cope with any image of herself as subject to natural forces or other people's views. Such a fear of dependency and loss of control requires that others fit into her emotional scheme. Manipulation in the name of generosity can only sharpen the animos-

ity around her. Three Coca-Colas and a plate of crackers are offered the
boys to influence their conduct, but they scorn her insipid fare, which
only whets their hunger to ride the horses and make sport of the place.
Their power feeds on Mrs. Cope's unpalatable bribes. In the morning
after a night in the field doing what they please, the invaders know that
they have Mrs. Cope where they want her when she resorts to the
obsequious charge of etiquette. " 'I expect you to act like gentlemen' "
(144), she pipes, after they reject her offer of breakfast. They have
already nourished their starved malice by drinking milk out of the
dairy cans and by racing the horses bareback.

Mrs. Pritchard is on hand to remind her employer, Mrs. Cope, that
ladylike courtesy fails because a sunny outlook does not square with
things as they are. Things are disastrous, and she has massive evidence
to prove it. One of her kin, seventh or eighth cousin removed, conceived
and delivered a baby while in an iron lung, and was laid out in a coffin
with her arm around the child. The story (part of a repertoire) has just
the right mixture of sex, pathology, oddity, and death to reveal the
calamitous nature of the world. This large woman has a ferret's skill in
unearthing the unpleasantness that Mrs. Cope glosses over. Distasteful
as Mrs. Pritchard and her stories are to Mrs. Cope, they give Mrs. Cope
enough illusion of success in dealing with misfortune for the two
women to have a working relationship. This symbiosis comes at a price,
however. In return for the delight of abrading Mrs. Cope with morbidity,
Mrs. Pritchard must tolerate Mrs. Cope's condescension. On the occasion of the boys' visit, Mrs. Pritchard's cynicism even yields a salutary
precaution. She would not be surprised, for instance, if they carried a
gun in their black suitcase. She may be wrong about the means but she
is right about the result. For what little wisdom it provides, the accu-
racy of Mrs. Pritchard's intuition issues from an emotional violence
that is alarming. She welcomes destruction. Arms folded, she surveys
the place with raging eyes that flatten "these fine hills to nothing" (134).
Mrs. Pritchard understands the hoodlums because she shares their
demolishing impulse.

The setup is ideal for Lucifer, who works best through sneaky
collusion. The boys, agents of the light-bearer, act out Mrs. Pritchard's
imagined ruination. Since others do the dirty work, she can sit back to
watch the place struck by devilment without feeling involved. Mrs.
Pritchard's detachment sanctions the added glee of taunting Mrs. Cope
with having been warned; and should foresight not prevent trouble, as

when Mr. Pritchard's stabling the horses does not stop the boys from abusing the animals, then Mrs. Pritchard gleans evidence of youthful stealth outfoxing adult initiative. Her gambits to ratify sinister assumptions vary, but their effect is always to harm her own soul. Mrs. Pritchard needs to reduce a situation to a futility agreeable to her dourness. She can then flaunt a blamelessness that gets rid of the need to examine her share in evil, in the same way that fire removes the need for the boys to think about the farm after they have sent it up in smoke. Arson, emotional and chemical, satisfies the urge to burn something that might give others pleasure or might stir guilt in oneself.

For all the dramatic possibilities inherent in fixation on doom or in avoidance of evil, Lady Cope and Dragon Lady Pritchard are not the main interests of "A Circle of Fire." O'Connor takes up a proprietress's conversion through Mrs. May in "Greenleaf," and the fate of an envious defamer through Mrs. Shortley in "The Displaced Person." Readers who insist upon the centrality of the two women in "A Circle of Fire" cause themselves disappointment over the negligible change in Mrs. Cope and Mrs. Pritchard (Gentry 54). It is, rather, precisely the women's shortcomings that further O'Connor's aim to bring Sally Virginia into womanhood. The girl's reaction against the feeble crudity of Mrs. Pritchard and the edgy primness of her mother defines the action of the story. Neither adult exemplifies the kind of woman the girl wants to be. " 'Leave me be,' " Sally Virginia snaps when her mother scolds her for wearing overalls and two pistols over her dress. " 'Just leave me be. I ain't you' " (150). The tomboy sheriff is out to find the force to combat the evil encroaching on her life. "A Circle of Fire" shows the twelve-year-old finding the good woman she can grow up to be—intelligent in recognizing evil for what it is and willing to resist it.

As the boys' playful vandalism unfolds, Sally Virginia moves to a position of structural determination. The story's ending perfects the focus. The girl is fed up with the outsiders pushing her mother around on her property and holding the place hostage to their will, and she proposes to beat the daylights out of them. Firearms holstered to her waist and a man's felt hat on her head, she singlehandedly stalks the "enemy" (150). So long as her search remains imagined, the officer of the law can carry out her duty. A cluster of bare-trunked pine trees four times her height are not too big for her to practice on. " 'I'm going to get you one by one and beat you black and blue. Line up. LINE UP!' " (151). Targets hit, she storms through the woods toward the real opponents.

When a thorn vine catches her skirt, there is a warning that she may encounter a menace that is larger than she is. Sitting on a stump to cool off, she hears the boys' ugly laughter while they bathe in the cow trough, and later, having eased toward the pasture, she sees the three males naked. The sexuality of the meeting is powerful, overwhelming to the degree that Sally Virginia cannot grasp what has struck her. And she is assailed. To a pubescent girl there is sexual astonishment, if not the real fear of assault, which she may be too frightened to admit. When a friend called O'Connor's attention to the sexual overtones in the scene, O'Connor found it "a very perceptive comment," acknowledging that on reconsidering the story she saw the child's exposure to sexual threat but noting that "the attack takes another form" (*Letters* 119).

Actually, the attack takes two forms, both physical, one against the land and the other against the girl. Being unclothed frees the boys to bare their greedy pleasure. " 'It's ours' " (152), asserts the smallest; this cry of ownership sends three wet glistening bodies dashing twice around the field, drawing a circle of their necromantic rights. With the place declared their own, the little boy goes the limit of his greedy imagination to boast that he would " 'build a big parking lot on it, or something' " (153). Powell, the mastermind, comes up with the something. As they begin to dress, Powell takes matches from his pocket, and the plan to torch the place spreads wordlessly among the three. They enter the dry woods that lie just ten feet from the pine tree hiding Sally Virginia. The orgy of jubilant destroyers with their sins, their genitals, their swagger, and their cabal besieges the girl. When the boys laugh, the shock pierces Sally Virginia's flesh, making her "prickle-skinned" (151); after the flames soar, the blow sinks into her central nervous system before settling in her bloodstream as a visceral contact with evil. There is a double disrobing here. Arson strips the revellers down to exposed fiends, and their hideous crime tears away the child's meager defenses against humiliating perdition. It is in keeping with the sexual tension of the scene to say that the sally of fire despoils the girl's virginal notion of peril.

Humanity's acquisition of sexual knowledge and that of good and evil has involved, since primeval times, a tree, the natural sign of fecundity and absolute reality. In "A Circle of Fire," a tree, the stately Georgia pine which O'Connor reveres as the native wood of the cross, physically marks Sally Virginia's new moral understanding. As she presses against the tree to watch, the bark of the pine trunk makes a swollen red and white imprint on the side of her face. First the thorns smarted, and now the rood itself brands Sally Virginia's flesh with the sign of suffering, just as the nun's crucifix embosses the girl's face in "A Temple of the Holy Ghost." The pine tree delivers the sacramental sign of confirmation, the communication of the Spirit. The spectacle waxes shrill and frenetic as the bacchants-turned-Apaches-on-the-warpath "whoop and holler and beat their hands over their mouths and in a few seconds there was a narrow line of fire widening between her and them" (153). The display stupefies the child, who tries to run away but remains stuck by "some new unplaced misery." When she does reach her mother, incredulity disorients the child's alarm. " 'Mama, Mama,' " she mutters, " 'they're going to build a parking lot here!' " (153).

The twist of tongue is the child's last remark. The rest is listening and vision. Sally Virginia hears her mother shriek over the fire she has dreaded, and scream for help; then the woman's face acquires a look the child has never seen before but recognizes as an expression of the "new misery" weighing her down. Though the sorrow is new for Sally Virginia, she can tell that the grief on her mother's face is "old" and "might have belonged to anybody, a Negro or a European or to Powell himself" (154). The features of sorrow do belong to all; the lines come from and go back to the sign of the rood pressed into the heroine's face by the pine bark. On her mother's face, Sally Virginia gazes into the root of the matter: pain under all pains, common woe born of shared sinfulness. Sally Virginia seems to know, among other things, that she is part of the various faces from which she feels estranged and to which she will always be joined. Her spiritual growth lies in applying this new perception of herself in others to the new misery she feels. The composite face that she sees is a human face, scoffed at, blindfolded (Mark 14:65), and marred (Isaiah 52:14); but the face bears the stamp of God (Hebrews 1:3), the image of the good woman and the good man.

The sacramental gift of the heroine's confirmation is suffering. It is not an evil to be avoided; nor is it a disaster imposed by fate. Suffering is demanded by the girl's personal destiny in love. Thorns and pine tree assign her the work of the crucifixion by annealing her flesh with the image of the good woman as guide. The compound face also reveals that strangers and enemies must be included in her suffering for it to have meaning. If suffering turns the sufferer back into herself or himself, as with Powell, then it creates self-pity and hatred and fear. Grace, however, works the other way. It turns useless misery into creative sacrifice.

The concluding sentence of "A Circle of Fire" shows how this conversion can come about for Sally Virginia: "She stood taut, listening, and could just catch in the distance a few wild high shrieks of joy as if the prophets were dancing in the fiery furnace, in the circle the angel had cleared for them." In the biblical story of Daniel alluded to here, God sends a messenger to three imperiled loyal believers to deliver them from the torment that Nebuchadnezzar brings upon those who refuse to worship him as lord. Instead of consuming the three, the fire cleanses and refines them. If one suffers in faith, as do the brave Jews, the fire of tribulation can lead one to God.

This fire smolders unceasingly. O'Connor makes a point at the end of the story to note that the column of smoke rising from inside the treeline widens "unchecked." Mrs. Cope's clamor will not quench it; Sally Virginia's guns will not snuff it out. Having spread from Daniel's Babylon to Mrs. Cope's place, the flame will continue to burst forth wherever the will to conquer subjugates others. The best defense is no defense at all. Trust aided by angelic intervention keeps one unsinged.

Within the boys' fire there glows the divine action that alters the destructive course of their malice, but one must look to charity to find it. If Sally Virginia sees the humiliation of her and her mother as an occasion to experience God's love, then the boys' holocaust will serve as a burnt offering to her spiritual growth. Divine love not only cuts, as we saw with the pine bark, it also comes, as Moses explains to Israel, through a "devouring fire" (Deuteronomy 4:24). This ardor destroys all that is imperfect, all that is self-centered; and it does so already for Sally Virginia by turning her awareness toward the will of God, which commands that she accept her duty to bear the displaced misery of others—Negroes or Europeans or builders of parking lots.

II

The most joyful communion established through suffering for others in *A Good Man Is Hard to Find* arises in "The Artificial Nigger." In this story, grace enriches the lives of the country poor upon their finding the good man on a city outing. Mr. Head takes his grandson, Nelson, to Atlanta for the day. Nelson was born in Atlanta and uses his birthplace to boast of his importance. Such impudence rankles Mr. Head, and so he plans the city trip to teach the boy a few things about authority. Once in Atlanta they get lost. Exhausted, and terrified by the massive confusion, Nelson accidentally knocks down a woman, who screams for justice by threatening Mr. Head. Frightened himself by the specters lurking in the urban maze, Mr. Head denies knowing the accused boy. The old man's betrayal estranges grandson from grandfather. However, as they walk single file toward the train that will return them home, they see a battered statue of a Negro. The plaster figure unites them, and they arrive back in the country reconciled in mutual forgiveness.

The excursion has elicited from critics a number of suggestive analogues for the protagonists' experience. We have expositions of Nelson's rite of passage (Martin 112–16), of Mr. Head's bigotry (Asals 79–92), of their joint reenactment of the fall (Feeley 120–24), and of their descent into hell (Muller 71–75). O'Connor's personal enthusiasm for the story sanctions these and even broader interpretations. She appreciates one reader's observation that Peter's denial seems to underlie Mr. Head's failure in duty (*Letters* 78); on another occasion she courts a rare overt political valuation when describing the statue as "a terrible symbol of what the South has done to itself" (*Letters* 140). Satisfied that her writing meets the formal requirements of the action of the story, she can enjoy with detached pleasure meanings others find that she does not understand (*Letters* 140). "I suppose," she remarks to "*A.*," " 'The Artificial Nigger' is my favorite" (*Letters* 101). Others can do the musing. Where O'Connor does spell out an intention, her definite view places all possible readings under the authoritative example of the good man. "What I had in mind to suggest with the artificial nigger," she states to Ben Griffith, "was the redemptive quality of the Negro's suffering for us all" (*Letters* 78). Through this agony flows the "apparent action of grace" (*Letters* 160) that changes Mr. Head and Nelson.

The intrusion of God's favor by means of the statue has been anything but apparent to many readers. Critical consensus translates the figure into the opposite, finding it the instrument of punishment. One scholar reviews the critical reception of "The Artificial Nigger" to show how far astray the assertions of imprisonment and ironic salvation have taken us from O'Connor's stated understanding (Napier 87–92). The attitudes generating the quarrel are instructive, however, because they reveal a great deal about the resistance O'Connor's art meets, and because they point to the precise signals in the story that are evident to O'Connor but equivocal to the audience.

Since the ending of the story does not rush the reader to the barricades of civil protest, the social activist will be disappointed with this version of the South's tragedy. Even the reader with larger moral interests is left pondering how the statue acquires its saving purpose when all we have is a quiet homecoming to an all-white backwoods. Were the story political, the question would be superfluous, since the urgency of reform is built into the stereotyped figures of oppressed black and onerous white. O'Connor, however, is not one for ready-made liberalism. Meaning for her comes through what is shown, and she then goes after a significance beyond sociology and psychology. Asals is sensitive to her aim, yet still has reservations about the outcome of the story: "What after all have the Heads really learned by the end of 'The Artificial Nigger'? How have their attitudes toward blacks been altered?" (91).

If we require a political answer, we will miss the story's depth, which *radical* in its political denotation cannot touch. The root of Mr. Head's change is O'Connor's source of human dignity, the cross. Mr. Head's recognition of the need for sharing in the pain and mercy of other persons alters more than a racial attitude. It transforms his view of himself, others, and God. The result unites Mr. Head, Nelson, and the artificial nigger into a single invisible body. A writer with a theological turn of mind not only takes shortcuts through social history but reverses the direction of analysis. To the historian, injustice, bigotry, and anguish all cause human psychological disorder. To O'Connor the spiritual writer, however, racism is not the cause but the result of an inner disruption. Human exploitation is another manifestation of the spirit's refusal to know itself and to accept its own suffering. Racism, seen by this light, is a disease of the soul that spreads out into human affairs and the body politic. What seems to gratify O'Connor is how "The Artificial Nigger" forces her special kind of spiritual inquiry through a burning political surface into the fallen center of the human condition.

The sore point between sixty-year-old Mr. Head and ten-year-old Nelson is their need for each other. After his wife dies and his daughter runs away only to return with Nelson before she herself dies, Mr. Head becomes the sole parent of one-year-old Nelson. He raises the boy to be independent and strong-willed, attributes that make the hard job of raising a young grandson easier. Mr. Head succeeds so well, however, that Nelson becomes a feisty competitor. They clash to preserve their valued independence. Atlanta is a ruse. The distant city allows them to assert their particular authority in advance without upsetting the balance of domestic caretaking that they strike with each other. They can argue about Atlanta and remain vulnerable in the daily ways that count. On the day they see the real Atlanta, old man and young boy see the rare gift of love they take for granted in the hills.

The story provides early signs of the journey's importance. O'Connor compares Mr. Head to Vergil going to Dante, "or better, Raphael, awakened by a blast of God's light to fly to the side of Tobias" (103). Raphael, whose name means "God heals" in Hebrew, signifies Mr. Head's sense of his moral guidance of Nelson through the strange city. As things turn out, the old man's humiliation does instruct the boy, but only after the healing angel removes the film of self-sufficiency from the eyes of both. Angelic intervention comes in the nick of time. Rivalry is wearing the two males down to reflections of each other's willfulness, looking like brothers "and brothers not too far apart in age" (105). From the moment they awaken, they battle. Nelson has corn pone cooking and meat fried before his grandfather rises at 2:00 in the morning. As they eat breakfast, each stares at "a fiercely expressionless face" (105) that does not budge.

Racism emerges not out of any direct contact with blacks but rather out of this unexpressed challenge. Since the boy has a head start on the day, the man recovers his control by asserting the one bit of knowledge he has about their destination. Atlanta will not please Nelson, Mr. Head declares, because " 'It'll be full of niggers' " (105). Since blacks were run out of Mr. Head's county twelve years ago, Nelson has never seen a black person. *Nigger* for the boy means the power Mr. Head holds over him that the boy must overcome. What Nelson hates is his own weakness. He calls that shadow self *nigger*. Hating the shadow permits him to ignore the actual peril of susceptibility. Racism works the same way for the old man. The boy's brashness and the natural self-doubt that a rural man feels about the big city can be put aside by having a *nigger* on whom he can heap all his fear and denial. The word *nigger* justifies a meanness that Mr. Head would judge inconsistent with "that calm understanding of life that makes him a suitable guide for the young" (102).

On the train, Mr. Head manages to allay his apprehension about Atlanta. He uses Nelson in the same way that he uses the shadow of the black person. " 'He's never seen anything before,' " the old guide announces across the aisle to a bleary-eyed stranger. " 'Ignorant as the day he was born, but I mean for him to get his fill once and for all' " (108). When a black man escorts two women down the coach, Mr. Head basks in expertise with the quiz, " 'What was that?' " Nelson sees the man as the man he is, apart from racist projection; but innocence cannot withstand shame. Mr. Head advertises to the sleepy stranger across the way that Nelson missed " 'his first nigger' " (110). Feeling it a blow to appear green before Mr. Head, Nelson finds an object outside himself to concretize his pain: "He felt that the Negro had deliberately walked down the aisle in order to make a fool of him and he hated him with a fierce raw fresh hate" (110–11). Cruelty, the mask of weakness, curtains responsibility. The guilt Nelson incurs from ill will dissolves in his false accusation of the black passerby. Now the black person owes Nelson something for making a fool of him. Ego defense institutionalizes racism.

The dining car brings out the intimidation that the country pair try to conceal. Mr. Head decides to show Nelson the kitchen, but a black waiter stops him. To save face before the black man's rebuff, Mr. Head shouts out that cockroaches would keep him out anyway. Such quick wit before sudden rebuke impresses Nelson, who feels that he will need that ready protection against the prohibitions of Atlanta. As they approach the city, Nelson appreciates that he "would be entirely alone in the world if he were ever lost from his grandfather" (112). Neediness is that part of Nelson that will not be lied to; it speaks to him now about his love for the old man. From this openness in the boy rushes an impulse to seize the man's coat. The boy unfortunately holds back. He loves but has no way to show it. The price he pays for not acknowledging Mr. Head's indispensability is loss of the comfort he needs.

In town the bedeviling fear of getting lost comes true. The emotional impact goes deep because *lost* in "The Artificial Nigger" is more than a hillbilly's paralysis in a department-store maze, more than forfeiting a lifelong reputation of competence in the backwoods. At stake is a basic security. Direction involves the heart's inclination between grandparent and grandchild. The biblical source for Dante's journey suggests how we are to take their being lost in Atlanta. Those who leave the straight path "walk in the ways of darkness," runs Proverbs 2:13–14, and they "rejoice in doing evil and delight in the perverseness of evil."

Many signs indicate that Mr. Head and Nelson move in Dante's eschatological footsteps in *The Divine Comedy*. The concrete dome of the railroad terminal, like the sun in Dante's purgatorial climb, holds the geographical center of the city trip. It points homeward. Before O'Connor's Vergil brings his charge to any purgatorial zone, however, he loses the focus by turning "to the left" (115) and left and left again until the suitable guide for the young misguides the youth committed to his care. Left (*sinistra*) is Dante's sinister way in the *Inferno;* as the two wander, the landscape confirms a hellish detour by growing treacherous. The strange woman indigenous to the underworld presses the allure of the region on the gullible young visitor. As Dante negotiates hell in circles, so O'Connor's wayfarers proceed through Atlanta in circles. For them the circular passage traces anew their old feud. As grandfather and grandson sink lower, their competition sharpens until they live out the dire prediction of Wisdom in Proverbs that those who stray from the commandment to love will take pleasure in evil. Mr. Head and Nelson come to enjoy malice when each strikes at the other's weakness with satanic precision. " 'This is where I came from!' " (115) taunts Nelson. With rancor equal to the attack on his authority, Mr. Head shoves the boy's head into a sewer; and the old codger once more transfers his fear of the city onto the boy, now imposed through images of rats and pitch-black tunnels. Having learned that accusation overcomes terror, the frightened boy shifts blame back onto his guide: " 'I don't believe you know where you're at!' " (116). When a black man appears, the boy's newfound racism provides a self-congratulation merely by pointing to " 'Niggers' " (117). More versed in racial hatred, Mr. Head can momentarily gain the upper hand by turning the boast into sarcastic pleasure: " 'Anybody wants to be from this nigger heaven can be from it!' " (118).

Their delight in hurting each other culminates when Nelson dazedly runs down an elderly woman. Other women mill around to be sure that justice is done. The old woman on the pavement screams that Nelson's " 'daddy'll pay' " (122) for her broken ankle. At her shout for the police, Mr. Head reluctantly edges forward from his hiding place, where he startled Nelson into dashing out in the first place. Terror of the litigious females triggers Nelson's need for paternal aid, and so he clings to his grandfather's hip. The old man's inner demon, however, has a tighter grip on him. Afraid of city police and trapped by avenging furies, Mr. Head refuses to pay what he owes his grandchild: " 'This is not my boy,' he said. 'I never seen him before' " (123).

When panic strikes, Wisdom cautions, "calamity comes like a whirlwind" (Proverbs 1:27). The tumult bears retribution, for "they shall eat the fruit of their way" (Proverbs 1:31). Accordingly, the arrogant must swallow their pride and taste humility. O'Connor's action is true to its biblical inspiration. Vainglorious Mr. Head becomes abased;

stubborn Nelson bends. Having lunged headlong at each other for so long, they now in a strange city get back what they gave out. Nelson repays Mr. Head's betrayal by staring through him, denying his presence, disdaining an offer of water to ease his thirst. Pride speaks to pride. The atmosphere chills as the whirlwind buffets both in the gnawing cold generated by their mutual scorn. Nelson's mind freezes "around his grandfather's treachery" (125). Then the cityscape becomes the heroes' mindscape. They wander into a grand suburb where mansion after mansion appears "like partially submerged icebergs" (126) and where sidewalks vanish. For guidance, they have only driveways spinning "endless ridiculous circles" (126) that torment the protagonists with evidence that the terminal dome is irretrievably out of sight.

Meteorology confirms the sojourners' feeling that they have fallen into the abyss. The affluent suburb duplicates the climate in the pit of Dante's hell, the origin of sin where Satan is locked in ice at the farthest remove from God's warming love. The chill of the large white houses invades the countrymen. Mr. Head realizes in his bones what Dante means in warning those entering hell to abandon all hope. When the love of his grandson whom he loves and has raised turns into hate, Mr. Head has "lost all hope" of the filial respect that makes old age endurable. The boy's eyes "piercing into his back like pitchfork prongs" (124) subject the old man to the classic sentence upon the damned. The falling afternoon light gives him the "ravaged and abandoned" (125) look of a Dantesque shade. In this suburb of punished pride, the bitter cold seems impervious to thaw. Not even Mr. Head's cry of dereliction ("'Oh Gawd I'm lost! Oh hep me Gawd I'm lost!'") melts the boy's icy retaliation. Nelson's eyes remain "triumphantly cold" (126), witnessing his guardian's utter humiliation. Both suffer intensely and without relief, for where the devil rules, pain freezes to stone in one's heart. Pride is its own punishment.

"The Artificial Nigger" lingers in Dante's inferno, but it also moves swiftly on to his purgatory and paradise, the realms that complete Dante's wondrous structure and that fulfill the mystery of O'Connor's presentation of God's plan. For O'Connor, affliction itself holds the way out of punishment to deliverance. By observing the physical posture of Mr. Head and Nelson, we can see how O'Connor embeds grief and expiation in one condition. The necks of both males bend forward to nearly the same degree; their shoulders arch to an identical curve. Something seems to weigh on both grandfather and grandson. Their unseen burden recalls the heavy stone of self-elation pressing down on the proud in Dante's *Purgatorio.* Atonement of pride involves bowing down to see examples of the submission they have lacked.

An abased state also prepares Mr. Head and Nelson to value humility when they see a lawn statue about Nelson's size sitting bent over on a brick fence. Drawing on the charm of plantation revival art, the designer meant to depict a carefree, grinning Negro savoring a watermelon slice; but chance has marked the statue with a chipped eye that throws off "a wild look of misery" (127) as the entire sculpture hovers on the verge of toppling over. This sentimental decoration, twisted into a bogeyman, puts the fear of God into the lost heroes. Whether vandals or the elements have deformed the work, the ruined form appeals to the old man and boy for aid and moral understanding. They know the need expressed by the statue's look of desolation, for their own tilted bodies send out the same mute cry for help. Sorrow twists all three human forms out of shape, chisels away differences in race and age to make one timeless figure of hardship. Adversity forges a bond that contentment persistently strains. The chastened white man and boy see their need for rescue in the artificial version of the black person they help to oppress. Mr. Head and Nelson must be saved from their idea of being superior, of being good men. The good man is before their eyes. The unrestrained misery on his face points the way to goodness by exposing the wounds received from their displaced suffering and that of untold others. The action of grace in the heroes' lives, in their humbled condition, brings them to experience the guilt they have repressed. Such is the way of retribution embodied in the good man.

The Atlanta trip does not end with mere hints of repentance. Mr. Head's contrition comes with Lear's intensity—a flourish that is rare in a collection of stories that usually leaves to the imagination the effect of the truth gained by the various searchers for the good man. Mr. Head sees for the first time in himself the corruption he has attributed to the outside world. Innocence lost in old age goes with a searing blast. The fire that King Lear summons to purify nature of unkindness rages in Mr. Head. The flame cracks the mold of his temperament and leaves him with no sense of entitlement. Back at the railroad junction, Mr. Head regards his safe return as an undeserved lenity. It is. Pierced by compunction about what has happened, the old man "burned with shame" that he could bring his Maker at death so little humility. A penitent heart enables him to withstand the circle of healing fire that has spread from Mrs. Cope's place to a nameless railroad intersection: "He stood appalled, judging himself with the thoroughness of God, while the action of mercy covered his pride like a flame and consumed it." Cauterized of pretense to virtue, Mr. Head can bear with great gladness the knowledge of "his true depravity" (129).

Even the postponement until sixty is a blessing. Only in dotage can Lear, who knows the anguish of betraying a loved child, accept love; only at sixty can Mr. Head take to heart the gift of mercy. Mr. Head's acceptance of grace arises from gratitude, and extends in a startling way. Grace alters his understanding of the pain of being lost. His agony, he knows, goes deeper than the city's sewer system; it goes beyond Nelson's arrogance and even his own pride. Suffering is part of the saving plan that guided him to safety, and he participates in the plan by emulating the good man. With God's aid "no sin was too monstrous for him to claim as his own." Mr. Head goes so far as to acknowledge having "conceived in his own heart the sin of Adam." Forgiven now, he can admit betraying his child. Forgiving, he can win the boy's trust. Through quiet contact with "poor" Nelson, the mercy given to Mr. Head becomes homage rendered to God, Who "from the beginning of time" paid Mr. Head's debt. Mr. Head will repay his portion by suffering for sins he did not commit. The image of sage-guide transforms into that of submissive servant—the good man's reflection. The hell of Atlanta behind him and the purgatorial fire of the railroad junction fortifying him, Mr. Head feels "ready at that instant to enter Paradise" (129).

The auspicious end of this perilous journey is in the air from the beginning. When Mr. Head awakens at 2:00 A.M. for an early departure, moonlight fills his bedroom and carpets the floorboards with silver. Everything glows with a "dignifying light" of nobility. From Mr. Head's shaving mirror, the moon seems poised "as if it were waiting for his permission to enter"; yet for all its courtesy, the lunar face is "grave" (102). Before the old man invites the moon into his house, the moon patiently accompanies him and his grandson during the day to Atlanta. The moon, of course, illumines the night when the sun does not shine. It is the guiding influence in darkness, the night guidance Mr. Head needs to make his way through his sinfulness. The influence seeing the two wanderers through their moral darkness in Atlanta is not the terminal dome; nor is it the sun. The governing power is God's will. Though providence controls with lordly forbearance, the stern aspect of the moon notifies the travelers that they will have to rise to the occasion of His command.

When Mr. Head feels his safe return to be miraculous, gratitude grants God a way into his heart. Everything changes. Praise calls forth thanksgiving throughout creation, and the moon springs from a cloud and floods the clearing with light. The moon rolls out a silver carpet of reunion as Mr. Head and Nelson detrain at the junction. The moon itself is restored "to its full splendor" (128), welcoming the conversion in Mr. Head. Moon, sage grass shivering in shades of silver, gigantic white clouds: all these details of nature compose a living doxology that attends the royal entry of the Spirit into Mr. Head's life. The hidden—as the moon is hidden during the day—but formative control over the old man's life shines fully. Mr. Head's one-day exilic wandering can be seen in this light as a preparation for a return home. Home is the new temple housing the royal caller, the Spirit's most welcome guest.

The story does not bring Mr. Head to his home but leaves him in the powerful state of anticipation. Before he can reach home, he must go all the way back to where the human story begins. O'Connor at the end remands him and Nelson to within the protecting "walls of a garden" (128) formed by the treetops at the railroad junction. The train coils past them "like a frightened serpent" (129) and vanishes. The garden bears the features of two opposite states of consciousness. It is Eden where sin is discovered, and it is Gethsemane where sin is overcome. A habit of being emerges from each habitat. Adam is the first sinful person, and he tries to repudiate guilt by hiding from God and covering himself up out of shame. Gethsemane reverses the impulse to escape guilt. Jesus is the first sinless man, and He takes for His own the guilt of all sin. He is the first person to expose His spirit to the glare of God's light. At the junction, Mr. Head gains the knowledge of Eden and the promise of Gethsemane. He is brought to the garden at the time he accepts his sinfulness. The proud grandfather sees that the disobedience of the grandparent of sin is his own disobedience. Mr. Head stands exposed to himself, to Nelson, and to his Maker. Uncovered, he stands in dignity "ready at that instant to enter Paradise" (129). Such is the humility he finds in old age that he considers himself a nonentity. Such is the obedience he gains that God gives Mr. Head the grace to drive the train away like a frightened demon.

In O'Connor's art the joyous aspect is usually the implicit one. The final tableau of "The Artificial Nigger" presages in its explicitness more than the usual joy of entering God's purpose for creation. The boasting is gone from Mr. Head and Nelson. Their mouths quiver. When they were lost, both were glib. When they recover their moral direction, they say but a few words, and these words are to make amends for past injuries. Nelson's face brightens beneath his hard-hat brim. " 'I'm glad I've went once, but I'll never go back again!' " he declares. So go the final words of the story. Harangue ends in quiet. The pair's agony has been as acute as that of the protagonists of the other stories in *A Good Man Is Hard to Find*, but the physical maiming and death that underscore the endings of the other stories are absent here.

The mercy that touches Mr. Head also tempers the ending. Grandfather and grandson are in sorrow, but not as orphans or victims. The poetry of O'Connor's ideas endows the Atlanta trip with the depth of eternal experience. In this profound moment, Mr. Head and Nelson stand still, balanced in their momentary victory over the fleeing serpent. They share the happy conviction that they are on the way home. For O'Connor, their intimate communication in the garden is a hieroglyph of the good man's submission that opens a way into the life of faith.

Mr. Head may come late in life to acknowledge his share in the suffering of others, but in opening himself up to mercy at sixty he is precocious next to General Sash. George Poker Sash-turned-General Tennessee Flintrock Sash of the Confederacy (Tate 99) takes longer than all the other characters in *A Good Man Is Hard to Find* to grow up. He is 104 years old, and it is not until he is struck dead that he feels the presence of anyone beyond himself. After more than a century of stalemate, General Sash is pulled into "A Late Encounter with the Enemy."

"Late" understates the General's resistance to any encroachment on his life. If the "way to despair" for O'Connor "is to refuse to have any kind of experience" (*Mystery and Manners* 78), then General Sash shows what life is like at the end of the line. He is twenty-five times older than Harry Ashfield of "The River" and far less mature and venturesome. At four or five, Harry wants to count, and plunges into the river to find the source of counting. General Sash, on the other hand, pouts in his wheelchair—a baby hitting his high chair with a spoon to demand attention. " 'God damm every goddam thing to hell,' " he drones (163). Dejection has so molded his nature that the rhythm of his curses matches the beat of his heart. By denouncing life General Sash reduces the possibilities of grace. In the life of the spirit, grace rather than years determines growth, and grace is another opponent the old soldier has been fending off.

Like all children, General Sash believes that the world revolves around him. History has no meaning, even though his imagined identity as superior military officer derives from the past. His dead children, though he fathered them, do not matter. His wife is totally forgotten. The living are no different from the other dead. Sally Poker Sash, the granddaughter upon whom he depends, is an adjunct to his grandiosity. The one pleasure left for General Sash is playing General Sash, sitting on any stage in full Confederate regalia and being his "very handsome" (156) self before an audience. His first taste of being a public spectacle came when he was ninety-two. Mr. Govisky of Hollywood decked him out in fancy army clothes for a movie premiere in Atlanta. " 'It was,' " the General is quick to declare, " 'a nashnul event and they had me in it—up onto the stage' " (157). Until the publicity stunt, he was just another Civil War veteran and most likely a foot soldier; after Mr. Govisky, he is a general. Two beautiful Hollywood girls complete the remembered picture of General Sash's great moment.

The old veteran fights to remain in that moment. He preserves the victory by lending himself out as a display property for parades. The General aspires to the fossilized permanence of the mummy in *Wise Blood* that Enoch Emery trots out to entertain the Taulkinham public. Immortality in a cage satisfies the old man. There, life amounts to death, unchanging and limited to the self: "Living had got to be such a habit with him that he couldn't conceive of any other condition" (155). Like people, time is an extension of Sash's ancient childish ego. One is never too old to sin, and to think of the human world with limits is to replace God with self. General Sash, O'Connor's oldest hero, commits the oldest sin of all by believing himself to be the source of life. His 104 years on earth, then, have two implications. They suggest the primeval nature of his guilt, and they point up how long spiritual immaturity can linger.

General Sash's armor falls at the August graduation exercises of Sally Poker Sash. Sally finished normal school many years ago and has been a schoolteacher ever since, but when the state changed its standards to require a college degree, Sally was forced back to school. True to the Sash family style, she expresses her irritation with the regulation by taking her own sweet time. After twenty summer sessions at the state teacher's college, she fulfills the requirements for a degree. Sash that she is, she sweetens her revenge against the impositions on her will by arranging to have her grandfather, the Southern General *par excellence,* on the platform to show *"them"* (156) what she stood for that ought never to change. Her imagination works out the rebuke: " 'See him! See him! My kin, all you upstarts! Glorious upright old man standing for the old traditions! Dignity! Honor! Courage!' " At sixty-two, a few years before retirement, Sally achieves the double victory of graduating from college and giving the newfangled world a piece of her mind for unsettling "the ways of decent living" (156).

No one deserves the honor of representing the past more than does General Sash, and the stage is the right battleground for his last stand. Theater has given him rank and identity. The past, however, is more complicated than his brave gray costume suggests. Story for O'Connor unfolds in depth as well as in time, and it gathers richness beyond personal conflicts in a universal drama. "Behind our own history," she remarks in her lecture on the regional writer, "deepening it at every point, has been another history" (*Mystery and Manners* 59). Even the ludicrous anecdote of the Sash family impinges on this sacred history.

O'Connor's title locates the story's essential history in chapter 15 of Paul's first letter to the Corinthians. The subject is the resurrection through Christ. To explore the mystery, Paul evolves a procession of glory, with the resurrection as the crowning event: "But each in his own order: Christ the first fruits, then at his coming those who belong to Christ" (15:23). Before Christ brings the elect to His glory, He reveals His mission by putting "all his enemies under his feet" (15:25). The final fruit of the resurrection will be made known by the perfect triumph of Christ over humanity's enemies. Through Christ's risen life, humanity gains victory over sin, Satan, and death: "The last enemy to be destroyed is death" (15:26).

General Sash in his own order will take his place in Paul's triumphal ascendancy. A private commencement exercise within Sally's public graduation ceremony marks the old man's entrance into the sacred pageant of history. The proceedings begin with academic pomp. A strong sun brightens the occasion; the General sits hatless in the heat, waiting to be wheeled indoors to his special place on stage. The tide of graduates and faculty in heavy black robes marches into the auditorium. As the heat sweats out the "last beads of ignorance" from the graduates, the sun bores through the last barricade of the General's spiritual resistance. He feels "a little hole beginning to widen in the top of his head" (164) while a young relative whisks him into the building. The sun conquers the General. The past, for which he had no use, comes back

to him through the hole in his head. When the commencement speaker
utters the requisite salute to the old days—"Chickamauga, Shiloh,
Johnston, Lee" (166)—the words from years ago bombard him "like
musket fire" (167). The flintlock ignites dark places in the General's
brain, and this time he cannot escape experience. The enemy stalks him
fully armed. As the expansive graduation music swells, his entire past
opens. Repressed memories pour over General Sash, causing the same
anguish Mr. Head feels when his betrayal strips him of his moral rank
over Nelson. Permeated with "sharp stabs of pain" (167), General Sash
collapses.

Agony clears his sight. From within the black ceremonial flow of
graduates, there emerges a succession of phantoms who "had been
dogging all his days" (167). The mortal enemies turn out to be his
closest kin, whose accusatory expressions summon up moral obligations still unanswered. His wife's narrow face stares at him critically;
one of his bald-headed sons squints as though still straining to find his
neglectful father; and his mother runs to him with a look of anxiety. In
the conflict between responsibility and detachment, the General did not
pass muster. Involvements mean pain; like Hazel Motes, General Sash
spends most of his life trying to avoid suffering, and succeeds in making
others suffer. Central Casting offers a momentary reprieve through
cinematic identity, but finally symbolic derring-do yields to actual
duty. The truth Hazel Motes learns is that living costs and avoidance
increases pain. The lesson applies equally to General Sash. As the
graduates cross the stage to receive their scrolls and to shake the college
president's hand, General Sash clenches his sword on his lap "until the
blade touched bone" (167). The sword is the old man's scroll, a roster
of experiences refused and compassion owed.

O'Connor prepares for General Sash's fortunate defeat through a
gradual disclosure of his opponent. At the beginning of the story,
"enemy" means death. As Sash's family history unfolds, "enemy" becomes
synonymous with "everyone" and "every place." The more O'Connor
goes into the General's mind, the more we see his stance of denigration
that conceives of the world as contained within his dejection. Such
egoism excludes creation and its Maker. General Sash comes through
not just as cowardly and ungodly, but as an enemy of God. Those who
reject love are "enemies of God" (Romans 11:28), and in rejecting his
family Sash aligns himself with these hostile forces. Besides scorning
his family, he appropriates creation for himself; in doing so, the old

man stands against the Kingdom. His ultimate enemy is God. This kind of enmity lies in Sash's willful estrangement from his Maker. For the sinful person, one who relies entirely upon herself or himself, God has become an enemy (Romans 5:10).

O'Connor's eye for anatomical detail makes it clear that the General has no chance against his foe. His mind may be unable to conceive of its own extinction, but his "feet were completely dead" (161). The power Sash thinks he has to put his enemy under his foot belongs to God, Whose might is being felt. Sash's subjection turns out to be the action of grace. As pain brings awareness, defeat brings hope. "For God has consigned all men to disobedience," Paul recognizes, "that he may have mercy upon all" (Romans 11:32). Sash confronts his disobedience in the faces of betrayed family members, rushing at him "as if the past were the only future now and he had to endure it" (167). In this array of faces, Sash finds the image of the good man Who holds the mercy that will allow the General to endure the future. At long last, the lonely and depleted 104-year-old veteran is taken into companionship with God.

Despite General Sash's obstinacy, the outcome of his late encounter with the enemy, like that of similar encounters in *A Good Man Is Hard to Find,* is on the side of ultimate union. The river lifts Harry Ashfield out of his fear. Mercy consumes Mr. Head's shame. The black procession carries General Sash to life. When the ceremony ends, Sally Poker Sash goes out in the sun again to wait for the honored General. Sally's B.S. in elementary education lifts her spirits one degree higher. In the meantime, John Wesley, the young relative in charge of wheeling the General around, speeds him out the back door to get a drink. As John Wesley bounces the corpse to the Coca-Cola machine by the side of the auditorium, Sash in death sits "fixed and fierce" with "his eyes wide open" (167) on the mystery overtaking him. The old trooper, like Sally, receives a degree in elementary education. He is schooled in guilt, suffering, and mercy. This new knowledge accompanies Sash out of his shadowed night into the vivid August sun, herald of the light to come.

III

O'Connor's first suite of short stories comes to a close with "The Displaced Person." The story tells about a man worthy of God who comes to live among a group of Georgia farm people. With his hands he immediately improves things, and by his presence he eventually unmakes the place. The changes occur, as they do in *Wise Blood,* in the aftermath of World War II, which lurks behind O'Connor's fiction as the historic passion of our time.

Mr. Guizac, his wife, and their two children escape from the Nazi occupation of Poland, and arrive in America to work for Mrs. McIntyre. Mr. Guizac is a master mechanic whose skill revives a marginal operation. The old silage machine runs as never before; a new drag harrow and a tractor with a power lift hum for the first time. The Pole's work delights Mrs. McIntyre but threatens the other hands. Mrs. Shortley, the wife of the hired hand, quits the farm one early morning with her family to protect her husband from dismissal. While departing, Mrs. Shortley dies of a stroke.

Without the Shortleys, the place thrives. Mrs. McIntyre basks in new prosperity until she discovers that Mr. Guizac has arranged a marriage between his sixteen-year-old Polish cousin, who has been detained in a refugee camp for three years, and the young black employee, Sulk. Not even profit overrides Mrs. McIntyre's racial convictions. Since it is better to do oneself in than to be a party to miscegenation, she decides to get rid of the Pole. She is spared dismissing him by Mr. Shortley's timely return to do her dirty work. Mr. Shortley kills Mr. Guizac. Bloodguilt stains the soil. Mr. Shortley sneaks off that evening. The blacks follow suit. Mrs. McIntyre becomes bedridden with neurological disease. The cows are auctioned off. The place goes to pieces. The old priest who brought the Guizac family over for a new life visits Mrs. McIntyre once a week. And a lone peacock, surviving with two peahens from a group of twenty or thirty fowl, continues to parade around the premises. The king of the birds prevails.

The metamorphosis accomplished by Mr. Guizac's arrival and execution provides a coda to *A Good Man Is Hard to Find* by bringing the good man into full view and then rounding out the consequences of the dejection and the compunction provoked by his presence. The first of the three sections shaping "The Displaced Person" shows the fate of a hardened will. The example is that of Mrs. Shortley, who responds to distress by clinging to her own strength as though all that is possible for her comes through herself. The story opens with Mrs. Shortley ascending a hill like a giantess in defense of her terrain. She rises "with the grand self-confidence of a mountain" (197) to survey the potential danger in the arrival of the Displaced Person from Europe. Arms folded, the massive but frightened woman lays claim to the prominence, oblivious to a white sun drifting behind a ragged cloud and to the peacock following her. When she reaches the hilltop, the peacock stops to elevate his tail. He pulls his neck backwards as if to focus on something far off which only he sees. Jeopardy so encases Mrs. Shortley that she remains unaffected by even the conspicuous appeal in the white sun, the ragged cloud, and the bird. Even if one reserves judgment on Mrs. Shortley's insentience to the theophany in scenic beauty, one senses foreboding in her apathy to nature's plain loveliness.

Peril there is in the woman's short sight. Only fear awes Mrs. Shortley, and it is people least given to harm who most elicit her dread. An unassuming priest of more than eighty years, who escorts the immigrant family, enters her field of vision as an insect, "black-suited" and "long-legged" (198). When Mr. Guizac bows with European formality and greets Mrs. McIntyre by kissing her hand, Mrs. Shortley jerks back her hand as though stung by venom. The Pole is exposed to the basic hardships of exile—he is homeless, unable to speak English, bereft of possessions, and responsible for the support of a wife, son, and daughter. His vulnerability does not reach Mrs. Shortley; the danger he represents, however, does. The Pole is the Displaced Person, a subhuman category in which she projects her many resentments. Her grudges settle on Mr. Guizac as a predator would descend on the nearest prey. Cast-off furniture and feed sacks that Mrs. McIntyre scrapes together for the shack where the Polish family will live make Mrs. Shortley feel cheated. More for others means less for her, and she wants everything she can get. Greed prompts her to see the new people as devious interlopers. Bitterness requires that the foreigners' gentility be seen as a pathogenic carrier of contagion infecting America with Europe's unreformed religion. That the newcomers are victims of persecution who are deserving of hospitality does not enter Mrs. Shortley's conscience; instead she injures them anew, continuing the oppression the Nazis began.

Despondency expresses itself through defilement. Repeated interiorly all day long, detraction becomes for Mrs. Shortley as spontaneous as breathing. She descends from her elevation to scrutinize the Poles "the way a buzzard glides and drops in the air until it alights on the carcass" (201). Her instinct reduces any creature to worthless remains for her picking. In her imagination, the big-nosed priest becomes embroiled with the Guizacs in a newsreel clip of mangled corpses at a death camp. After the old priest admires the " 'beauti-ful birdrrrd' " unfolding his " 'tail full of suns,' " Mrs. Shortley depreciates his delight, scorns the peacock as " 'Nothing but a peachicken' " (202), and discards the bird of glory onto the spoils of her exterminating will.

The fanatical need to project her own evil onto some enemy is disquieting evidence of Mrs. Shortley's humiliation. Besides having to conceal her own malice, she has the shiftlessness of her husband, Chancey, to fob off as virtuous industry. Attentive to neighborly decorum, she wants everyone to know that Chancey is not available to meet the new people because " 'He don't have time to rest himself in the bushes like them niggers over there' " (201). Accusing Astor and Sulk of idleness deflects attention from Chancey, who probably can be found polluting milk by taking his cigarette break in the dairy barn. He may as well neglect his dairy work since he takes his real job to be making whiskey in a remote corner of the farm. Though Big Belly, as the blacks call Mrs. Shortley among themselves, complains about Astor and Sulk behind their back, in their presence she turns solicitous to recruit allies against the Polish menace. She repeats Mrs. McIntyre's warning that the Pole will put " 'the Fear of the Lord into those shiftless niggers!' " (204). Big Belly of course will stand up for her country and for Negroes against "Gobblehooks" (199) sent over from "the devil's experiment station" (212).

Mrs. Shortley establishes a bond with Mrs. McIntyre on their shared feeling of deprivation. People poach on Mrs. Shortley's dignity; the help swipe Mrs. McIntyre's property, the basis of her esteem. For over thirty years a series of white trash and blacks have stolen from Mrs. McIntyre, draining her dry. Within three weeks, however, Mr. Guizac's dedicated energy strains the confidence between the two women by taking away the main reason for Mrs. McIntyre's discontent. Mrs. McIntyre has the decency to be grateful, the capacity to feel pleasure. " 'That man is my salvation!' " (209), she says brightly to Mrs. Shortley. Without bellyaches to keep her close to the proprietress, Mrs. Shortley feels alone. She begins with a slow burn over Mrs. McIntyre's indifference to Chancey's three years of service and erupts into paranoia when Mr. Guizac discovers Chancey's still.

The more the place flourishes, the more desperate Mrs. Shortley becomes that the Pole is replacing her in Mrs. McIntyre's favor. To protect herself Mrs. Shortley intensifies her projections of blame. Instead of feeling through the situation, Mrs. Shortley as a good Christian turns to the Bible for help; but living life through scripture rather than approaching God through life exaggerates the woman's terror. Now her offhanded caution to Mrs. McIntyre to be wary of the devil who brings good fortune becomes reality. Mr. Guizac is the Whore of Babylon. The Apocalypse and the prophets yield messages that Mrs. Shortley needs, sending back up-to-date scriptural versions of the newsreels showing the wicked nations being butchered. She reads scripture as she views the sun and the peacock, imposing her dread on Book and creation alike. The sky of her mind sends back the promise to get even with the Guizacs, children of wicked nations.

The desire to oppress is Mrs. Shortley's self-destruction. To avoid the indignity of being fired like white trash so that Mrs. McIntyre can increase Mr. Guizac's wages, Mrs. Shortley packs her family and goods to escape. The trip goes beyond her expectation. She passes through the gate of the farm into a vision resembling spinning planets in the peacock's tail. Heat swells Mrs. Shortley's body; her heart stops; a spasm twists her body in agonizing death. When the violent thrashing subsides, however, her "fierce expression" relaxes into "a look of astonishment." One eye draws inward as the massive corpse rolls against the car seat. In death her power of sight does not project a world, but receives the real one in depth. With new eyes as clear as glass, Mrs. Shortley "seemed to contemplate for the first time the tremendous frontiers of her true country" (223). Vehement animosity brings Mrs. Shortley to find the good man when he arrives; at the end, his disruptive presence proves to be her deliverance, for Mr. Guizac opens the gate for her entrance into a secure home.[1]

Though Mrs. Shortley's fate troubles readers with ambiguity, O'Connor's description shows that justice probes Mrs. Shortley at the last moment to initiate a hurried purgation. Her apoplectic disfigurement is payment for the heap of massacred bodies she assembles of Poles, priests, and other foreigners. God's will to remove the defilements caused by her will is also imprinted in her attitude. The radical uprooting of the Guizacs, for which she feels no sympathy, expresses the condition that finally commends her to mercy. As she covets scraps of goods as though they confer distinction, she becomes "displaced in the world from all that belonged to her," and the experience is "great" (223). Displacement, she learns, results from suffering. It does not, as she fears, cause pain. With this corporeal reception of knowledge, the act of repatriation to her true country brings a resettlement of guilt to its rightful claimant—Mrs. Shortley herself.

It makes sense that Mrs. Shortley's urgent grief elicits a saving response. With her biblical rantings, preoccupation with evil, desire for justice and dignity, wandering, loneliness, and sinfulness, Mrs. Shortley has been living on the borderline of the divine all along. Contemplating its frontier amounts to being aware of what is always true of human life but with an awareness corrected by charity. O'Connor puts this truth before the reader's eye in the dawn marking Mrs. Shortley's death: "A dark yellow sun was beginning to rise in a sky that was the same slick dark gray as the highway" (222). The human path darkened by sin's gloom passes not only close to the sacred but also in unison with the movement of creation. The half-light of dawn endows Mrs. Shortley's wrath and pain with depth as it leads her to a lasting stronghold against the torment of judging herself.

Before O'Connor more fully considers this presageful light, she extends the pattern of displacement in Part II by developing the effects of Mr. Guizac's appearance on Mrs. McIntyre's fortune. Her lot has been declining since the Judge, her first husband, died thirty years ago. There is a second husband, Mr. Crooms, now in a mental institution, and a third, Mr. McIntyre, probably drinking in a Florida hotel room. A flock of tenant farmers also passes through like migratory birds. The Ringfields, the Collinses, the Garrits, the Herrins, and the Shortleys snatch what they want and fly off. Nothing marks the decline more vividly than the peacock population, which Mrs. McIntyre tolerates as useless; with only a cock and two hens now, she at least saves feed. Her response to her overall bad luck is resentment. Each wave of loss increases her sense of deserving more than she gets.

Mr. Guizac's arrival is the good luck that compensates for Mrs. McIntyre's previous raw deals. Prosperity brings out her sense of entitlement. " 'I've spent half my life fooling with worthless people,' " Mrs. McIntyre asserts to old Astor, " 'but now I'm through' " (224). Magistracy suits her. Paying bills equals assigning human worth, since the source of money is for Mrs. McIntyre also the source of being. The blacks are dependent on her yet act " 'like the shoe is on the other foot' " (227). An independent attitude in her employees pilfers her authority. She may have married the old Judge for his money, she may have benefitted from her workers, but envy makes it she who is taken advantage of. When she recalls the years of being done in, she cries. The restitution that Mr. Guizac's labor provides is her due.

The rights of Mr. Guizac lie beyond Mrs. McIntyre's understanding, in the realm of accounts receivable. Only after she learns of his plan to marry his cousin to the half-witted black, Sulk, must Mrs. McIntyre come to grips with him as a real person; and she does so by retreating to property rights of a landowner. She withdraws to the closet-like space in the back hall that houses the Judge's old ledgers and bank books in the sacred hush of historic mores. She can reflect on a moral matter where business is conducted. She quantifies the dilemma to the bottom line of self-interest. The result is the old self-sorrow that has nagged her for thirty years. The empty safe is the tabernacle of her pity, sanctifying the feeling that nobody in the world is poorer than she. The disgruntled tenants who flee, the two blacks who cannot, the Guizacs who should, the Polish cousin in the detention camp: all of these people exist outside her compassion. Her failure to feel for others, more than the untruth of her being the world's poorest person, defines her weakness, because it approves her spiteful ways. Prayerful attention leads her to confront Mr. Guizac to forbid the marriage. She rules that his attempt to free his orphaned cousin from custody by marrying one of her blacks is malevolent. As owner she can impose her will on her hirelings.

Ownership is just one way, however, of thrusting her ego on others. Dread is another. In an ambivalent moral situation, Mrs. McIntyre takes the easy way out because of fear that chaos might result, and here she arrives at the same image of Mr. Guizac that Mrs. Shortley in her terror projects. He is for both women the fiend of disorder. " 'What kind of monster are you!' " (234) cries Mrs. McIntyre. Freedom for the young Polish detainee defrauds her order: " 'I will not have my niggers upset. I cannot run this place without my niggers' " (235). The blacks are calm enough about the prospect, but her niggers need appeasing. Moreover, it is the Guizacs and their cousin who are at fault for being victims of war and tugging at her conscience for a braver response. As the dutiful man turns his other cheek and gets ready to work for the woman who scorns him, Mrs. McIntyre adds in an unguarded afterthought, " 'I am not responsible for the world's misery' " (235). Pity shows through only to be tamped down by personal and social fear. By exempting herself from responsibility for the world's suffering, she risks exacerbating that misery.

Part II ends with Mrs. McIntyre mounting the top of the slope with her arms folded, confident that she can rise above a Guizac just as she has overcome his predecessors. That her triumphal climb duplicates Mrs. Shortley's ascent issues a warning. Mrs. Shortley feels equal to any threat and explodes like a volcano. Volatility also underlies Mrs.

McIntyre's expectation. She may have stopped Mr. Guizac's arrangement with Sulk, but her heart nevertheless "was beating as if some interior violence had already been done to her" (236). Two emotional forces intrude on her well-being. The loss of Mr. Guizac will be an economic setback, and she has put into words the dismaying notion of universal affliction. Responding to the world's distress would make her feel anew.

Part III shows how pity can and does shake the foundation of Mrs. McIntyre's world. A succession of three scenes in this final section dramatizes the interplay between justice and justification that makes up the whole drama of "The Displaced Person." The first scene takes place one month later with the old priest, Father Flynn, to whom she owes an explanation of her decision to fire Mr. Guizac. Doubts do qualify her selfishness: "There is no moral obligation to keep him, she was saying under her breath, there is absolutely no moral obligation" (237). Defensiveness also makes her reluctant to state her racial prejudice as reason for banishing an exile anew, and Father Flynn addresses her inchoate decency with an assumption of fair play: " 'Dear lady, I know you well enough to know you wouldn't turn him out for a trifle!' " (238). Since she would dismiss him for an untenable motive, she falls back on her feeble excuse: " 'It is not my responsibility that Mr. Guizac has nowhere to go' " (239).

It is during Mrs. McIntyre's protestation that Father Flynn becomes taken by the peacock in a special way. What he sees and what he says express the guiding theme of "The Displaced Person" and the suite of stories it draws to a close. As the priest prepares to leave the house, three peafowl reach the middle of the lawn. The cock stops and spreads his tail. Small fertile suns float depth on depth in a feathery penumbra of green-gold around the cock's head. The sudden display amazes the old priest, who bursts out in unabashed joy, " 'Christ will come like that!' " As though appreciative of the attention, the cock holds his tail unfurled as he delicately steps backward for the priest's benefit. " 'The Transfiguration,' " murmurs Father Flynn (239).

The transfiguration of Christ is the decisive moment that reveals Jesus to be the Son of God (Matthew 17:1–8; Mark 2:8; Luke 9:28–36). Jesus leads Peter, James, and John up a high mountain where He is "transfigured before them, and his face shone like the sun, and his garments became white as light" (Matthew 17:2). He appears talking with Elijah and Moses, whose presence identifies Jesus with law and prophecy. While Jesus is speaking, a voice announces from a bright cloud that " 'This is my beloved Son' " (Matthew 17:5). The sight and sound daze the disciples. When they lift up their eyes, they see no one but Jesus. They are brought back to actuality, and the extraordinary experience can only be reported as a dream vision. The effect is to make revealer and revelation one.

The signs surrounding Jesus' transfiguration come from celebrated moments in Exodus. The mountain, understood by tradition to be Mt. Tabor, evokes the events of Sinai to show that they are reenacted in the life of the new Moses. The brightness around Jesus intensifies the association with Moses by recalling his luminous face that requires veiling after the Sinai theophany. The bright cloud is the Shekinah, the visible sign of God's presence and the same billowy mass through which God speaks to Moses. These Old Testament details indicate how much of the old story Jesus fulfills. The Gospels give more such details. On Tabor the voice speaks of a deeper reality than that of the Law given through Moses. The new appearance of Jesus describes a change of His body into the likeness of glory He comes to accomplish in His passion and death.

The light of glory shimmers through the slick gray dawn of Mrs. Shortley's new life and in the blue of the peacock's long neck and extended plumage. Wherever it flashes, the glint manifests the good and divine in creaturely life. The invitation to find the godly within the human comes to Mrs. McIntyre through Mr. Guizac, whose quiet dedication and patient suffering shine forth the saving way. The refugee does not force his secrets upon her. He does not force his loyalty upon her. His grace, like that of Jesus, comes hidden and revealing. The power of Mr. Guizac impinges on Mrs. McIntyre as a challenge to the insentience that she confuses with virtue. The spiritual affinities of the displaced Pole are made obvious when Father Flynn shakes Mrs. McIntyre's hand good-bye. Still absorbed by the peacock and the desire to instruct the woman, the old priest says, " 'He came to redeem us' " (239). The words refer to Jesus but describe Mr. Guizac.

Several weeks later, Chancey Shortley returns to reclaim his job and presses his case with the flawless logic of moral displacement. He reckons that the Pole killed his wife because he knew that he came from the devil, and figures that he has the dairy job coming to him as payment for his wife's death. As a native American veteran of World War I, Chancey deserves more than a foreigner. Mrs. McIntyre grasps

Mr. Shortley's reasoning, but economic interest and reluctance to confront her negative feelings outweigh his entreaty to fire Mr. Guizac. Suspicious of her ability to dismiss the Pole, Chancey takes his case to the blacks, the courthouse, the grocery store, and anywhere people will listen to his complaint about the Pole. For a person who denies blame, for a person who will not sympathize, there is justification through social shame; and where intolerant conformity rules, the appearance of breaching custom carries more weight than does truth. Unable to stand "the increasing guilt any longer" (248), Mrs. McIntyre sets out one cold Saturday morning to fire Mr. Guizac.

The coldness of the day also spurs Chancey to act. Having waited for the hand of God to strike, Chancey this morning adjusts the brake on the large tractor to slip and push the small tractor over Mr. Guizac, who is lying underneath the machine making repairs. Mr. Shortley sets the brake to fail, but all are responsible. Just before the tractor moves, eyes seal a pact. Mrs. McIntyre "felt her eyes and Mr. Shortley's eyes and the Negro's eyes come together in one look that froze them in collusion forever" (250). Mr. Guizac may have escaped the Nazis, but he is no match for this group of conspirators. His execution has the casual brutality of a nightmare and the inevitability of heinous calculation.

The despised and innocent foreigner lies splayed on the icy ground, sacrificed on the bone-crushing coldheartedness of the place's owner and workers. Whereas compunction for the man's plight would have valued his dignity, evil disfigures his wholeness. The gospel account of the transfiguration prefigures the paschal death, and the preceding disclosure of Christ's glory in Father Flynn's appreciation of the peacock anticipates Mr. Guizac's earthly participation in Christ's suffering. The sacrificial slaughter of Mr. Guizac exemplifies the message he brings on arrival: the outlander is the "figure for our essential displacement" (*Mystery and Manners* 45).

The final scene of "The Displaced Person" shows that in our essential displacement lies the call to be evermore transfigured by the action of suffering. Mr. Guizac's death accomplishes "a kind of redemption," O'Connor explains, "in that he destroyed the place, which was evil, and set Mrs. McIntyre on the road to a new kind of suffering," one of purification. It is, however, the expiatory stage of Mrs. McIntyre's journey that raises doubts in O'Connor's mind about the conclusion's effectiveness. Having the peacock roam the grounds pleases her as a natural evocation of the Church's watchful eye over Mrs. McIntyre's final days, but the redeeming growth in the heroine's sickness seems to O'Connor not fully realized. In a rare moment of wistfulness, she wonders about Mrs. McIntyre: "Isn't her position, entirely helpless to herself, very like that of the souls in Purgatory?" (*Letters* 118).

The answer lies in the spiritual action of the text. Reparation for Mrs. McIntyre begins while Mr. Guizac receives viaticum, the sacramental provision for the crossing to his true country. As Father Flynn slips the Eucharist into the dying man's mouth, Mrs. McIntyre becomes numb. The woman who lacks fortitude to act with her tender heart experiences a failure of nerve. The man she decides to expel turns out to banish her to "some foreign country" (250) where she imagines the grieving family bent over the victim to be natives. The region where mourners reside in hopeful sorrow is purgatory; Mrs. McIntyre, now an exile on her own land, emigrates to that realm in her protracted illness.

Atonement at the end of "The Displaced Person" has Mrs. McIntyre take Mr. Guizac's place so that she can know the harm of her own worst faults. Sorrow arises through rigidity and restraint. While she watches Mr. Guizac fix the tractor that will kill him, "the cold was climbing like a paralysis up her feet and legs" (249); after the murder, the cold fills Mrs. McIntyre's body and confines her to bed. The icy ground on which the man, like the Eucharist, is broken and blessed becomes the ground of Mrs. McIntyre's conversion. Confinement to bed helps to relieve past encumbrances. She has been weighed down by property, the burden of which submerges the higher aspirations of heart and mind in worldly security. As justice cleanses the greedy spirits on the fifth terrace of Dante's Purgatory (Canto XIX) by binding them to their possessions, Mrs. McIntyre's prostration shows the effect of desiring material gain above other considerations. While outstretched and motionless, the ailing woman has her face turned up toward new knowledge. She learns that she is not made of money, just as she insists to Mrs. Shortley. Mrs. McIntyre can become a good woman without having a cent to her name or a business deal to offer. Covetousness unmakes her; poverty remakes her. When her material and physical resources give out, she can be received into her true country.

The poverty at the end of "The Displaced Person" is not the grinding penury that Mrs. McIntyre understandably fears or the abject misery of the Guizacs, which should be effaced from the earth, but the destitution that leads humankind to place complete trust in God. This is the stark need that Father Flynn answers at the end. The priest blesses

Mrs. McIntyre's poverty as he anoints Mr. Guizac's agony. The maternal eighty-year-old visits every week and, after feeding bread crumbs to the peacock, explains doctrines of his church. O'Connor does not specify which beliefs Father Flynn discusses, but two teachings that he favors, the incarnation and purgatory, give aid to Mrs. McIntyre's lingering sickness. Argumentative technicalities aside, the fact that God assumes human nature means that He deals with humans through flesh. Bodily illness in O'Connor's fiction reveals divine concern by forcing a character to ask about the ultimate meaning of life. The imminence of death has no parallel in her narratives in calling the characters to feel themselves a part of God's plan. In coming to the sick woman, Father Flynn does not leave the fate of her soul to chance. He nurtures the "possibility for interior development" (*Presence of Grace* 76), which O'Connor affirms as part of purgatorial pain.

Wisely circumspect about individual eschatology, O'Connor suggests the truth to come for Mrs. McIntyre through Father Flynn's attitude. He steadfastly attends the crippling slowness of the woman's dying because he sees that while becoming dumb, and almost blind and deaf, she remains vulnerable to love. Liminal hearing suffices for his weekly oral instruction. By supporting her last days with words of grace, the priest changes the heroine's oppressive habit of order-giving, now useless, into a message-receiving faculty that can aid her liberation from the burdensome world. Father Flynn knows with Paul that "faith comes from what is heard, and what is heard comes by the preaching of Christ" (Romans 10:17). Mrs. McIntyre's failing body is not a vessel of biological destruction but a viable form of prayer. At the very least, by ministering to Mrs. McIntyre's infirmity, the priest relieves her of the most severe burden of terminal illness, the feeling that she is no longer of any use. For the old priest, it is in her bodily impairment and lack of economic success that the heroine becomes sacramental.

The sacramentality of Father Flynn's anointing catechesis arises from O'Connor's Pauline frame of mind. "For you know the grace of our Lord Jesus Christ," Paul explains, "that though he was rich, yet for your sake he became poor, so that by his poverty you might become rich" (2 Corinthians 8:9). The incarnation and death of Jesus, irrevocably linked to resurrection and transfiguration, are an impoverishment that distributes the wealth of Jesus to the redeemed. Such "effects of redemption" (*Letters* 118) would be the signs of Mrs. McIntyre's conversion that O'Connor wishes were plainer in the story. However defective

O'Connor judges the final scene, its opacity makes theological sense, for there can be more darkness than light in revelatory experiences through which God grants Himself. This is the case with the gospel disclosures. As God in the cross of His Son draws very near humanity, His presence seems more profoundly concealed to the human mind. The riddle of suffering as intensified by the terror of being forsaken by God carries much that is obscure along with what is clear.

In the end, theology yields to poetry. O'Connor turns over to the peacock the mystery of human life drawing to fulfillment. "The peacock" are the first words of "The Displaced Person," and the last sentence of the story (and the collection) remarks his enduring presence. As Mrs. McIntyre lies in the priest's pastoral care, the rubble of the place and the remnants of its inhabitants' lives come under the reign of the king of birds. He has the last word, gives the sign of last things returning full cycle to the Creator. The technical word for the completion of this process is the Parousia, and the ordinary similitude for this new reality is the peacock. When the bird of glory lifts his tail, brightness radiates the pattern of sacred history. His feathery cosmos contains the inscape of Tabor, the transfiguring map for the journey to find, and in the search to become, the good woman, the good man.

NOTE

1. Entrance into O'Connor's "true country," which Mrs. Shortley gains at the farm gate, comes by means of Jesus. Jesus, the good man, is the true gate to heaven. A hymn of Thomas Aquinas entitled *"Verbum supernum prodiens"* ("The Heavenly Word proceeding forth") traces the course of this mediation from the Son's assuming flesh to opening the gate to the eternal *patria,* "our true native land." The last stanza goes:

> *Uni trinoque Domino,*
> *Sit sempiterna gloria:*
> *Qui vitam sine termino*
> *Nobis donet in patria.*

> —

> To Thy great Name be endless praise,
> Immortal Godhead, One in Three;
> O grant us endless length of days
> In our true native land, with Thee.

The Hymns of the Breviary and Missal, edited with Introduction and Notes by Matthew Britt (New York: Benziger Brothers, 1936), p. 188.

4

The Price of Love

The Violent Bear It Away

"Will you still say, 'I am a god,'
  in the presence of those who slay you,
though you are but a man, and no god,
  in the hands of those who wound you?"
Ezekiel 28:9

The Violent Bear It Away (1960) puts unusual demands on the
imagination. The pressure affects O'Connor at the outset. When only
fifty or sixty pages into the first draft, she alerts Robert Giroux in 1953
that her second novel will be a while in the writing. "It's a theme," she
explains, "that requires prayer and fasting to make it get anywhere"
(*Letters* 59). Judging from her discouraging reports to friends, one sees
that even humble submission to the job, a renunciation O'Connor
almost perfected, does not ease her through "the realm of the impossible"
(*Letters* 177) that she sets her sights to explore in *The Violent Bear
It Away.*

  Writing short stories simultaneously provides relief, and so does
preparing public lectures. Nevertheless, her "Opus Nauseous" (*Letters*
284) is "driving me nuts" (*Letters* 172). The effort is so involving that
putting the manuscript aside amounts to a parole from the penitentiary,
and yet not working on the novel is unthinkable. Sounding like Hazel
Motes at the typewriter picking his way word by word to the pinpoint of

light, O'Connor describes herself run ragged for seven years by the book. When the finished copy approaches the darkness of print, however, she brightens. O'Connor registers her usual scruples about minor flaws and anticipates that the book, perhaps seen by its creator as the prophet Jeremiah, will be "pounced on and torn limb from limb"; but she knows that she has made something that works. "I am pleased with it myself," O'Connor says, "everything in it seems to me to be inevitable in the economy of the situation" (*Letters* 342). Commenting with less need for modesty, Stanley Edgar Hyman sums up the strenuous undertaking in the total economy of her career as "O'Connor's masterpiece" (19).

Readers too have difficulty with *The Violent Bear It Away*. The theme that taxes O'Connor, readers find ambiguous. The biblical title that she thinks is the best part of the book, for instance, states flatly that physical force gains the kingdom of heaven. The affirmation of redeeming violence rings true to her previous fiction and extends her belief that one must "push as hard as the age that pushes against you"; O'Connor feels the shove of spiritual indifference in our age pressing to the degree that the kingdom is taken by violence "or not at all" (*Letters* 229). Yet there is a counter meaning in the Matthean title that promises a dispensation after John the Baptist, namely, with Jesus, when humility takes the kingdom. Some arguments take up this other view of O'Connor's theme. These revisionist commentaries lead to persuasive readings of the novel as "an allegory of the Church" (Hyman 24) and a reenactment of the mystic's quest (Mallon 54–69). This constructive view will find even more in the text to work with. All the human relations and much of the dialogue concern love, but love darkened by stronger motives. The opacity of the subject is in large part a result of O'Connor's negative approach, which she takes to the edge in her second novel.

O'Connor's supreme work does have a strange way of presenting love. The story concerns prophets, who are known more for their anger than for their emotional warmth. They are inspired preachers of God whose job is to denounce the moral conditions before them. They excited derision when they appeared on the scene about three thousand years ago, and with their imperishable sensitivity to evil, they continue to endure ridicule for their antagonism. In prophetic outburst and the outcast state incurred by it, O'Connor finds the hard push that gets the message of God's compassion through to a people resistant to the holy.

The disturber of the mind who causes all the trouble is Mason

Tarwater. He is an eighty-four-year-old Tennessean who lives in the hills with the Bible and the Spirit. Mason is the good man for our dark time. His archaic, austere life does justice to the forbidding reputation established by his predecessors. He wants others to know of God's personal interest, but his caustic manner impedes the message. He is also determined to perpetuate his mission, and so he kidnaps a nephew and later a grandnephew to succeed him. His harsh upbringing tries the students. The nephew refuses to be a laughingstock and decides instead to serve the society his uncle scorns. The grandnephew also tries to get rid of his heritage to serve God, but he fails. The consequence of his failure is that he must spend the rest of his life in the estrangement imposed on God's messenger. And so, to the very end, what O'Connor deems worthy she also fills with horror.

The novel does show more tolerable ways of life. Alongside the family of prophets, the story has a cadre of devils who ingratiate themselves with winning advice to get ahead in the world. Their suavity confounds success and failure, friend and foe, right and wrong. In the name of reason, the devils promote such acts as arson and murder as feats of conscience. Finally, as the demonic influence bears down on the grandnephew's action and his destructiveness becomes more reprehensible, the hero experiences ordeals that force the reader to reconsider an easy antipathy toward him. O'Connor, in sum, does not allow for clear emotional affiliation in *The Violent Bear It Away*.

All this ambivalence meets with the controversy it seeks. Expositors go back to provenance in early drafts and in O'Connor's library to see how the novel comes together, and there is a lively argument from various critical perspectives over O'Connor's technique and meaning. While a number of particular scenes and minor figures receive close attention, two issues especially preoccupy readers. One is the satanic presence. John Hawkes's 1962 essay, "Flannery O'Connor's Devil" (*Sewanee*), is the catalytic statement on her use of satanism to demolish the modern trust in reason. O'Connor herself protests that Hawkes exaggerates the devil's contribution to the novel (*Letters* 456 and 507) and that he mistakes her Lucifer, a fallen angel of God, for his own Manichean figure of God's dark equal; but her disclaimer falls on deaf ears. Hawkes's devil has his partisans, who measure the novel's effectiveness by how true O'Connor remains to the "devil of reduction" (Hendin 20) that amply furnishes her with barbs. A recent study brings the adversarial line full circle to complain that O'Connor is "desperate" (Kessler 93) because she relies on stereotypes of the devil rather than exploring the rich individuality that the embodiment of absolute evil possesses.

The other issue takes up the old uncle, Mason Tarwater, and his grandnephew, Francis Marion Tarwater. Whereas those fascinated by satanism stress allegorical and satiric patterns, readers struck by the protagonists emphasize psychological verisimilitude. Their proper aim is to recover the novel's human drama by reacting against the emblematic. A student of human behavior finds much to analyze in this book. Mason at best comes across as a grouch whose "excess of egoism" may be excused because he takes his stance "from the self-righteous position of the elect" (Eggenschwiler 118). If one goes beneath geriatric quirkiness to diagnose pathology in prophecy, then the old man's fanaticism bespeaks great peril. Such hatred as he vents serves to expose the violent wrath of the South's "primitive fundamentalism," which amounts to "the denial and utter extinction of the possibility of love" (Rubin, *The Added Dimension* 65–66). Whatever the old preacher's value, he is for many a raving lunatic victimized by the violence and psychosis that curse the family's blood (Hyman 24). Given the genetic stock, it follows that in assuming Mason's mission young Tarwater bears "the fruit of irreversible psychological damage" (Shloss 85).

The studies of the two Tarwaters are more cogent and nuanced than a passing observation can convey. For all their contemporary language, however, the findings of emotional imbalance echo the familiar charge of madness and hysteria made about the ancient prophets. Whether probed by symbolism to yield allegorical import or by psychological determinism to manifest inner disturbance, the meaning of *The Violent Bear It Away* seems cut and dried. In dealing with the novel's paradoxes, all parties to the debate invoke the realism O'Connor espouses to invalidate the realism she believes that she achieves. She is clear in her letters about having no regional or denominational or psychic model for her prophet: "The true prophet is inspired by the Holy Ghost" (*Letters* 407). The Spirit of God is love, and remains the most elusive of the divine persons. Mason's character takes its integrity from this intimate mystery. Accordingly, the verisimilitude of the novel finds its coherence in the invisible world of the Spirit—O'Connor's realm of the impossible.

A letter of 27 August 1962, which came to light after the publication of *The Habit of Being,* offers guidance in understanding O'Connor's characterization and realism. "Tarwater is not sick or crazy but really called to be a prophet," O'Connor writes plainly to a teacher who passed on a student's puzzlement; and the ending "can only be understood in religious terms" (see Appendix). Psychology helps us understand the prophet but tends to deduce prophecy, the religious terms, exclusively from behavior; in doing so, it disregards inspiration, the source beyond the prophet's awareness that O'Connor says is crucial. By the same token, there is the opposite danger that arises from approaching the prophet through dogma. If we consider only the supernatural origin of the prophet's word, we miss the very human person and predicament that are the stuff of O'Connor's art. The achievement of *The Violent Bear It Away* lies in the individual experience of inspiration, the human struggle to respond to the revealing message that impinges on the person called to speak for and with God. The hero's consciousness remains in flux (Desmond 110–16).

Francis Marion Tarwater embodies the clash with divine revelation. A boy of fourteen, he is the hero of *The Violent Bear It Away.* Through his resistance and ultimate capitulation we understand what it feels like to hear God's word. The prophet's coming of age provides the theme O'Connor refers to in her letters as "the violence of love" (382). To avoid implications of softness, she prefers to call this charity by the name of grace. Nevertheless, if we keep in mind her shy approach to tender feeling and joy, we will find in O'Connor's second novel fresh evidence of her "thinking more and more about the presentation of love and charity" (*Letters* 373).

II

One way into O'Connor's thinking about the presentation of love is through the structural features she uses to trace God's action on her young hero. His story has twelve chapters to recall the twelve disciples chosen and taught by Jesus to help Him in His mission. These twelve go back to the twelve tribes of Israel previously called to spread the divine message. The number twelve designates the human contribution to the total plan of salvation, and the twelve chapters of *The Violent Bear It Away* signal the merging of Francis Marion Tarwater into the line of those enlisted to share the work of God. The boy will make his contribution as a Christian prophet; to observe this aspect of his vocation, O'Connor gathers the twelve chapters into three sections, layering unity upon unity, depth upon depth. Twelve flowing through three records the continuity of divine initiative from old to new covenant. In particular, the triadic movement aligns the events of the novel along unbroken trinitarian lines as Francis Marion Tarwater, despite his disobedient will, proceeds *to* God the Father, *through* Jesus the Son, *in* the Holy Spirit. Three subsuming twelve celebrates the mystery of divine mandate and prophetic reaction, with the power of the Spirit holding everything in balance. Love expresses human participation in God's trinitarian action.

This large design throws into relief the ultimate meaning of the here and now in Tennessee. The plot is simply Tarwater's attempt to run away from the responsibility of being a prophet. He circles from Powderhead, his homestead, to the nearby city, and back to Powderhead. Encounters along the route constitute the action that brings the boy to the threshold of prophecy. O'Connor has a chronology to match the spatial simplicity of the story. She limits time to one week—the seven days completing the hero's preparation—to highlight the moment of his dawning awareness. Since active prophecy lies in the past with Mason, who dies just before the story begins, and in the future with Tarwater, who assumes the role after the story ends, the duration spans an interregnum between acceptances of the Lord's call when the world lacks a Tarwater committed to shout the saving news. In its brevity, the novel measures the decisive change in the fleeting moment that we call life; and in the stolid finiteness of a remote patch off a Tennessee dirt road and a dark city, O'Connor surveys the condition of our material creatureliness through which we encounter God.

Part One of *The Violent Bear It Away* treats the transference of prophetic duty from old to young Tarwater. This part has three chapters. In each, a tempter coaxes young Tarwater to renounce his Tarwater legacy; together, the enticements pull the boy further away from his obligation. The increasingly urban terrain indicates the inimical direction of Tarwater's movement. He kicks the dust off his shoes in Powderhead (Chapter I), hits the road (Chapter II), and reaches the city (Chapter III). The trip takes one day, as the hero spends the morning in Powderhead, departs at midnight, and arrives in the city in the morning darkness of the next day. We know that the boy has strayed very far from the ancient truths of Powderhead when we come to the last word of Part One. Tarwater meets his cousin Bishop; the idiot child, whose smile radiates unalloyed love, appears to Tarwater as his "adversary" (93).

"Adversary" brings us back to the first words of the novel, which provide clues to where foe and friend are found. The opening sentence, which so pleased O'Connor, runs in full: "Francis Marion Tarwater's uncle had been dead for only half a day when the boy got too drunk to finish digging his grave and a Negro named Buford Munson, who had come to get a jug filled, had to finish it and drag the body from the breakfast table where it was still sitting and bury it in a decent and Christian way, with the sign of its Saviour at the head of the grave and enough dirt on top to keep the dogs from digging it up." The sentence gives in miniature a paradigm of how to respond to God's commandment to love and how to trespass it. Buford Munson comes to buy whiskey and stays to give himself. From noon to sundown the black man toils to finish the spadework Tarwater abandons. Mason rests in peace thanks to Buford, whose work of mercy is freely given and unassuming, as great acts are made in O'Connor's fiction. From Buford's selflessness there flows an outpouring of spirit that spreads into a eucharistic vision at the end of the novel.

Buford's sacrifice emerges from Tarwater's self-indulgence. The boy tries to dig a hole for Mason's massive corpse but finds the solid brick earth covered by sandy topsoil a burden he will not bear. After deciding to disregard Mason's final request, Tarwater tries to eradicate his bad conscience by getting drunk, and then tries to get rid of the corpse by setting the place on fire. The boy's destructiveness takes its meaning from Mason's teaching. Since the old man believes that the validity and fulfillment of his body awaits the resurrection, Tarwater's conflagration shames God's loving promise to restore the world and humankind to His glory. Tarwater's refusal to fulfill his duty to Mason incurs a debt to Buford Munson and then increases Tarwater's debt to God by adding to the irresponsibility that Mason teaches the hero to indict and correct. By torching Powderhead, Tarwater replaces God's plan with his egocentric will; the subsequent horrors in the novel issue from his self-love. At the outset, then, we see that Tarwater is his own enemy.

The first sentence is a Faulknerian head start on the hero's encounter with himself through others. It rushes with adverbial clauses and expansive *and*s to encompass the entire drama by speeding along through so much happening so soon among three characters whose connections are not yet firm in the reader's mind. To deepen the panoramic sweep, the texture of the language at once endows details with ultimate meaning, as when the corpse of the nameless uncle acquires "the sign of its

Saviour." The sentence exhausts and overwhelms. And yet, these very intensifying techniques set the burial of Mason's body as a fixed idea in the reader's mind so that one feels what young Tarwater feels in the weight of Mason's past teaching and in his dead bulk in need of a ten-foot grave. In a flash O'Connor prepares us to go behind the young hero's brows, where the essential conflict takes place.

The second paragraph moves into Tarwater's consciousness. The bereft fourteen-year-old grapples with the prospect of being alone after Mason's death by reviewing the Tarwater family history. By far, the most determinative influence is Mason's. Mason shapes the way the hero sees the world, and therefore he must be overcome for Tarwater to cut his ties and be himself. Tarwater declares his independence with the decision to steer clear of the folly that turned Mason into "a one-notion man" (39). The obsession is Jesus. The stench or sweetness in ordinary things could send the old man ranting about the day of judgment because Jesus pervaded his experience of places and persons. To avoid this hidden power that seized Mason, Tarwater decides to keep his eye on what lies in front of him. If he can keep physical facts from getting mixed up with invisible forces, then he can thwart the "threatened intimacy of creation" (22) that attends the habit of feeling Jesus in this red furrow or that mule's hindquarters or that idiot child. The mystical bent of Mason's mind is to Tarwater the cause of a world of angry fantasy.

Tarwater wants his world sharply divided between matter and spirit; and egoist that he is, the boy wants his god abstract, a function of his thought. Then, should the Lord call, Tarwater will know for sure because the signs are worked out in his mind, where dirt and dust and flesh do not mar divinity. The Lord will summon him in "a voice from out of a clear and empty sky" backed by "wheels of fire in the eyes of unearthly beasts" (22), as is His communication with Ezekiel. The boy likes God abstract, the call, univocal; and he wants the vehement marvels he finds in the Bible. The effect of such idealism is Tarwater's permission to God to dwell in the comfort of the boy's mind. Behind egocentricity lies Tarwater's understandable fear of "the hard facts of serving the Lord" (6). Mason's training aims to destroy the boy's use of abstraction to shield him from God: " 'It's no part of your job to think for the Lord,' his great-uncle said. 'Judgment may rack your bones' " (10). Mason knows from experience that those who do not put faith in the Lord's mysterious ways will be given over to the lust of certitude.

Mason's distrust of the mind proves wise. As sin is born out of the head of Milton's Satan, so the devil appears in the novel by taking his usually comfortable position in Tarwater's mind. The guardian devil begins as a voice rumbling with challenges to defiance that give the boy just the protection that he seeks from digging the grave and following the old man's orders. The voice is too shrewd to reveal its true intention of gaining an ally in its hateful activity. Instead, it plays to the boy's desire for freedom and need for companionship. Tarwater's enemies are the voice's enemies; and with increasing sympathy for the boy and deepening indignation at the deprivations imposed by the old man, the stranger vows his willingness to liberate Tarwater from "this empty place" (36). Though this devil does not incarnate himself in a snake, he still coils his way around the boy with seductive eloquence to create the intellectual intimacy the boy favors. To flatter the hero's self-image of maturity, the voice debunks Mason as immature and foolish and tyrannical. Mason, the voice argues, used Tarwater to carry mash to the still. Tarwater does not owe Mason a thing; rather, Tarwater has consideration coming to him. At the root of the voice's concern lies the narcissism that turned Lucifer against God in the first place and that marks the rebellious angel's steadfast purpose. He praises the hero's intelligence in order to undermine his faith: "Ain't you in all your fourteen years of supporting his foolishness fed up and sick to the roof of your mouth with Jesus?" The lure of Tarwater's being his own person paves the way for his being his own god. The choice before him, says the stranger, is not between good and evil, as Mason teaches: "It ain't Jesus or the devil. It's Jesus or *you*" (39). In one stroke the devil tries to deny the boy's sense of responsibility and evil and to get him to think himself equivalent to the Jesus Whom Mason raised him to serve.

The crisis showing the effectiveness of the strange voice occurs at noon, when Buford Munson and a tall, Indianlike woman arrive to buy whiskey. Both are moved by the fact of Mason's death because death carries meaning for them, and because the old man lived so that his suffering helped others. " 'He was deep in this life,' " Buford says as he reaches out to touch the hero, " 'he was deep in Jesus' misery' " (48). Buford's companion also feels Mason's death deeply; she crosses her arms and wails in sorrow. A gentle touch and feeling one's way through loss run against Tarwater's effort to numb himself to grief. He dismisses the woman's warm regard with a coldness worthy of the devil: " 'I'm in charge here now and I don't want no nigger-mourning' " (43). Tarwater puts down the shovel, runs off to the hollow where the bootleg is stashed, and gets drunk. Firewater completes the devil's work as it carries inebriating self-interest through the hero's gut and to his head.

The intimacy between Tarwater and his guardian devil is now physical. The stranger pants over the boy while he pulls away a stone to get the bootleg, in order to swallow from the jug. Then, the devil's "burning arm slid down Tarwater's throat . . . reaching inside him to finger his soul" (45). With slippery ease, the stranger penetrates Tarwater's inner being, reducing him to an object and knowing him more deeply than he knows himself. Tarwater thinks that he is drinking liquor and forgetfulness, but we know that fire and death are ravishing him. The full implication of the devil's intimacy in the hollow will emerge after the homosexual assault at the end of the novel. For now, O'Connor shows narcissism's appeal to Tarwater, setting the contentment of egoism against the background of love's violence. Tarwater is becoming enamored of himself, the danger of which also becomes known. O'Connor has the devil entering Tarwater at the head and then fingering his soul to dramatize how evil is at first charming but at last disgusting.

The hour underscores the peril. Tarwater stops digging the grave at noon, when the sun crosses the meridian. Noon is the critical time of judgment, when the human person resolves to act. In addition to drawing on a common scriptural symbol, O'Connor would know the tradition, reaching back to Hugh of St. Victor, that the Fall, the expulsion from Eden, and the death of Jesus occurred at the biblical sixth hour, or midday. Milton provides a suggestive analogue. Eve heard the devil's "persuasive words, impregned / With reason" as "the hour of noon drew on" (*Paradise Lost* IX 737–39). At noon in a Tennessee hollow those provocative words ring in Tarwater's ears while the cozy stranger encourages the boy to savor the forbidden drink from the black jug. The devil gratifies the boy's appetite. After noon, Tarwater is beyond reason and beyond burying the corpse. By evening, he ceases "to have any feeling in his legs" (47).

As the sun wanes and the stranger guides his gullible young friend into moral darkness, we see that the devil's gambits are toward the single end of removing any sense of guilt in the boy. Self replaces others and God. With guilt suspended, the devil can deliver the final blow with tender caress: "I wouldn't pay too much attention to my Redemption if I was you." After noon, the devil's deceptions are concentrated on a single word. He renders the concept of redemption so trivial that the word comes to mean no more than an obstacle to comfortable indifference. "Some people take everything too hard," he says (45). Demonic logic is flawless: no feeling means no debt; no debt, no guilt; no guilt, no need for Jesus; no Jesus, no redemption. If successful, Lucifer can deprive humankind of the divine presence that he lost and can never regain.

In *Paradise Lost,* when Eve plucked the fruit, "Earth felt the wound" (IX 782). Tarwater's taking the liquor causes a comparable reaction in *The Violent Bear It Away.* The sun keeps an eye on Tarwater's dealings with the devil, and the fallen angel of light, who is aware of his celestial opponent, goes out of his way to mock him as "that dwarf sun" (36). The narrator, who holds a distance from the characters, alerts the reader at the moment Tarwater pulls out the black jug that the sun appears as "a furious white, edging its way secretly behind the tops of the trees that rose over the hiding place" (44); and when he swallows the drink, the sun turns "angry" (45). The sun manifests God's all-seeing presence. Throughout the novel, the sun—high in the firmament over the devil's and Tarwater's head—exposes and judges them.

The sun's emissary brings judgment before night falls. Concerned that Mason's body remains unattended, Buford goes to the hollow to find the boy, who, in his blurred drunkenness, sees Buford's face where the sun would be in the fading sky. The charred black visage speaks for the sun: " 'This ain't no way for you to act. Old man don't deserve this. There's no rest until the dead is buried.' " Buford's "two small red blistered eyes" (47) remind the boy of the honor and pity he owes Mason, and Buford tempers the rebuke with a physical touch of sympathy for the boy's grief. This laying on of hands, the first of a series in the novel, overwhelms the boy's guarded ego: " 'Nigger,' the child said, working his strange swollen tongue, 'take your hand off me' " (48). O'Connor shifts from *boy* to *child* to mark the spiritual regression set off by the menace of Buford's compassion. Self-absorption makes Tarwater too weak to be loved. To protect the courage borrowed from alcohol, he projects his self-hatred onto Buford for reminding him of his duty; and in sloughing off his guilt, Tarwater works his way into the devil's role. Buford accepts the insult as he bears the boy's negligence because he knows that choosing Jesus involves the risk of touching the wounded child, digging the grave, and sweating over the old man's moldering corpse.

Late that night Tarwater awakens from a stupor to a night bird's screeching. Hung over and angry, he fumbles his way back to the shack, careful not to turn his head to the section of the yard where he began the grave. Dejection becomes a beacon lighting the way across a desert of emotion until he reaches the shack, where he thinks Mason's body remains, and begins to set small fires beneath the structure. The pyre rises "up through the black night like a whirling chariot" (50). This flame does not transport Elijah-Mason, whose body rests in the ground. Rather, this fire sends the hero on his way. The "chariot of fire and horses of fire" (2 Kings 2:11) are vehicles of divine fury in judgment (Isaiah 66:15) at the same time that they act as a visible protector of the man of God. The chariot of fire unites judgment with protection. Judgment Tarwater deserves; protection he needs for the journey ahead. Under the cover of midnight and with the sun on the other side of the earth, the hero leaves Powderhead. He can avoid the sun by keeping to the dark side of life, the world inhabited by those who avoid the violence of love by comforting themselves in their own snug needs.

As though waiting for Tarwater to begin his trip, a "rutted face" (52) driver coming from Mobile picks up the hero the moment he reaches the highway. The stranger is named Meeks. Meeks is the Charon of the Southeast, the grim coachman who ferries travelers down the direct black highway into the lower world. Whatever a boy setting out in life needs to know, this swashbuckling businessman in a cowboy hat can tell him. He sells copper flues throughout the region, and with Tarwater he can act as a channel conveying the flame of the boy's ardor to reach the city ahead. If experience teaches Meeks anything, it is that love is "the only policy" that works "95% of the time" (51). Love sells flues, and Meeks has a book filled with affectionate notations, usually medical and preferably morbid, about his customers to give his business a personal touch. His sycophancy bears a family resemblance to the smooth style of the devil when he greets Tarwater in Powderhead. Both are placating and upbeat on the surface but scheming and bitter at heart.

Meeks is a tour de force for O'Connor the cartoonist. She makes him the flattest possible character, speaking in the flattest possible language and inhabiting the flattest possible moral setting. It is difficult to take this caricature seriously, but it is dangerous to pass over him lightly, as he would like us to. His genial sales talk coats a despiritualizing cynicism that makes love and human contact mere commodities. After boasting that his notebook has reminders of his customers' private lives, he quickly says that he is pleased when a customer dies because each dead person is one less to remember. Forgetting the dead may be expedient for a busy salesman, but for the hero it involves his destiny. The word *dead* triggers in Tarwater an automatic attack on his great-uncle's teaching that " 'the world was made for the dead' " (16). " 'You don't owe the dead anything' " (51), the boy blurts out in an attempt to justify his not burying Mason. Such insensitivity hardly shocks Meeks, the rogue apologist for a world without moral responsibility: " 'And that's the way it ought to be in this world—nobody owing nobody nothing' " (51).

Nobody and *nothing* bespeak the void remaining after guilt disappears and love turns inward. To an ordinary country boy, Meeks, with his telephone charm, say, announcing his arrival to the lady Sugar, may seem knowing; but Tarwater has the sense to distrust the roving cavalier. The boy tunes him in and out. Meanwhile, Meeks drones on about commissions and his success, and O'Connor keeps the traveling salesman in the perpetual motion required to sustain his imagined power. " 'And I know where I'm going,' " he declares (52). He goes next to the city, the place of doom where his inner darkness shelters him from seeing the obligation he might incur to another person. To preserve his self-importance, Meeks numbs his sense of guilt and feigns a vocabulary of love, the result of which is delusion and dejection. As he titillates Sugar with news of his return, "an acid smile" begins "to eat at the corners of his mouth" (81). Unfeeling corrodes his humanness into cartoonographic residue. " 'So long, son,' " Meeks bids with paternalistic ostentation, and hands the boy a business card for a future " 'deal' " (84); but Meeks's real gift is his presence, which warns of the despair that comes with severing oneself from consequences.

During the ride, Tarwater thinks about his responsibility as he reflects on the two most important people in his life: Mason, his great-uncle, and George Rayber, his uncle and only remaining blood connection. The bond among the three goes to the core of what it means to love. The lonely hero even fantasizes that he and his uncles might have lived together had they felt the same way about love. But they do not. The standard of love for Mason is the crucifixion, and he equates love with his own willingness to risk danger to prepare others for the glory Jesus purchased for them. The old man uses blustery means. He kidnaps his nephew and then his grandnephew to teach them about the Lord, beats on his sister's door to warn her of the Lord's justice, and whips himself into paroxysms to drive sinners into the Lord's forgiving arms. Prophetic love expresses itself in willingness to proclaim the divine word before others at any personal cost, and Mason typifies the prophet's loving obedience. Society may spit and snicker and lock him up in an insane asylum for four years; every member of his family may reject him; still, the old man goes on hissing and moaning about the mercy that burns. O'Connor refers to his recklessness as "mystical love" (*Letters* 484). *Mystical* seems a peculiar adjective to describe the stance of her explosive, down-to-earth mountain of a man, a mason skilled in the materials of common clay; yet in his unlimited embrace of life he is mystical. The great-hearted Mason knows the depth of the physical.

Though Mason instills the disposition to boundless love in George Rayber by raising him to be a prophet, Rayber cringes before such exposure to experience. The portrait of Rayber that Tarwater brings to the city is one of an emotional coward who has many ideas but no ability to carry them out. We understand from Mason that Rayber's ideas are his defense against flesh, blood, nerves, and feeling. He removes the bearable idea from the threatening actuality. By responding to the idea of people and things instead of people and things themselves, Rayber gains control; but his power impoverishes life. The ideals he seeks make the world spiritless. He tries to make a life out of thought by becoming a schoolteacher; then life gives him a son with Down's syndrome to show the impotence of abstraction before the implacable urgency of physical caring. Rayber can no more love his son merely in his mind than he could change the child's pants in his head. The sadness of Rayber is that his desire to love does not break through pedagogical cant.

Part One of the novel ends with Tarwater arriving at Rayber's home in the city. Filled with pride for having freed himself from the old man's power, as Rayber did years ago, Tarwater stands ready to be congratulated for his boldness. What greets the hero, however, are two visions that disappoint his great expectations. Rayber comes to the door as though in a trance, and remains stolid while Tarwater announces Mason's death. Where Tarwater anticipates praise, he finds impassivity. Then Bishop, Rayber's deformed little boy, shambles into view. A harnesslike strap crisscrosses his chest and restrains him around the neck. Though bound by his controlling father, the little-understood Bishop, who rules by a power so gentle that it passes as repugnant weakness, reaches out to touch Tarwater. In a world where one lives in and for oneself, such tender contact menaces. Tarwater knocks Bishop's hand away, and the friendly child retreats into bellowing grief. " 'I won't have anything to do with him!' " the hero protests (93). Bishop's soft love causes a seismic upheaval in Tarwater's soul.

III

Part Two is a sequence of refusals. This middle section of *The Violent Bear It Away* (Chapters IV–IX), the longest of the novel's three parts, passes over the uneventful early days of Tarwater's visit with Rayber to take up the fifth and sixth days of his flight from Powderhead. During these two pivotal days, Rayber tries to educate the country boy in the ways of the modern world, and Tarwater tests the validity of Mason's training. To do so, the hero must rid his mind of Mason's habit of bringing every action back to one's relation to God. The challenge to Tarwater's independence is the old man's instruction to baptize Bishop. The flow of this middle section is one of ever-increasing apprehension over what form Tarwater's rebellion will take, until it erupts with his drowning Bishop in a lake. Tarwater the arsonist and shamer of the dead of Part One becomes in Part Two Tarwater the killer and, by force of Mason's training, the baptist *malgré lui.*

O'Connor prepares for Tarwater's fall into murderous hatred through a succession of scenes depicting the rejection of love. During a night-time Pentecostal worship, Lucette Carmody, a crippled evangelist of twelve, shouts the theme when lamenting the dire consequences of the world's habitual failure to recognize love in its midst; then, while Bishop plays in a water fountain, Rayber and Tarwater demonstrate that very deficiency in their abusive treatment of the loving child; and finally, the killing of Bishop makes vivid the anguish caused by the lovelessness that Lucette bemoans. Within the deepening gloom of Part Two there also arises in each incident a disclosure of divine attention. The poetry of O'Connor's drama shows that the greatest motive of God's charity is to answer the needs of human persons. In fact, the sharper the need and sorrow, the greater the hallowing. God becomes protector of the unprotected, friend to the friendless, father to the orphan, bread to the hungry, living water to the drowned child.

One force promoting the evil in the second part is Rayber's plan to empty Tarwater's mind of God and such rot as Mason put in it. Out of his love for Tarwater, the schoolteacher will provide the country boy a decent education so that the backward but intelligent youth can lead " 'a normal life' " (103). Rayber will lift the "terrible false guilt" (106) weighing on Tarwater's conscience for destroying Powderhead, and replace the insane business of prophecy with "the duties of a good citizen" (108). Escalators and airplanes will serve to expose the silliness in the conviction of rising again to everlasting life.

The gimcrack novelties of modern technology, however, bore Tarwater. They no more fulfill his imagination than the ravioli at a city restaurant could satisfy his hunger. The goal of Tarwater's desire lies beyond his consciousness, and it is not until he steals into town at night after an unpalatable dinner that an urgent need takes organic form in him. He stops at a bakery window to stare at a forgotten loaf of bread, physical nourishment that is also a reminder of the appetite that Mason aroused and that only God appeases. All along, the remembered appeal on a poster he saw earlier to "Hear the Carmodys for Christ!" pulls Tarwater into a dingy garagelike tabernacle where Lucette Carmody is the featured attraction. The inducement for Tarwater is to prove to himself that he can resist this " 'horse manure' " (109), but the girl's sharpness pierces his cussedness and speaks to his longing.

Like Reverend Shegog's Easter sermon in Faulkner's *The Sound and the Fury*, Lucette Carmody's inspired language forges the events of *The Violent Bear It Away* into proclamation. Her subject is love: " 'Do you know who Jesus is?' she cried. 'Jesus is the Word of God and Jesus is love' " (130). Beyond this assertion of the central message of Christian faith, nothing else about her performance is orthodox. In fact, the show comes with revivalist pyrotechnics that almost cloak the truth the girl speaks. Lucette is not yet twelve, the scriptural age of maturity; yet for six years the crippled girl has endured hardship and pain to evangelize among hostile strangers around the world. She is frail and wears a black cape turned over a shoulder to reveal a red lining and a short skirt to highlight her twisted legs. Youthfulness, anguish, and the peculiar sources of inspiration bear on the larger meaning of O'Connor's novel. These conditions define Bishop's role to bring others to God, and point toward Tarwater's future task as a teenage prophet. Whereas the world holds children in contempt, as with Herod's slaughter or with the disregard of a consumer society, God sees fit to assign children to be messengers of His word. Like little Samuel (1 Samuel 1–3) and young Daniel, Bishop embodies, Tarwater resists, and Lucette receives the word of God to pass it on in their individual ways.

Lucette's way is very much her own. With a bravura reminiscent of Mason's sweeping narrative from Adam to the rising of the dead, Lucette recounts two histories to her audience. The history of God is the history of love, presented from the moment of its creation through its crowning by the incarnation to its fulfillment in the resurrection. As Lucette speaks, her arms stretch to reach the power of God which draws her voice upward: "She held her arms over her head for a moment. 'I want to tell you people the story of the world,' she said in a loud high child's voice. 'I want to tell you why Jesus came and what happened to Him. I want to tell you how He'll come again. I want to tell you to be ready. Most of all,' she said, 'I want to tell you to be ready so that on the last day you'll rise in the glory of the Lord'" (129–30). The human story paralleling that of God is the story of unreadiness for love. Of this deficiency Lucette blasts a warning: "'If you don't know what love is you won't know Jesus when He comes'" (130).

Lucette offers no soothing reassurance that love comes in congenial forms. On the contrary, she goes out of her way to caution against trivializing love by expecting it to meet our expectations. To expect too much desensitizes us to love. Lucette is most conscious of a God with the virility to be angry, to shear away egoism, and to bring humankind to His will. The world expects a king as its savior, and receives a lowly child in a cold manger, a vulnerability that the world cannot acknowledge as love. Humankind wants love on its own soft terms, and thereby remains too weak to receive the love that comes. Lucette also laments this failure:

> "The world said, 'Love cuts like the cold wind and the will of God is plain as the winter. Where is the summer will of God? Where are the green seasons of God's will? Where is the spring and summer of God's will?'" [132].

The freshness of Lucette's language guarantees that she speaks from an experience that explains O'Connor's understanding of the violence of love. Love is not a cultural nicety; it does not ratify one's desire; nor does it make one fit in or feel good. Love is God's self-communication through Jesus, the Word made flesh; and in human affairs, love is the absolute will that calls forth each person to God. Love reveals the individual's duty that furthers the divine plan for all creation. This winter will, plain and perennially out of season to tepid human expectation, cuts and burns to prepare for the glory to come.

Lucette's words are not only about the cutting of love, they also cut an opening in the defenses of Rayber and Tarwater to expose their need for love. As Rayber spies on the service from outside a window, the girl's words make him experience the pain of his early years when he needed to believe and to be loved. He sought protection in his father and found a man indifferent to spiritual desire. His father's lovelessness came to characterize the negligence of the world. Rayber was left only with Mason's uncompromising guidance. The schoolteacher's anger over the unhealed wound of his childhood distorts Lucette's presence into a confirmation of his being duped. He brings everything back to himself by making others into functions of his petulance. All children are victims—Bishop, by his daily existence; others, by their disposition to trust. The pain of unanswered love in childhood is sharp enough for Rayber to taste now. It "laid again on his tongue like a bitter wafer" (130). The communion of bitter remorse nourishes Rayber. Acrimony numbs his feelings. He finds a way to fulfill his desire to love through a deluded fantasy as "an avenging angel . . . gathering up all the children that the Lord, not Herod, had slain" (132). Rayber is eager to get away from "the atrocious temple" (124) where Lucette preaches on love and back to the sedative of his home, where he can sink into his bed.

For Tarwater, the ramshackle church marks a spiritual crossing. He enters pridefully armored and departs humbled by a shock suffered during the ceremony. He is too stunned by Lucette's achingly pure voice for O'Connor to describe how he feels, but she shows the effect of Lucette's charisma. The boy's submissive eyes tell the truth that the blasphemy from his convulsive lips tries to hide. He feels vulnerable. He would even allow his uncle to touch his shoulder. Clearly, Tarwater is becoming more human, coming of age. Extending the image of cutting that O'Connor uses to explain love and that she evokes in the sharp sound of Lucette's name, we can say that Tarwater undergoes the rite of emotional circumcision as the girl's preaching cuts the covenant in him to accept the burden of experience. In the moment when the prepuce of Tarwater's heart is cut, he is ready to see Rayber through affection. As we might expect, Rayber cannot discern love in the boy's "drained but expectant" face (137). The scene ends with the failure of love. Rayber walks home trapped in his habitual rage over Bishop's deformity. Tarwater walks behind him, unseen by Rayber; and at home the boy lingers on another threshold, this one the physical entrance to his bedroom, hoping not to be alone in his pain.

By morning, Tarwater's face hardens again. To compensate for an "opportunity missed" (139), Rayber decides to take control of his nephew. The schoolteacher plans a day at the museum of natural history, where his textbook knowledge will give him the upper hand. He can impart the scientific truth about human development and dispel the erroneous biblical notions that Mason put into Tarwater's mind. By ten o'clock in the morning Rayber sets out with his two charges for the museum. But they do not reach their scheduled destination. To reach the museum they must walk through a park. The park has a fountain, and the trip ends when Bishop gets his feet wet in a shallow pool and must be brought home for dry shoes. The unexpected snag is a telling break.

Revelation is in the air from the outset. The trees in the park stop Rayber short by reminding him of Powderhead, the ancestral haunt he wants driven from his mind. As Rayber sits down to rest from the disturbing association, Bishop climbs onto his lap to have his shoelaces tied. Then the grinning little boy fits his white head under his father's chin, and the insupportable tenderness of love cuts into Rayber: "Without warning his hated love gripped him and held him in a vise" (141). If the pang of love strikes unexpectedly, it can be conquered by a habit of refusal. Memory supplies the ritual for Rayber to wrench numbing ease out of torment. He has learned to use love against love. He can contain the impulse to love by limiting his responsibility to loving only his child, and then caring only for the boy's physical needs. This technique of restraint was learned several years back when Rayber tried and failed to kill his son. The disclosure of infanticidal urges in a father who professes to love his son, and who in fact does love him, must affect even the most callous reader.

It was May, on a day filled with sun, as days highlighting Bishop's life are described in the book. Rayber is at an ocean beach two hundred miles from home. With only the imperturbable sky watching, he swings his joyful son in the air and then below the water's surface with the intention of holding him there. Suddenly, a force greater than the child's instinct to breathe surges against Rayber's hands; he releases his pressure, pushes down again in anger, and loses his grip on Bishop to an undertow that catches the child. The rescuing current also pulls Rayber back to his senses as he sees the consequence of his attempted murder. The serene expanse of blue sea and sky guards the child and indicts the father.

As Rayber recalls the attempted killing, the act that was to free him of his hated love redoubles his guilt. Anger drives him to plunge the boy down, and frenetic selfishness makes him snatch the body from the undertow; but not the slightest concern for Bishop's anguish mollifies Rayber's will. Rayber's guilt no more brings him to atone than his love brings him to love. He rationalizes killing his deformed son as an improvement of the scientific order. Only a strange twist of the call to unlimited love that Mason drilled into Rayber stops the slaying. When the undertow retrieves the body, Rayber pictures the future without Bishop; and he panics. Without the yoke of Bishop to anchor him, the pull in Rayber's heart toward boundless love might overtake and drown the schoolteacher in misery. If Bishop makes life difficult, he also makes life possible for his father.

At stake is Mason's teaching. His influence underlies the episode in the park with the same unseen energy that retrieves Bishop along the shore. As Rayber and Tarwater continue their shadowboxing with Mason's ghost, Bishop receives their punches because he is the breathing reminder of Mason's univocal commission to baptize others into the life of redeeming love. By scoffing at Bishop, Rayber and Tarwater try to deny their shared history of injured feeling for ignoring Mason's command. " 'All you got to do is nurse an idiot!' " sneers Tarwater. " 'I nurse an idiot that you're afraid to look at,' " counters Rayber (143). The dare activates Tarwater's essential dread, which he masks with gratuitous insult: " 'I'd as soon baptize a dog as him' " (143–44). Both Rayber and Tarwater resort to the satanic habit of propping up teetering positions of power with the pain of an innocent victim.

The scornful exchange ceases when Bishop scampers off to the stone fountain sculpted into a lion and surrounded by a concrete circle. The water splashing from the lion's mouth forms a shallow pool that attracts the delighted child. Rayber perceives in a flash that Bishop in the water offers Tarwater the perfect opportunity for a quick baptism. Alarmed by the sacrament he discredits as an "empty rite" (146), Rayber snatches his son from the water. As he did on that unforgettable day in May, when the avenging angel in him became Pharaoh drowning an innocent child in the Nile, Rayber spares Bishop a calamity of Rayber's own making. The episode ends with Tarwater walking off alone. At the time, we do not know his intention at the fountain. Later, in Chapter VIII, when at the Cherokee Lodge he reflects on his response, the reader learns that Tarwater is torn between Mason's order to baptize Bishop and the devil's behest to kill him. The hero's divided will and the premature termination of the trip to the museum give Chapter VI an inconclusiveness that is undermining in a meticulously crafted novel. Enigma, however, makes a point. In a world that awaits the final gathering of the crosses, all human actions are half measures; and with figures such as Rayber and Tarwater, who are skilled in resisting the invitation to grace, there can only be infirmity of purpose. As Tarwater recalls his indecision in the park, he senses that the atmosphere is "being purged for the approach of revelation" (163); accordingly, O'Connor brings *The Violent Bear It Away* to its midpoint not with explanation but with mystery.

Disclosure emanates from the lion occupying the center of the fountain. Mason warned the hero to " 'watch out for the Lord's lion' " (24) at the time he gave Tarwater burial instructions. The lion tested Daniel's faith, and it tested the loyalty of Mason when he was thrown into the insane asylum. The lion also pursues Tarwater. The ferocious cat lurks in the hero's self-will. It shows itself in the fire set to cremate Mason, and will menace the hero's work in sly ways—both as pride from within and as animosity from without. From time to time, he will feel overcome. One such moment is at the fountain. When Rayber whisks Bishop away, Tarwater walks past the pool with his back bent "as if he were being driven away with a whip" (147). He is struck; but it is love, not the trainer's rod, that lashes Tarwater. In Chapter VI, the hero advances from the temple where Lucette warns of love's cut to the lion's den where he feels the severity of love in a preliminary trial. A boy raised to be a prophet does well to know the torment of the lair, for such knowledge can teach him to stay the might of the whip.

The lion story in the Book of Daniel (6:16–23) assures the vulnerable Daniel that faith will bring divine aid. A king of Babylon casts Daniel into a lion's den for refusing to worship him as a god. Daniel remains loyal to God, Who sends an angel to close the lion's mouth, and Daniel stands unharmed. Mason counts on that help in his struggle against current Babylonian idolatries. In fact, Christian reflection in the Latin church has developed the tableau of Daniel standing untouched among the lions into an emblem of the resurrection of the body—the risen life through the risen Christ that Mason works for. The lion, then, gains power by both belligerence and submission. It forces change to meet the needs of faith.

At times, the violent lion bears witness to the kingdom. Matthew (11:12) reminds us of such an era in the epigraph to *The Violent Bear It*

Away. After John the Baptist, the same passage suggests, meekness carries the power of faith. The new dispensation of the cross makes the Messiah the Lion of the tribe of Judah. " 'Weep not,' " consoles one of the elders in Revelation, " 'lo, the Lion of the tribe of Judah, the Root of David, has conquered, so that he can open the scroll and its seven seals' " (5:5). The seer in Revelation expects the lion to disclose the fixed purposes of God that are sealed in the scroll, but the creature that appears to the seer is "a Lamb standing, as though it had been slain" (Revelation 5:6). O'Connor's revelation in the park borrows both images. There is the lion and there is Bishop, who will be slain.

The revelation climaxes with an example of the mysterious power of meekness. What is the lion's den for Tarwater becomes a sacred font for Bishop as the Lion of the tribe of Judah protects the idiot boy. The lion's guardianship first comes to our attention in the ordinary light of day that sifts through the trees around the fountain before touching Bishop. As he wades in the water near the fiery majesty of stone, the sun shines "brightly on Bishop's white head." The rapt child stands there absorbed with "a look of attention" (145), saluting what is always above him; and through his natural wonder he recognizes that the light accepts him as he is. There is no mistaking O'Connor's poetry. The fiery presence is a sign of glory. The courtesy of God approaches the little, humble idiot through beauty and power. The glory of God recurs as a sphere of transcendent purity. This light appears in Ezekiel, in Isaiah, and in Paul; and it radiates in a comparable way in *Wise Blood*, "The River," and "The Displaced Person," to cite telling instances among many in O'Connor's fiction. The indelible traces of glory in *The Violent Bear It Away* illumine the divine presence in Bishop, and show us how to know Who love is when He comes. The sun in the park manifests His son, the dim-witted child, awaiting immersion into the life of the Son. For a moment Bishop bathes in the fountain and in the source of life that secures him from danger. The circle of divine wholeness rings him in peace. When in the water overseen by the lion, Bishop is content. The concrete circle replicates the sun, rays and all, which are again repeated in the heraldic lion.

The full splendor of sun and water and lion in mystical union comes in Chapter VIII, where O'Connor represents the scene through Tarwater's sensitivity. He, unlike Rayber, feels "the approach of mystery" as the three walk into the park. Mason's education attunes Tarwater to the divine power in nature with which the prophetic commission is allied. Again O'Connor wants the reader to see the sun tacking from cloud to cloud before it emerges above the fountain. When it does alight on the statue, a theophanic brilliance glitters: "A blinding brightness fell on the lion's tangled marble head and gilded the stream of water rushing from his mouth" (164). Solar light makes gushing water appear as a breath of fire crowning Bishop's white head; and when he watches his reflection in the water, his round face mirrors and enlarges the sun. O'Connor's use of images shows that the beginning of recognition lies in knowing what to expect and in considering that the least likely may be the best material for love. God, we see by this light, has already marked Bishop for glory; and so when Tarwater kills the child and inadvertently utters the baptismal words, the drowning is a confirmation of the divine relation that Bishop always enjoys.

The revelation ends abruptly when Rayber grabs Bishop from the pool. When yanked outside the protective domain of the royal lion, Bishop howls. Though his doleful outcry subsides into a soft wail, Bishop's face turns "red and hideously distorted" (147). He feels the pain of separation from origins, longing for the true parent and light from Whom Rayber kidnaps him. Removal from the dignity that is conferred by glory results in Bishop's ugly transformation, a change that forces Rayber to turn his eyes away from the agony he causes. Drastic alterations in facial expression are common in O'Connor's fiction, but nowhere is the cause clearer. Without the brightness of spirit to shed luster on his humanness, Bishop—everyone—becomes a grotesque.

O'Connor completes the episode by returning the point of view to Rayber's tunnel vision, from which the suffering and distortions emerge. Blindness to love also blurs the sense of responsibility. Rayber sees no more cause for blame in his behavior in the park than he does in his attempt to kill Bishop years before. The schoolteacher blames God for the crying child; and he curses Tarwater, the "Goddam backwoods imbecile," for going off alone. Though palming off guilt on others allows Rayber a vicarious absolution, Mason's old threat scrawled on the back of the educators' journal in which Mason was reduced to a case study rises before the angered schoolteacher: "THE PROPHET I RAISE UP OUT OF THIS BOY WILL BURN YOUR EYES CLEAN" (147).

There is no telling when the fire will be lit under the boy by God; but the incandescent lion, aglow with its blazing ally, the sun, guarantees that one day the secret flame will ignite. With this evangelical forecast comes the promise of apocalyptic comfort given by the lion to the lamb (Isaiah 11:6). Those chosen for the purifying heat can hope to prevail. Lo, the Lion of the tribe of Judah will also be at hand, as he presides over the fountain in the park, to wipe away the tears.

Before the lion and the lamb meet at the climactic baptism, Rayber returns to Powderhead. He wants only to fill his car with gasoline for the planned trip to Mason's place the following day, when he will cure Tarwater of the spiritual sickness he picked up from the old man; but the schoolteacher's car, like Hazel Motes's Essex, can be driven by another will, which takes Rayber down the deep red embankments he knew as a boy. Whereas Bishop, who accompanies his father, gapes in open-mouthed wonder at the magnificence around him, Rayber swells with anger as the car crests at "an entrance to a region he would enter at his peril" (183). Powderhead activates dormant emotions. Rayber's heart beats frenetically, as it did when he walked this patch of ground with Mason; now, to check his expanding heart, he tries to reduce the wood of Powderhead to board feet that would pay for Tarwater's education. The autonomous beauty of the trees, however, serves to remind him of his personal failure. Here Mason stirred in Rayber the tendency to love without limit; and amid the woods that never budge from loyalty to the Creator, Rayber feels the disparity between Mason's legacy and his own impoverished lot. Life is synonymous with defeat, and disappointment leads Rayber to quail before experience and to dignify his decision "to resist feeling anything at all" (182) as stoical wisdom. Powderhead impugns this attitude by wrenching Rayber's heart, but the violent emotional twist alters nothing in him. This chance visit, his last to Powderhead, is Rayber's farewell to the past and to the possibility of love. That evening his heart constricts into hard muscle impervious to love's cut.

The final scene of Part Two occurs thirty miles from Powderhead at the Cherokee Lodge. The resort is a ramshackle warehouse made into a lakeside guest house, an architectural conversion that O'Connor favors to mark the transitional point where God intervenes to build a future edifice out of feeble human structures. The small lake near the rickety lodge is not much to look at, but on first sight Tarwater feels that "it might only the moment before have been set down by four strapping angels for him to baptize the child in" (167). The setting reinforces Tarwater's fear of approaching Mason's orders to christen Bishop. The trees surrounding the sacred font form a crown of thorns in recognition of the spiritual store of Jesus' life that the old man wants Bishop to share in. Special protection adds to the mystery. One of the four sturdy angels is on hand to watch over Bishop. On their arrival, the heavy woman at the desk warmly greets the child: " 'What's your name, Sugarpie?' she asked" (152). When Tarwater cruelly rejects the child's friendly touch, the receptionist is there to make Tarwater feel that he has profaned the holy: " 'Mind how you talk to one of them there, you boy!' the woman hissed" (155). This vigilant angel gets her message across, for when Bishop sits on the steps to have his shoelaces tied, Tarwater ties the laces with unexpected kindness. Later, the receptionist sees Bishop amble down the dock and runs after him to save him from falling in the water.

For Bishop the lake is pleasure, but for Tarwater the lake as baptismal font obstructs his freedom. He senses that here he must act decisively to put an end to Mason's power and to cross over into independence. The lake is Tarwater's Jordan. The River Jordan bears on his destiny in several ways. It is featured in the reports of miracles by Elijah and Elisha, from whom Tarwater expects unearthly signs to guide him; and it is the place where Jesus, through baptism by John the Baptist, receives His mission to go forth to teach the world, the task that Tarwater tries to avoid. The specific link is with Elisha, who takes up the mantle of prophecy from Elijah on the bank of the Jordan. Where Elijah's mantle falls, it strikes water; and the spring confirms prophetic succession (2 Kings 2:13–15). The lake set down in Tennessee by O'Connor's four strapping angels flows from this fountainhead. The act of immersing Bishop in this water is Tarwater's crossing the Jordan of reluctance and his coming into possession of Elijah's mantle. True, he drowns Bishop to preclude his membership among the sons of the prophets, and the mantle falls uneasily on him; but then Tarwater's fate is always opposed to his desires and passions. The singular traits of the Jordan also suggest a way for O'Connor to take this paradox into account. Though the modern mind would think of the most important river in Palestine as a beauty of nature, people in biblical times dreaded the Jordan as a dangerous barrier because of its dark, muddy waters. From their point of view, the river was almost completely useless. *The Violent Bear It Away* follows the divine precedent of putting the unwanted into service. The stirring of the miraculous into the tarnished and violent water provides the right mixture of supernatural current in her hero's action for O'Connor to name Tarwater after the Jordan's tarred waters.

The actual murder of Bishop comes to the reader in a restrained style that barely keeps itself from weeping or screaming. O'Connor wants horror to carry its own judgment. Since the physical universe holds fast to an allegiance to God's self-communication established in the days of creation, O'Connor can step back and trust nature's operation to pay the needed moral attention. Earth, air, fire, and water objectify the will of God. To begin with, the sun that keeps an eye on Bishop in the park issues an alarm when Tarwater leads him down the lakeside dock to the kill. A "weird light" intensifies every color in the pink twilight and transforms each weed sticking out of the ground into a "live green nerve" most sensitive to pain outside its protective sheath: "The world might have been shedding its skin" (197). Had the world become Bishop, as Rayber and Tarwater fear, it would again have come together in the radiance of the sunlit lion. But now Rayber's self-hatred and Tarwater's self-conceit fatally impose their will on Bishop's body; and at the hour of his death, the anatomy of the world becomes satanic, at once serpentine and infernal. Rayber sends his son to execution by passively watching Tarwater, "the surly oarsman," ply his human cargo "to some mysterious destination" (198). The red globe reacts by exploding the purple sky into darkness.

Nature's dark also reifies the unnatural night of Rayber's mind, through which O'Connor initially presents the murder. She adopts the schoolteacher's point of view because she wants us to know that in giving Tarwater the idea of drowning Bishop to prove independence from Mason, Rayber is an accomplice to the murder. In addition, O'Connor wants the reader to feel the trial of love preceding the shutdown of Rayber's heart. Hearing aid turned off and eyes closed to nap on his bedroom cot, Rayber congratulates himself on achieving an indifference toward both son and nephew. Dignity in a miscreant world requires apathy. The man called to mystical love ends up celebrating a puny credo, "To feel nothing was peace" (200); the incantation romanticizes his failure. Disturbed by the moon, "a pale messenger" (202) delivering an ultimatum to respond, Rayber switches on his hearing aid, which picks up the rising and falling of a garbled bawl. Though the fierce struggle causing the sound is unseen from the lodge, the cry is clearly his son's. The bellow claws his heart, but Rayber remains still, lets no sound escape his set jaw. His collapse serves as a self-judgment of his life. "He makes the Satanic choice," O'Connor states, "and the inability to feel the pain of his loss is the immediate result" (*Letters* 484). Rayber ends up a monster of containment.

For all the terror of the climactic scene at the lake, the narrative never raises its voice; the passion and exaltation of dying child, homicidal cousin, and crushed father are set forth with transparent simplicity. The one caring witness is the moon, which counterbalances the horror and rejection dominating the end of Part Two by revealing a presence of compassionate lucidity. Before Bishop dies, the moon flushes with apocalyptic ire, and, to borrow Habakkuk's description of a parallel moment in salvation history, bestrides "the earth in fury" (Habakkuk 3:12). When Bishop is beyond human pallor, the moon too loses its color and hews a rescuing path on the water: "The sky was a hollow black and an empty road of moonlight crossed the lake" (202).

The watery trail of moonlight maps two topographies. One is a new course for Tarwater, who sets out for home armed, he believes, with proof by water that he has escaped the call of prophecy. The other is the new life that comes with Bishop's death. However mysterious these paths, the ultimate effect is one of lucidity. As the colors of twilight and the bellows of Bishop die away bit by bit, stripping down the violent texture of the drama, the moonlight swath of God's love across the cataclysmic night becomes increasingly understandable and unmistakable.

IV

As Tarwater makes his way back to Powderhead, shadowy figures cross his path to hasten him along. First, a weary trucker speeds him through the night, evicting him at a point ten miles from Route 56, where there is a dirt road home. Near the crossroads, a man cruising in a lavender and cream-colored car picks up Tarwater. Tarwater gets drunk and raped and discarded. He labors on to Powderhead. Thirsty and battered, he meets a large woman leaning against a store where he and Mason traded. She beams black, judging eyes on him. He takes in her accusation that he shamed the dead, and pushes on. Like Jesus entering Jerusalem on an ass, Buford then appears on a mule. The humble black servant greets Tarwater with a rebuke for not burying Mason, and announces that he has dug the grave himself. Tarwater goes to the grave that he was too selfish to dig. As darkness falls and the new moon rises again, the wood across the head of the grave shows Tarwater that he has not won his independence from God: he failed both to destroy Mason's corpse and to disprove the truth of the resurrection that

Mason lived by and placed on Tarwater. These defeats constitute Part Three of *The Violent Bear It Away.*

Tarwater's drubbings are best understood through the Old Testament cycle of apostasy, enslavement, repentance, and deliverance. When Israel does what is evil in the Lord's sight and forsakes the God of its fathers and mothers, it provokes the Lord to wrath. In anger the Lord gives His people over to despoilers, who take by force whatever Israel possesses and values. After Tarwater commits the grave sin of killing Bishop, the Lord's anger, kindling in the red moon, strikes Tarwater in a similar way by putting him under the power of his enemies lurking about the road to Powderhead. When Tarwater escapes from one assailant, the hand of the Lord remands him into the control of another and another, until the hero who thinks himself a young god feels his powerlessness and learns that he is free only when loyal to the Lord. Tarwater's enemies systematically tear from him aspects of self-love that stand in the way of his loving God. Part Three, in sum, shows the empowering of love—the love to which nothing counts but love.

These reverses occur from nightfall to nightfall. The biblical day is lunar, and within the two risings of the new moon Tarwater lives "the lifetime of a man" (220) whose calling goes back to ancient Near Eastern legends. For prophets, self-realization is always abrupt because length of time matters less in their work than does depth of choice. However rigorously taught by Mason, Tarwater's service to God depends upon his own free assent. That decision for O'Connor cannot be grasped as a slow inner growing. Her reliance on drastic moments to further the action and young Tarwater's maturity squares well with prophetic records, which are filled with shameful indignities and frightful visions seizing their subjects. Prophets live under the judgment of destruction that God has them announce. They become lonely, poor, castigated, assaulted. Knowing that the education of a prophet is harrowing, O'Connor spares her teenage prophet-elect none of the terror.

Above all, the making of a prophet entails Tarwater's feeling the cold-bloodedness of slaying Bishop. If Tarwater does not feel the emotional source and consequences of his acts, his guardian devil, whose counsel is toward callousness, can retain the upper hand. The first despoiler makes the hero feel both the devil's lack of feeling and his helplessness before it. A "huge and skeletal" (207) auto-transit truck glides in to swallow him up on the highway. The wiry driver looks like a citizen of a world that has shed its skin. A "sharply twisted" (208) nose wrenches between the man's heavy-lidded eyes. His voice comes from another section of the country. So does his humanity. Somewhere on the run between Detroit and Tennessee he seems to have lost emotional contact with people. He wants it known that he does no favors for anyone and that a rider must supply talk, preferably of gore and sex, to keep him awake. Tarwater, unaccustomed to meeting cheap demands on his sensibility, is a disappointing source of stimulation. Matters of the soul that surround Bishop's death totally absorb him. His terse comments on being born again and the bread of life make no sense to the man with the serpentine nose. The truck driver's dejection flattens everything into moral tedium. The slaying of only one boy bores the morally fatigued trucker. All the mechanical helmsman can do is drive on to deeper zones of unfeeling, and his direction points toward the dullness of heart awaiting Tarwater if he persists in his willfulness.

When the tired driver pulls onto the shoulder of the road to rest, Tarwater dreams back to the drowning of Bishop and relives the defeat that his mind tries to erase. Arms flailing in an attempt to extricate himself from any indication that he is not in control, the fated fugitive recalls that he did after all cry out the words of baptism. The Lord has trapped Tarwater in the cab of the huge truck to teach him that he has been snared for His plan.

The truth of this lesson, however, requires experience for it to take hold. For now, the Lord gives a sign. Caught, as everyone remarks, like reluctant Jonah in the whale's belly, Tarwater witnesses in his dream a plateau of red sky on the eastern horizon. The plateau widens until the sun rises "through it majestically with a long red wingspread" (217). The wingspread is Pentecostal and sacrificial—a figuration of the life emerging out of Tarwater's inadvertent christening. The airy plumage visually transcribes Jonah's name, which means "dove" in Hebrew. In scripture, preaching becomes the sign of Jonah. In Tarwater's novel, O'Connor unites word with person to make the red dove over the lake the sign of Tarwater. The red dove is the Spirit as harbinger of mercy, the mercy that Tarwater denies Bishop and begrudges Mason and therefore must bring to others.

Before Tarwater can awaken others to God's compassion, the claims of love must tear away the assurances of intellect that block divine forgiveness in himself. This realization begins when the woman at the store off Route 56 chastises him mercilessly for leaving Mason's body exposed and burning Powderhead. The woman whom Mason found as refreshing as a shade tree on a hot day receives Tarwater like a sentinel. Large and sturdy, her imposing presence is cut from the same rock out of which O'Connor carves the park lion. Black eyes peer from "her stony face" with a knowledge of Tarwater that rattles his confidence. She puts before him the facts that she learned from the blacks: he " 'shames the dead' " (225). The huge wings that O'Connor envisions folding behind this woman become her, for the imaginary wings point upward to the source of her message and power. Each charge begins with *And;* each *And* strikes like a hammer. The indictments are in the present tense to nail Tarwater with the judgment of his evil as ongoing and still active. The litigious *And*s demolish Tarwater's alibis and level his sins to the eternal ground on which the woman stands. Her last words, " 'And scorns,' " bolt Tarwater to the obligation of living for the last day, the duty he thought he sank with Bishop in the muddy water at the Cherokee Lodge: " 'And scorns the Resurrection and the Life?' " (226). The rock-faced storekeeper lets the prodigal boy pass into the loneliness that his actions create. Exhaustion wrings his eyes; terror shrinks the skin of his face. Trying to escape from God wears him down to a tight, dry shell.

Tarwater's unsightliness does not deter a ready satan from lending a hand. The boy's guardian devil dons a lavender shirt, black suit, and panama hat; then he tools his matching lavender and cream-colored car down the road to Powderhead to pick up the hero. As at the grave site in the beginning of the novel, where a devil first comes to the rescue, the importuning cruiser encourages Tarwater to get drunk during the ride back to Powderhead. Eager to disobey Mason's warning against demon rum and rides with strangers, Tarwater gulps down the liquor. The boy, already tipsy over killing an idiot, wants to be deprived of feeling the impact of the murder. The taker of life is ripe for the taking, and self-indulgence opens the way for his capture. The satan rapes Tarwater in the secluded woods.

Though many readers do not seriously consider Tarwater's molestation as sexual encounter, O'Connor plans the rape as carnal and repulsive and indispensable. A letter of 27 August 1962, which came to light after the publication of *The Habit of Being,* clarifies her intention. A teacher writes to convey a Catholic student's puzzlement that O'Connor should use so ugly an act as rape to bring Tarwater to his mission. Sympathetic to the moral freshness prompting the student's aversion, O'Connor states amiably, not defensively: "It was a very necessary action to the meaning of the book . . . and one which I would not have used if I hadn't been obliged to." Her explanatory kindness (a peacock feather accompanies the letter) resolves three nagging questions about *The Violent Bear It Away:* "Tarwater is not sick or crazy but really called to be a prophet"; it takes the homosexual in the fancy car to make the young hero "see for the first time what evil is"; and the ending, which "can only be understood in religious terms," would be "merely a dishonest manipulation" without sexual indignity preparing for it (see Appendix).

Rape culminates the barrage of physical ordeals that Tarwater sustains after his great-uncle and protector dies. Mistress of form that she is, O'Connor times the rape to explain the components of the sinful disobedience that is building in Tarwater and threatening to lock him into the satanic choice. O'Connor's strategy comes to the hero in the car's cracked window, in which he "could see a pale reflection of himself, eyeing him darkly" (228). By turning the salacious stare into sexual penetration, O'Connor brings out the unacknowledged egoism of Tarwater's conduct. It is self-love that motivates his action from his first swill of whiskey taken to avoid digging Mason's grave. The same involvement generates his wandering in self-admiration as he demonstrates that whereas others talk, he acts. The homosexual assault near the end of his dereliction vivifies his spiritual narcissism and accomplishes the reverse of what he expects for his decisiveness. Tarwater is stripped bare by the personification of self-love, the master-narcissist, Satan ("enemy," in Hebrew) or the devil ("slanderer," in Greek). By name, the *adversary* is condemned to be gratified by referring every thought and act against God to his desire for revenge. As antagonist in Tarwater's battle of wills, the lavender devil is the ultimate despoiler and the last of many complements showing the hero's negative self. Satan's homosexuality forces the boy to have intercourse with himself and with himself in another simultaneously, so that Tarwater learns the hard way that by following his own inclinations he is raping himself of true worth.

My language here, however, misleads if narcissism is understood as metaphor and rape as philosophical act. O'Connor is not concerned with personality disorder; she would never cushion rape with clinical understanding. She makes the effect raw. She wants the reader to know that forced sexuality makes the hero feel uncovered parts of himself with excruciating immediacy. While the demon has unrestrained privilege over Tarwater's body, both devil and hero know Tarwater at the core of his vulnerability. As he sins with his body by destroying Bishop and burning Powderhead, so his body must experience sin as annihilating and torrid. The gut is O'Connor's shortcut to the heart. If the hour Tarwater spends with the satanic incubus is a hurried maturity, it must also be a protracted physical anguish.

Sexual congress while he is sunk in alcoholic stupor leaves Tarwater numb. Like Milton's satans who lie stunned from the fall at the beginning of *Paradise Lost,* Tarwater's dazed slump renders his mind useless in grasping fully the blow he has received. Propped against a log that lies between two tall trees, he cannot appreciate that the crosspiece ties him to the cross. Awareness will come as he feels the experience gradually but acutely, and his recognition will be all the truer for emerging from the unconscious, where the red dove hovers. What little Tarwater can acknowledge now comes in a waking groan torn out of his racked, naked body. Punch-drunk, he savagely grabs his trusty matches to purify "the evil ground" (232) of the stranger's touch and sappy odor. His instinct is keener now, and his nostrils are able to pick up the rot. The rapist's hand strikes deep enough to help Tarwater mediate his opposing wills: while not yet saying Yes to his vocation, he says No to the stench of Satan. In a world where Satan passes for a friend, the identification of evil constitutes a negative knowledge of good.

It may seem mad to torch "every spot the stranger could have touched" (232) if we do not see that control has been Tarwater's last remaining source of integrity. His autonomy had to remain pure, or its value as justifying murder would be undermined. Rape makes him experience what the reader has known from the first sentence of the novel: he is not an independent doer and blameless defier of Mason's orders. No longer is Tarwater wise in his rebellion. On the contrary, he has been in bondage, tied by a lavender handkerchief of amour propre. He is stupid because he has lived in Satan's deception, and he is profane because his liberty is made possible by the obscene sacrifice of Bishop's body. He does not give himself life, but has life on loan from the dead. He was born in a car wreck that killed his mother, grandmother, and grandfather; he survives on the corpses of his family, one of whom he killed to prove his separation from Tarwater blood; and he lives a constant debasing relationship to the enslaved self he despises. And now this terrible vicariousness continues as "a violet shadow" hangs "around his shoulders" (237), exuding the sweet stink that putrefied the ground where he was raped. To shake off this airy caress, Tarwater must repent of self-adoration.

Rape is the heinous means of turning the hero's will Godward, away from the nuzzling shadow-self; but the shock does not immediately bend Tarwater's egoism. He still wants to be his own man by escaping two foul alternatives; he wants to get rid of the saccharine presence but not to take in "the sweat and stink of the cross" (8). His will, in fact, lags behind a determination made by his body, for olfactory aversion to this devil reaches Tarwater's brain directly, and, through corporeal transfer of knowledge, fills his body with revulsion. His swoop of disgust triggers thirst and shoulder-ache, which signify that the hero is already capitulating to the unappeasable demands of the cross. Rape hurls Tarwater into the passion that will convert the fourteen-year-old baptist-murderer into a prophet *malgré lui.*

Tarwater's howl embraces the passion by echoing Bishop's dying grief, which blared out "after centuries of waiting" (202). Tarwater tramples on Bishop's trusting love and gets back what he gave by being crushed in rape. For one hour with the rapist, Tarwater takes Bishop's place to feel the mortal helplessness that was suffered by God's child in Tarwater's sadistic hands. This hour brings him to his essential poverty. He has replaced God with himself, and with Satan he cannot help himself. The entreating stranger who is alluring at the beginning turns out to be abhorrent. The same is true of Tarwater's plan for independence. His ego, having put its faith in the illusion of self-mastery, is destitute when the devil rips away the appearance. Self-loathing results. The terrible clarity of repugnance burns. Groaning parches his lips, and his inward gaze singes his eyes so that he can see the murdered Bishop as part of his personal need for merciful love. One counsel of the hero's truly great great-uncle is already coming to pass. " 'Judgment may rack your bones' " (10), Mason warned. Rape marks the beginning of judgment, with ultimate humiliation preparing Tarwater for final purgation.

V

The cleansing shock strikes Tarwater in Chapter XII, and this development makes the last chapter of *The Violent Bear It Away* important for an understanding of love's violence. The closing segment follows Tarwater from dusk on the road to the secluded clearing where Mason's house once stood and back at midnight to the road, where the seven-day adventure ends. Here O'Connor does not miss the chance to give a magnificent description of grace searing Tarwater. Hour by racking dark hour, she has three illuminating appearances cauterize his spirit.

Fire surrounds all three visions. A mammoth Tennessee sun works up its full redness, which animates the scene as Tarwater walks along the faint path to the charred remains of his little holocaust of a week earlier. Powderhead feels different to him than it did before. The scorched Eden of his past does not receive him as a victor claiming his spoils or as a lost son returned home. The place stops him in his tracks, possessing him rather than yielding to his possessiveness. The disturbance comes from the heated breeze of the satan wafting over Tarwater's neck. In familiar, conspiratorial first-person plurals, the devil importunes his boy to claim Mason's place: "It's ours. We've won it." Velvety whispers pledge loyalty: "now we can take it over together, just you and me. You're not ever going to be alone again" (237). The lavender odor is fresh enough in Tarwater's nostrils for him to recoil from his consort; and to put an end to their partnership, Tarwater sets a match to a pine bough to erect a wall of flame between himself and "his adversary" (238), who disappears into his own fiery leer.

Out of the dusky atmosphere Buford Munson appears. Like Jesus entering Jerusalem on an ass, Buford arrives on a mule. The man who bore Tarwater's burden approaches on the burden-bearer. Motionless, rider and animal "might have been made out of rock" (239). The image of stony material is consistent in the novel and fitting theologically as a sign of refuge and moral steadfastness. Rock is the attribute of the Lord. "Rock" (Hebrew ṣûr) is a divine title bestowed on the lion in the park and the woman at the store, whose belief and action have the power of defense against devils. Buford epitomizes what these other figures of faith stand for: namely, the personal responsibility to alert others to the moral dangers afoot. Buford reminded Tarwater before the boy got drunk and stopped digging Mason's grave that the old man " 'was deep in Jesus' misery' " and " 'needs to be rested' " (48). Buford foresaw Tarwater's betrayal, and at the end stands guard over the fresh grave that he himself dug and marked with a rough cross.

Buford's words are few. They speak not of the pride that he takes in doing Tarwater's job but of the additional guilt Tarwater incurs in trying to destroy Mason's body, which the old man believed was made for the resurrection. For all their force, however, Buford's words are less powerful than the concrete results of his action, which the black man now projects with his eyes. Three times within the span of five brief paragraphs (240) O'Connor uses the verb *watch* ("watching," "watching," "watched") to depict Buford observing Tarwater from the mule. He watches until, good lookout that he is, Buford smells smoke and turns the mule down to the woods to deal with the latest danger, this one too of Tarwater's making. Through Buford's vigilance, O'Connor develops the prophetic charge that Tarwater's training prepares him to receive. He will be a watchman. The assignment goes to the heart of prophecy. Ezekiel sees the need with especial clarity and defines (33:1–33) the role that Buford fulfills in an everyday way. Ezekiel sees the social order of Israel as doomed through idolatry, and calls for personal responsibility to fill the moral vacuum. The person who sees peril must warn the people of judgment. The prophet who fails to warn the people of disasters bears the guilt of neglect and the additional guilt of doom that befalls the people. The prophet-as-watchman distinguishes Ezekiel's contribution to the prophetic tradition, and provides the basis for O'Connor's expansion of the figure into riven seers—one of whom, Hazel Motes, is even blind—who are the eyes for the modern world that cannot see devils for what they are.

Not another word is spoken in the novel after Buford's terse announcement of Tarwater's guilt. The concluding pages delineate the sights that the young watchman-to-be takes in: the grave, a meal, and a fire. Now Tarwater's eyes go deep to see the eschatological reality for which the watchman mounts guard. What makes the hero see anew is the divine light that pours out after his confession of guilt. Defeat teaches Tarwater by anguish the obedience he had been unable to learn by love during his time with Mason and Bishop. He comes to fathom creation by means of what he owes the Creator. His obligation to God takes the form of envisioned multitudes to whom Tarwater must answer. The spectacle constitutes the inaugural vision of Tarwater's ministry, and comes as the sun sinks behind the blazing trees. As the scriptural new day begins with sundown, Tarwater's day of awareness begins with dark setting in. Moreover, *to watch* means to relinquish a night's sleep. So too, Tarwater must stay alert in order to survive in the night without succumbing to its darkness.

First, Tarwater rivets his eyes downward on the grave. The cross acts like a living tree guiding his stare down through the soil "to where its roots encircled all the dead" (240). The boy who could not bury one great-uncle now digs with his moral sight a universal grave. Mason taught him that the world was made for the dead, but how could

Tarwater imagine that he was made for their deliverance? Can love entail this insupportable job? Suppose he again backs away from the assigned task? The prospect of being accountable to both the dead and the living is awesome. But so is the aid. The power that the great-hearted Mason rants about has exposed its source, the cross, which provides the sap for physical growth and for the final resurrection harvest.

This spiritual nourishment takes eatable form in the next scene, where another multitude, a throng of feasters appearing on the field that Buford just crossed, presses the feeling of accountability on Tarwater. They sit on a slope, reclined as they would have dined in biblical times, taking food from one inexhaustible basket. Tarwater surveys the crowd for his great-uncle and sees the old mountain of a man on the expiatory mount, leaning forward in starved anticipation of the fishes and loaves in the basket. Before Tarwater's eyes is the marvel that brings the "look of complete astonishment" (10) to Mason's face when he dies before having breakfast. The complete meal is laid out. While O'Connor alludes to the gospel account of Jesus' feeding of the five thousand, her interest lies not in the miraculous but in the basic appetite that the messianic banquet satisfies. The meal of the end of time identifies the all-sufficient food that Tarwater's persistent hunger needs. Nothing less than redemption will fill his longing.

The nature of this food is that it increases the hunger it satisfies. As night dissolves the supper vision into darkness, Tarwater's hunger rises—"through time and darkness, rising through the centuries . . . in a line of men whose lives were chosen to sustain it" (242). The lineage of prophets, Tarwater's ancestry, is before him. What links the line of prophets in their strange wandering is sacrifice. The surge issues from the blood of Abel, the first murder victim, whose death cries out for atonement and whose sacrifice Yahweh receives with favor. It builds through the countless other sacrificial victims, the most notable of whom hangs on Calvary, and the most recent of whom floats in the lake by the Cherokee Lodge. The blood from these sacrifices transcends time to illuminate a "red-gold tree of fire" glowing along the property's treeline, where it is about to consume the darkness in "one tremendous burst of flame" (242). This is one fire that is not of Tarwater's doing. He may have set it with the pine bough, but the Lord's will transforms the fire into a furnace of judgment that chastens as it expands. Tarwater will be fuel for the divine fire.

The burning tree reveals God's will not by giving dogma or by imparting knowledge of higher worlds. The purpose of this sin-consuming fire is to open wider the already scorched eyes of Tarwater to the coming events, to the concrete realities in the day-to-day world that will test his loyalty. The nature of God was not Mason's concern, just as abstract theology never troubled the prophets of Israel; nor will God's nature interest Tarwater. Like Mason, Tarwater must deal with plain facts, the corporal works that represent a merciful God—answering the needs of hunger, thirst, nakedness, homelessness, sickness, imprisonment, and of the dead needing burial. The message determining these acts comes to Tarwater silently and to the reader in stark capital letters on the page: "GO WARN THE CHILDREN OF GOD OF THE TERRIBLE SPEED OF MERCY" (242). Tarwater hears the order with his being as he lies on the ground with his face in the soil of Mason's grave. Everything that is active, that stirs and sprouts, that enriches the plenitude on the beatific slope and fills the tree-lined sky, comes in these words. Whereas self-adoration destroys, the command for self-donation creates. The words are incarnational—"seeds opening one at a time in his blood" (242).

The blood seeds of mercy are not foreign to Tarwater's being. From the moment he finds Mason in need of burial to the rape and back to Powderhead, Tarwater has been plumbing his inner weakness. Though he boasts of being in charge, downfall after downfall shows that his one and only help lies in what the Lord can do and say. The headstrong boy is too weak to be loved and too afraid to love until rape so weakens him that he cannot resist. Schooled by evil, he learns what mercy means. Then the Lord stands ready to help, and the speed of mercy offsets Tarwater's reluctance. It is as though the Lord is so eager to love that the moment Tarwater feels worthy, the Lord rushes to the rescue, forcing His love upon the boy before contrition, as it invariably does, turns to pride.

Tarwater dedicates himself to God with an act of eligibility. He stoops to gather a handful of dirt from Mason's grave and smears the dirt on his forehead. This one self-effacing deed in the penultimate paragraph of *The Violent Bear It Away* palliates all the brutality that leads up to it and will fall from it. The gesture is instinctive, made with commitment rather than with will, and gains power from the invisible world O'Connor draws upon. In the biblical background, the mark on Tarwater's head distinguishes him as a person of God. God mitigates Cain's punishment for killing Abel by branding the wicked man for protection (Genesis 4:15). Subsequently, God instructs Ezekiel (9:4) to mark the forehead of those who show signs of remorse for Jerusalem's abominations in order to spare them from impending doom. The saving seal appears again on the forehead of God's servants in Revelation (7:4).

The most relevant use of the mark comes from Dante, O'Connor's master teacher, who depicts the psychology of receiving the merciful stamp. Eager to ascend Purgatory, Dante flings himself at the feet of an angel (*Purgatorio* IX) and begs to be admitted through its locked gate. The guardian angel responds to Dante's rush of humility by carving seven *P*'s on his brow. Each *P* (*peccatum,* or sin) suggests one of the seven capital sins that are purged on the terraces above. The marks are unique to Dante. The souls of those on Mount Purgatory do not receive the *P*'s because they have already been absolved. For them the *P*'s represent the stain left by sin, the propensity toward evil and the resistance toward good that linger after sin is forgiven. The dirt that Tarwater spreads on his forehead is his anointing admission of guilt, the condition through which he must discover the meaning of his sins as he wanders on heathen soil warning of divine mercy.

The mystery of absolving love can be seen in the natural growth of Powderhead's landscape, where the flat cornfield thrives despite fire. Mason planted the field before he died; Buford plowed it; and now the corn stands a foot high and waves in fresh green lines across the field. The harvesting is left for Tarwater. The growing cornfield is a collective duty that depicts, like fire and cornstalk bearing upward toward their natural source, the natural inclination of human love rising toward its source in works of mercy. This organic movement holds the secret of the resurrection that Mason yearns for. O'Connor, in fact, gives her living version of the analogy Paul uses to explain the resurrection to the puzzled Corinthians. He exclaims in a grand exposition on future life: "So is it with the resurrection of the dead. What is sown is perishable, what is raised is imperishable. It is sown in dishonor, it is raised in glory. It is sown in weakness, it is raised in power. It is sown a physical body, it is raised a spiritual body" (1 Corinthians 15: 42–44). We sow a seed and reap something altogether unlike the seed and yet derived from it. The corn seeds that Mason plants in the ground and the loaves that he hungers for in the vision and the seeds that germinate in Tarwater's blood are one. The process of perishable grain yielding imperishable crop in Powderhead will be the measure of Tarwater's duty wherever he goes.

He must first go into the dark city to awaken the sleeping children of God. That eventuality disturbs some readers, for whom prophecy signals Tarwater's embracing of Mason's monomania. Presumably, such disheartened readers share Rayber's pipe dream that Tarwater attend college and become a solid citizen. O'Connor thinks otherwise: "They forget that the old man has taught him the truth and that now he's doing what is right, however crazy" (*Letters* 536). Mason's truth inverts our accepted social values and leads to a depth that fascinates O'Connor. Rather than sealing Tarwater's conflict off by severing him from his losses, she lengthens the perspective on his future through concealed danger. "I've left him right at the beginning," she tells John Hawkes. "I keep wondering about how the children of God will finish him off" (*Letters* 359).

The final tableau sends Tarwater into the dark unknown. Sober for a change, he emerges from the burning woods onto the highway determined to get on with his business. Beside him glides the "diamond-bright" (243) new moon, casting his body into a jagged shadow that slashes a path as though he is forging through a thicket. The gloomy mass will always be with the messenger. It is the dark tangle of sin, his and that of the sleeping children of God. And the moon guiding him with diamond brightness has the hardest possible edge, which is exactly what Tarwater will need to cut through sin's density.

Battered but not diminished, Tarwater sets his singed face on the dark city. Violence has strengthened him, but so too has humility. No visceral wound of rape, no emotional shock of finding Mason's body, however deep, can compare with the vehemence of contact between him and the sin of self-love, his sin, which is the genesis of his destiny. The encounter galvanizes the conviction to convert and to love, not to kill, and makes Tarwater realize that he is eligible for the resurrection.

This consciousness also makes Tarwater luminous as he approaches the city in the middle of the night. He acknowledges that he is in hock to God, for prophecy is, after all, a mortgage on his future. Things are at last out of his hands. The next and all subsequent moves will be God's. Surrender brings out the valiance that is in his very fiber so that it can go out to meet God's claim on it. *The Violent Bear It Away* ends with Tarwater exposed to the love that cuts like a cold wind.

5

Convergence

In the name of God the almighty Father who created you,
in the name of Jesus Christ, Son of the living God, who suffered
for you,
in the name of the Holy Spirit, who was poured out upon you,
go forth, faithful Christian.
Commendation of Dying

For God sent the Son into the world, not to condemn the
world, but that the world might be saved through him.
John 3:17

Everything That Rises Must Converge is a uniquely important
book for Flannery O'Connor. It is her second collection of short stories
and last book of fiction. In November 1962, she gives Robert Giroux a
progress report on the material that he is eager to publish: "I have seven
stories but I don't think there is enough variety in them to make a good
collection. I might as well wait and see what I come up with in the next
year or two. I'm not in any hurry. I still want to call the book *Everything
That Rises Must Converge*" (*Letters* 498). O'Connor's health is deterio-
rating from lupus when she writes these words, and the next two years
are her last; nevertheless, weak bones are creative incentive to craft a
memorable book. There is a sense in O'Connor's mind that this suite of
stories carries her farewell, for despite her own physical debility, and
whatever her collection's eventual contents, the title of the work-in-
progress rings words of hope and confidence. In its final form the

collection gathers together nine stories that span nearly a decade of writing. The earliest, "Greenleaf," appears in 1956 (*Kenyon Review*); the latest, "Parker's Back" and "Judgement Day," are finished just before O'Connor lapses into the coma that precedes her death on 3 August 1964. In 1965, *Everything That Rises Must Converge* is published posthumously with an introductory encomium by Robert Fitzgerald.

O'Connor tells us that the title comes from the French Jesuit Pierre Teilhard de Chardin (1881–1955), a scientist, philosopher, and poet. The phrase, O'Connor explains, "is a physical proposition that I found in Père Teilhard and am applying to a certain situation in the Southern states & indeed in all the world" (*Letters* 438). The comment refers to race and family relations in a story, "Everything That Rises Must Converge," which is sold in 1961 to *New World Writing* and which becomes the title story of the collection. In noting the global applicability of this exuberant proposal, O'Connor is also revealing the ideas that shape the celebratory disposition behind her maturest art.

Though the title publicizes O'Connor's turn of mind toward exultation, readers manage to circumvent her new direction. "The violence that dominates nearly all of these stories is the slow violence of disease," remarks one critic; it is "the physical or psychic weakness that binds children to their mothers" (Hendin 102). Another commentator tries to go beyond neuroscience but stalls at the precise point from which O'Connor leaps forward. Interpreting her last volume in light of her first, this reader sees death and destruction culminating the stories in such a way that convergence seems to be a possibility that is never quite fulfilled (Muller 69–71). These views typify the many readings of the individual stories and volume as a whole, and they keep alive the inference that O'Connor at the end of her career remains a seer into the shadowed realm where humanity is brought low.

Those who perceive O'Connor as a resolute teller of cruel tales miss the good hopes proclaimed throughout her last book. The allusive title is her way of registering the conviction that overriding awesome setbacks and painful depletions, the planet is on an advance toward future unity. Convergence bespeaks that joyous outcome, and the nine stories show how it comes about. Convergence further tells us that O'Connor comprehends the movement in the stories by its divine end, finding the meaning of choices and events in their results. This manner of thought, like the last leg of Hazel Motes's journey to God, follows a backward course. The late O'Connor story, then, is to be understood in the reverse of the way it is lived: not as causes creating an effect, but as an end integrating the sequence.

There is no getting around Teilhard in assessing this turn of O'Connor's creative intelligence. Each study of her work must explore anew the contribution of the Frenchman's theology of evolution. But since O'Connor is an artist who "merely enjoys" and "does not analyze" (*Letters* 45) the many intellectual texts galvanizing her mind, there is no need to force things up. She has a way in letters and reviews of striking the essential note and moving on. Her appreciation of Teilhard takes the form of discovery and homage. With the important features of her enthusiasm set before us, we can go on to the primary issue of O'Connor's artistry in *Everything That Rises Must Converge.*

A good place to begin considering Teilhard's bearing on the confluence of guilt and love is O'Connor's review of his *Phenomenon of Man* and of Claude Tresmontant's *Pierre Teilhard de Chardin.* It appears in the 20 February 1960 issue of *The Bulletin,* the local diocesan newspaper. O'Connor knows that the writing of a paleontologist who studies evolution to find its spiritual significance and who has his insights suppressed by his church will have limited appeal to conservative Catholic readers, so she cuts through intricate biological and mystical classifications in *The Phenomenon of Man* to extol the value of Teilhard's research. As a scientist, he appreciates that modern discoveries sever humanity from old definitions conferring dignity; as a believer, he seeks ways of giving hope that accord with the processes in creation. His search is for "a new way to sanctity" (*Presence of Grace* 88), which O'Connor believes is the pressing need of our age.

Teilhard's way is by "spiritualizing matter," and that is "actually a very old way" (*Presence of Grace* 88). The approach is personally and historically familiar. O'Connor identifies the strategy in every artistic effort to vivify the spirit in words. In fact, Hazel Motes takes this path to God in *Wise Blood.* As we noticed the tracks of St. Paul along Hazel's journey, we now see Hazel's creator recognizing similar traces in Teilhard's way. "Teilhard's work," O'Connor says, "is a scientific rediscovery of St. Paul's thought" (*Presence of Grace* 87). Teilhard's work is also a scientific corroboration of the Pauline ideas that O'Connor uses in her early fiction.

The link between Teilhard and O'Connor is Paul's theology of the mystical body. Paul envisions Christ uniting all creation in Himself, with the crucifixion as the victory that sanctifies the feeble body so that "in him all things hold together" (Colossians 1:17). Teilhard and O'Connor understand Paul's mystical body not as ct solution to a riddle about God but as a moral catalyzing explore the world in original ways as scientist and fiction v ilhard's evolutionary evidence of Paul's vision leads him to the t onvergence. O'Connor employs the process of supernaturalizii to tell the spiritual comedies of our time. While the applicati lhard and O'Connor differ, their faith in God's plan to unify a osmos into Himself remains the same.

The Teilhard proposal entitling O'Con collection, roughly explained, goes like this: the entire univers lways has been, in perpetual evolution toward cosmic conver o a single whole. The air, the earth, humankind—everythi eading toward a unitive perfection. That end is union with G h God's Son. The organic surge culminates with Christ manife self in all things. Christ is the Omega of everything. His pervas ce makes matter divine; this divination of the physical, the Pa gnals the fulfillment of convergence and the end of time. By such lights, faith is not at odds with science and spirit is not antagonistic to matter. On the contrary, Christianity for Teilhard complements the massive phenomenological mystery in nature by accounting for its thrust as a movement toward sacred wholeness. Other mysteries fall into place. The incarnation marks the invasion of flesh by the divine, and the resurrection proclaims the winning back of matter into the ultimate source of life. Teilhard is convinced that humanity, for all the evolved growth it has attained, remains to be completed in physical nature and that suffering, epitomized by the crucifixion, holds the secret of convergence.

It is possible to ignore these immensities and still appreciate O'Connor's last collection. What one will miss, however, is the story behind the stories: how a spiritual storyteller matures in depth without changing the essential pattern she discerns in the human drama. Teilhard, then, teaches O'Connor what she does. The startling endings of her stories in *A Good Man Is Hard to Find* show how spirit drives an openness to the infinite. With Teilhardian support, fresh attention to this design frees O'Connor in *Everything That Rises Must Converge* to enter more tender zones of feeling that this openness exposes. Gentleness becomes prominent in the last stories as O'Connor searches out "the hidden love that makes a man" (*Letters* 307).

The Teilhard title invites us to look to charity for explanations in cruel and destructive situations. The practice makes for a strange magnificence. Teilhard discerns a dazzling thrust turning in harmony within a turmoil of atoms, molecules, and cells. The contrast astounds him; the consonance enchants him. Each step of the progression impels Teilhard to rhapsodize. Though each person feels cut off from the others and from the vast systems of nature, Teilhard takes and gives heart. Humanity too is on the way to perfection. Faith tells Teilhard how: God is drawing creation into the embrace of His person. The gesture transforms. Illness heals, and pain eases into joy. Even death holds love for Teilhard. Death is a final descent into the depths of matter from which there is an ascent into life. Divine energy in the cosmos makes it superabundant with love.

Though O'Connor appraises everything by this cosmic love, she knows that the everyday constitutes the story. Humble efforts as well as sudden violence hold the invitation to grace. Accordingly, these nine stories stay close to domestic matters. The scale of O'Connor's fiction gains integrity by remaining small because the eternal resides in it, urging the recognition that every human act has some important end. The joy of fulfilling one's daily duty or the grief of not doing so makes life passionately interesting in the setting of small southern towns because that mundane duty carries ultimate importance. Every human effort builds up or pulls back the flux of convergence.

In *Everything That Rises Must Converge* guilt marks the entry point for each character's participation in Teilhard's convergent flux. Guilt provides the psychological impetus for the character to struggle for union with others and the world. And persevere everyone must. Creation depends upon each person's quickening the power that transcends and fulfills all. The sense of duty dawns at the end of O'Connor's stories, but in Teilhard's writing the injunction to serve the universe is pervasive. Whenever the motif of responsibility arises, a synonym for guilt (duty, obligation, payment) stresses its personal character. "If man is to come up to his full measure, he must become conscious of his infinite capacity for carrying himself further," Teilhard exhorts in *The Prayer of the Universe;* "he must realize the duties it involves . . . " (*Universe* 43). Duty is conceived here in the psychology of mysticism, which lifts behavior into a divine order. Where union with God marks the bounds of human striving, one must abandon all notions of narrow self-importance and put the divine in the ego's stead. Guilt transforms egoism into charity by helping the mind break the habit of centering upon itself.

O'Connor's high-toned scoundrels and overbearing do-gooders experience such a rupture in themselves. The hard effects of unwelcomed knowledge that strike in the early fiction, however, soften in the last book into an inner diminishment, a desirous void, which makes room for God. This accommodation brings new knowledge. There is self-understanding in knowing that the essential longing is for God; and when the overwhelmed sinners discover that they are made for God and not the other way around, they learn how to love. Typically, the protagonists love another, lose that person, hope to regain her or him, but succeed only in coming to themselves. As quiet ways call the characters to self-truths they are eager to forget, subdued touches and turns express their assent. A thin voice calls for help, a sigh dresses an incision of grace, a whisper sues for favor, a bruiser cries like a baby.

These and other muted gestures are attributes of a change not in setting but in spiritual milieu. *Milieu* is Teilhard's word for the quality in which everything is immersed. His use of the word describes the way in which O'Connor resets the stage of her early dramas in her last collection with more space and mystery, throwing all the light upon small acts of loving receptiveness. The starry sky shining like a vast construction project that remains unheeded in Taulkinham in *Wise Blood* drenches *Everything That Rises Must Converge* in a mystical ambiance that compels the characters toward the upper limit of spirit. The magnetism opens new lines of force in the action. The shock at the end of O'Connor's previous stories shows an individual conversion, but in the posthumous volume the same collision of love suggests a collective salvation. As they gravitate toward the divine milieu, the characters carry out their duty in unison with the fulfilling plan of all cosmic perfection, even though they may be out of step with the immediate need of the person they love. But what else should be expected of a community of wounded egotists when they feel their need for communion? The divine milieu may be vast and ineffable but its attraction is intimate. To a greater degree than is shown in the early stories, family and friends share in the protagonists' relationship with God.

With access to the divine milieu one has need of nothing; yet with equal urgency, one has need of everything. This paradox generates a warmth in *Everything That Rises Must Converge* that is not easily understood. It arises from the magnetism that draws out the intimate essence of each character, the godly likeness hidden behind human ugliness. What is most intimate coincides with what is ultimate. No one, it turns out, is indispensable to the holy evolution of the world's body. All are worthy of love and are en route to one crucial source. The mystery of convergence is renewed in each lifetime, a lifetime that comes once and only once. This transience and the pain that attends mortality are inexplicable, even abhorrent, if taken in the isolation of a single existence; but the cosmic view explains grief. It explains it well enough in O'Connor's late fiction to bring forth the added liberation of a broad grin over how much greater joy there flows from distress than the sufferer realizes. When we find the role of pain in the cosmos, Teilhard declares, "we can read its features and distinguish its smile" (*Universe* 73).

This comic recognition requires a turn of fate that O'Connor consistently depicts through conversion and that Teilhard calls *retournement,* a turnaround that directs one to God (*Heart of the Matter* 61). The overarching movement for Teilhard begins with a *retournement* that leads to preparation and culminates with fulfillment. This triadic progression provides a way into O'Connor's last book. With varying degrees of emphasis, the progression expresses the shape of the individual stories as well as the ensemble design they yield.

If taken in groups of threes, the nine stories of *Everything That Rises Must Converge* vivify a conscious habit of mind that O'Connor mentions in early 1960 to Andrew Lytle as her "thinking more and more about the presentation of love and charity" in her fiction (*Letters* 373). Like Elijah, to whose prophetic calling she compares her artistic growth, O'Connor feels that she is waiting for the Lord to speak through powerful forces only to realize that she must attune herself to the command issued in a gentle breeze. To linger in the O'Connor world, which in the end is lighted by Teilhard, is to observe the fragile adjustments made to delicate fiats of love as the Master of joy conquers troubled hearts. Now O'Connor shows love as loving.

II

Retournement

"Everything That Rises Must Converge" opens the collection, and "Greenleaf" and "A View of the Woods" follow. They make a widow-

widower group centering upon the anxieties of abundance. Each ends with sudden, ghastly death; but the result of each death by which the total narratives are to be read is an awareness of love that O'Connor is reputed to neglect. The turnaround begins in an event and closes with illumination, an experience Teilhard calls an "intoxicating wonder" (*Universe* 43). The very characters who seem set against tender feeling prove to be loving all along. Their predicament is not that they do not or cannot love; rather, their affection miscarries because they love too little by loving too much.

Take Julian's mother in "Everything That Rises Must Converge." She lives for her son. A widow for many years, she scrimps to give Julian everything. She lets her teeth rot so that the boy can have his straightened. With limited means, she puts him through college and now, one year after graduation, supports him so that he can spend his precious time writing. Her time counts for little. The fifty and more years of her life are donated to a fancy of herself, a dream with historic depth but no growth. It skips from being a little granddaughter of a former governor to being Julian's mother, a daughter of the old order who shows her worth by having a son who has attended college. Without Julian around as progeny, one would not know that the woman ever married. In late middle age she remains the child, the descendent of Grandpa Godhigh on her mother's side and of the less lofty Chestny line on her father's side. Julian's mother is nothing if not unassuming, and, really, is nothing because she is diffident. She wants to give herself to tradition and Julian, but can only throw herself away before both. Her cause is so godhigh, her maternal effort so great, that the language of religion fits her renunciation. Whatever name she acquires in marriage, and is therefore Julian's surname by birth, she relinquishes as a widow's mite to the cause of family dignity: her son will be a Chestny. She has the martyr's genius for turning sacrifices into pleasure. The sign of victory is her namelessness. We know her as "Julian's mother" (Hopkins 114).

By doing so much for Julian, the woman makes him helpless. Work does not agree with him. Selling typewriters part-time conserves his energy for writing, but the desire to write masks his fear of adult responsibility. He is too intelligent to be a success and not cynical enough to exploit dependency. His mother has excuses in advance of defeat so that he cannot even fail. Such protection from disappointment deprives him of self-awareness. As a result, Julian plays the emperor to conceal his feeling menial. His mother's largesse weighs on his conscience to the degree that he does not "like to consider all she did for him" (3). Julian is, after all, his mother's son, and knows his duty. But how does one repay a saint? He wants to love but languishes in finding a way to redress her profusion of kindness.

"Everything That Rises Must Converge" shows Julian's last attempt to repay his mother's love. His chance arises during one of those exasperating trips O'Connor uses to set things right. This journey is a bus ride downtown to the Wednesday night reducing class for working girls over fifty who weigh between 165 and 200 pounds. The atmosphere is charged with the social tension felt in a small southern town in the 1960s, when racial barriers are being torn down. Political action enhances Julian's attempt to be loving. The eve of his new relationship with his mother recapitulates their twenty-odd years of living for each other without discovering a way to express their affection until the widow dies. At the moment of death, Julian's mother finally mothers her son into love.

The excursion begins with ritual reluctance. Before Julian's mother can enjoy an evening out at the Y, she must turn recreation into medical treatment. If put under doctor's orders to lose twenty pounds to lower her blood pressure, she can indulge herself. She must also find a way of involving her son. Because buses are dangerous to ride at night now that they are integrated, Julian will need to escort her. With Julian at her side, the delicate widow can feel safe and take quiet pride in being with her son, the college graduate. As she adjusts a new floppy purple hat in the hall mirror, we can see that the mental gymnastics are important to her vulnerable self-esteem. How she goes places displays who she is. Impoverished now, she has self-sacrifice and remembered elegance to pit against the disorder of the modern world.

A lifetime of this prevarication prevents Julian from responding in an honest way. His mother means well but preempts affection by putting Julian's feelings on a level of guilt congenial to her sacrifices. The level is high; the guilt, staggering. Waiting for his mother to pin her hat, Julian "appeared pinned to the door frame, waiting like Saint Sebastian for the arrows to begin piercing him" (3–4). The wait is brief. Any sign of enjoyment from his mother wounds him. The hat that gratifies her taste repels Julian. He cannot pass unfavorable judgment any better than he can acknowledge his mother's generosity. Her self-denying love erects a wall of virtue that Julian cannot scale. Life would be tolerable for him "if she had been selfish, if she had been an old hag who drank and screamed at him" (5). What could be an agreeable evening out begins as an intense summary of their old feud and loyalty.

Their conflict is so long-standing and their gambits are so repetitive that Julian and his mother can anticipate each other's hostility and get right to the nagging issue: self-respect. " 'I know who I am,' " announces Julian's mother when he mocks her primness. Though she feels good about raising and educating Julian, for a full sense of self-worth she must look back to the time when her grandfather owned a plantation and two hundred slaves. What seems racist is nothing more than a desire for dignity displaced onto conventional antebellum nostalgia. History confers on her the distinction denied her in a messy modern world. The good old days, not political ideology, account for her pious condescension: " 'I tell you, the bottom rail is on the top' " (6). She wants merely to count, and confuses the progress of another—epitomized by the same need in blacks claiming their civil rights—with her feeling of exclusion. " 'They should rise, yes, but on their own side of the fence,' " she asserts (7).

Julian misses the torment causing his mother's defensive clichés and takes them as a call to arms. In the spirit of Saint Sebastian, he welcomes the blows to prove his faith. His faith lies in liberal reform, especially the kind that frees him from anger. Now he can enjoy the persecution of his mother's racism and substitute ideological guilt for the actual guilt produced by his mother's generosity. He will teach her about the real world. As one "unafraid to face facts" (12), Julian is equipped to wage theoretical war. Emotions must not enter to soften the attack. Though he sees himself as a martyr for an ideal, Julian is an emotional miser. In a conflict of ideas, he need spend no more sympathy on blacks than he squanders on his mother. The Negro is the occasion for an atonement that is not even his own. When riding a bus, Julian makes "a point to sit down beside a Negro in reparation as it were for his mother's sins" (8). The vanity of his amends remains hidden to him. Both he and his mother use the black race to avert the painful separation from each other and from society. Julian's mother puts on hat and gloves as armament. Julian uses cold malice.

The battleground is the bus, in which other passengers are inducted into the family ordeal. When a black businessman takes a seat, Julian makes his move by crossing the aisle to sit next to him. Julian's alliance is lost on the man, who is reading a newspaper, but not on Julian's mother, the intended target. Betrayed, she reddens with hypertensive ire. To underscore the lesson, Julian tries to strike up a conversation with the man; when the banter fails, Julian retreats into his head to complete the argument with his mother. The scenario calls for black friends (distinguished, naturally) and a black woman (seductively beautiful) to visit their home. The dream fades when a black woman with her little son boards the bus. The two black reflections of Julian and his mother do not check Julian's reverie so much as they complete it for him. A "bristling presence" (17), the black woman acts out the authority that Julian's mother dissembles. Whereas the white mother coaxes, the black mother orders her son Carver to comply. Carver's mother, also nameless, like Julian's mother uses her son to communicate power to the world. In the bus, Carver's mother wants to stop Julian's mother from teasing Carver with ingratiating asides. Instead of correcting the white woman, however, she slaps and scolds little Carver. Her indirection and all the other obliquity come to a halt when Carver's mother hits Julian's mother with a red pocketbook for trying to give Carver a bright new penny. All her life, Julian's mother has paid dearly for her affable charm; now she pays with her life.

The black woman's assault unleashes rage in Julian, who gives a grim twist to the strategy of blaming the victim for her pain. With his mother sitting stunned on the sidewalk, Julian's cowardice turns into boldness. " 'You got exactly what you deserved,' " he gloats (20). Shame shuts off Julian's consciousness. The effect of his self-protection is awful. His mother is victimized three times over: first, by her own sacrifices for Julian; then, by Carver's mother for her touchy pride over the bright penny offered to Carver; and finally, by Julian's punishing her for his helplessness in the moment of humiliation. Julian wants to rescue her from the assault, just as he wants to take her to the Y, to restore the decayed Godhigh mansion, and to provide for her. When she considers returning the new hat, Julian boyishly promises that some day he will earn enough money for her to buy what she likes. Despair over his capacity for success, however, nullifies any emotional effort to allay in both of them the penury of the heart. Fear of tenderness pushes Julian into his mind, where he binds his mother's physical wound with a lesson in race relations. As his mother wobbles dazedly down the sidewalk, Julian lectures: " 'That was the whole colored race which will no longer take your condescending pennies' " (21).

Nor will the white woman any longer have to endure her son's stern tutelage. The throes of a fatal stroke are sending Julian's mother on an emergency run for help. " 'Of course,' " she informs Julian at the beginning of the trip, " 'if you know who you are, you can go anywhere' " (6). She is onto a truth, expressing in her way an evolutionary idea proposed by Teilhard, who believes that human identity bears on direction. But to grasp the depth of her claim, Julian's mother must experience a *retournement.* And so she does. In doing so, she learns the converse of her precept: if one knows where one is going, then one knows who one is.

Julian's mother in the end knows where she is going. She tells Julian that she is heading " 'Home' " (22). Home is Grandpa's place, where unconditional acceptance conquers physical and economic poverty. Accessories are not needed for the return. Home is where she is loved as she is, where the arms of the old black nurse Caroline will embrace the widow-child. Since frailty recommends her, she need not worry about her hair coming undone or her pocketbook falling. A dumpy, expendable woman knows permanent love. Becoming a child is not a regression but an advance to true identity, the lovable destitution that points toward growth in the absolute.

The *retournement* in Julian's mother forces a reversal in Julian. Staring at the changed woman, he looks "into a face he had never seen before." Her new aspect effects in Julian a heartrending effort toward consciousness. He becomes present to his mother as he has never been. He repays the generous woman by feeling the anguish of losing her. The loss is so insupportable that he cries and begs and demands that she not leave him: " 'Mother!' he cried. 'Darling, sweetheart, wait!' " (22). But the loved woman is not about to delay her return home. On the contrary, with the confidence of knowing where she is going, she gives her spoiled son the final gift of her self-respect. She sizes him up with one focused eye, finds nothing, and dies. Her parting judgment reaches in Julian the deeper self that feels the duty to love. " 'Wait here, wait here!' " (23), he beseeches while running for aid. He does not want her to die before he can be good to her. His language of desperate endearment confirms that Julian, like his mother, takes love seriously. To each other they are darlings, dearly loved ones, and when too dearly loved, martyrs in the original meaning of the word as "witness." Julian and his mother are witnesses to love.

Though romantic imploring cannot reverse the tide of death sweeping Julian's mother from Julian, a simple sharing of their common life of pain can alter Julian's dread and can draw from his guilt the strength to move on. Julian will need strength. The cluster of lights guiding him to seek help is receding faster than he is running to it. The direction of his new growth is through darkness, the realm of guilt and sorrow into which his mother ushers him. Through her death, the widow weans her adult child into mature life. A frightened, lost son must find his way up a new road. He must roam alone through the darkness to which he must entrust himself in order that loss and grief may live and become spirit. His mother's sacrifices, which Julian scorns, show Julian how to die into manhood. By advancing through pain, the heart pays for its birth and growth. The heart owes such recompense to the flow of creation, which evolves from each person's restitution. As Julian's mother pays her final obligation on entering the flow, she prepares the way for Julian. Even if she babies him into financial dependency, she succeeds in teaching him to accept spiritual responsibility for another; and in the life of guilt and sorrow, charity, not capital, gauges maturity. At the end of "Everything That Rises Must Converge," Julian shares both a common life and a common goal. Both unities between mother and son signal the convergence which rises into contact with God.

"Greenleaf" tells of another sweetheart whose *retournement* leads to a rendezvous with God. The favorite is Mrs. May, whose appointed meeting is at once more amazing and more ludicrous than that of Julian's mother. Until the ending, Mrs. May is unaware of having a special appointment with God. The story begins with the latest of countless nuisances in her weary life. The sound of a bull chewing grass outside her bedroom window interrupts her sleep. The animal is no ordinary stray. The bull appears "silvered in the moonlight" like a "patient god come down to woo her" (24). The intruder arrives dressed to court. A prickly hedge-wreath crowns his horns, which he tips to the lady in her boudoir. For her part, Mrs. May has only scorn for the bull, even though she unwittingly is preparing herself for him. Peeking through the venetian blind in her nightgown, Mrs. May can be seen with her hair set in curlers and her face covered with egg-white astringent. Her bovine mien suggests that the bull has come to the right mate to make his suit. Even her outworn coquetry is fitting for this old and scrawny caller. " 'Some nigger's scrub bull' " (25), mutters the fine Mrs. May. If the visitation is a cartoon version of some ancient cultus, romance is nevertheless in the air. O'Connor in the end unites woman and animal in a locked embrace. One horn of the "wild tormented lover" (52) pierces Mrs. May's heart, and his other horn hugs her around her side.

The impaling is a challenge for O'Connor from the outset. "I am very happy now writing a story in which I plan for the heroine, aged 63, to be gored by a bull," she writes in January, 1956, to a friend; and "it is going to take some doing to do it and it may be the risk that is making me happy" (*Letters* 129). The ending of "Greenleaf" does satisfy O'Connor in bringing a necessary action to fulfillment (*Letters* 146). Scholars, however, do not share O'Connor's enthusiasm for "Greenleaf." The consensus holds that she does not master the technical challenge of getting the bull's horns into the woman's ribs so that the action embodies a definite meaning. Even a reader who is sympathetic to the spiritual thrust of "Greenleaf" finds the ending ambiguous because the heroine's discovery suggests both "the illumination of grace and her rejection of it" (Feeley 98). Less congenial discussions do not pause to consider the possibility of value, either ambiguous or explicit, in the goring. One reader turns O'Connor's theology into its opposite: the bull "may be Christ . . . yet his crucifixion of the lady on his horns results in a perception of nothingness" (Hendin 115). Another reader goes further to say that the piercing does not convey "the obvious Christian implications" that inform O'Connor's stories (Drake 28). Then there is the usual reduction of her complexity into one more grotesque finale that turns on a "dreadful stroke of irony" (Friedman 19). The grander evasions distill "Greenleaf" into allegory, making it either a tract on "Jansenist doctrines of original sin and carnality" (Driskell and Brittain 125) or a Snopesian tale of political change in the postwar South (Walters 138).

The most generous estimate of "Greenleaf" comes in a passing remark calling it a bridge between *A Good Man Is Hard to Find* and *Everything That Rises Must Converge* (Friedman 18). The observation is useful. Published in *Kenyon Review* in the summer of 1956, just after the appearance of *A Good Man Is Hard to Find* in 1955, "Greenleaf" is a watershed for O'Connor. Before she acquires Teilhard's *The Phenomenon of Man,* in which she writes "1959" after her signature, O'Connor is working along spiritual lines similiar to those of the French Jesuit. If we begin with O'Connor's judgment that "Greenleaf" is a fully realized story, we can inquire into the special passion of its drama at the same time that we see how she anticipates her valedictory proposal that everything that rises must converge.

For Mrs. May to rise, she must unlearn her disdain. Her superiority rests on her property. She is a proprietress and proud of it. An industrious widow, she labors fifteen years to make a go of a marginal dairy farm and to raise her sons, Scofield and Wesley. Turning the farm that Mr. May left her into a profitable operation is accomplished against great odds. The failing land, two hostile sons, debt, nature's vagaries, and a shiftless employee named Mr. Greenleaf conspire to make Mrs. May's work more difficult. Her effort, nevertheless, remains undaunted because her fear remains unabated. Loss of property is not, of course, the threat that she thinks it is; nor is survival the issue. Mrs. May is much closer to the end of her struggle than she is to the beginning of it, and even without the help of her selfish sons, she has more than enough to see her through. Some deeper uncertainty than money stalks her; some sharper alienation than being a city woman running a farm makes her cling to the land. And because she does not feel grateful for what she does have, Mrs. May dooms herself to feeling cheated. " 'I'm the victim. I've always been the victim' " (44), she sighs, simply because the bull's owners do not immediately obey her order to remove it. Practiced complaints elicit her sons' bored loathing, and with her sons Mrs. May can feel used to the limit. Self-sorrow is the heroine's real enemy. It separates her from everyone.

It does not occur to Mrs. May that the need for security and the desire to better oneself—the wish for transcendence, really—are common to human striving. She feels alone and defends her cherished uniqueness by projecting her natural but unexamined fear onto others, especially those who impose upon her hospitality without sharing in the cost involved. Her grievances crystallize in the name *Greenleaf*. Greenleaf is the name of her hired hand, and stands for all the last straws piled on her back. Mr. Greenleaf's sons own the scrub bull that reminds Mrs. May of all the hogs of other people that destroy "her oats," of their mules that roam on "her lawn," and of their bulls that breed "her cows" (26). Creation exists as so many objects to which she affixes the possessive *her*. She clutches her possessions as though her entire life were bound in her little house and acreage. From her besieged shelter, Mrs. May when distressed can look out any window to draw solace from her pastures; but the calm she finds comes less from the pastures' vital beauty than from the reflection she finds in nature of her own determined character.

The bull is a messenger sent to invade the fortress that Mrs. May has built around her narcissistic rule. No person or power has yet overcome her defense. But the bull has only to be itself for Mrs. May's paranoia to complete the task of destruction. Her fear turns anything under her control into potential loss. It can shape the message of the night. As she sleeps, the bull's chewing becomes an enemy gnawing away a wall of the house, an encroachment which swells into the force that has been devouring her energy since she moved to the farm. She controls what is not hers by making it a symbol and dealing with the abstract danger she assigns to it. In this instance, the bull, whose stud days are behind him, is more interested in grass than in Mrs. May's cows; but as a symbol, he is the menace of fifteen years with horns.

As a victim, Mrs. May feels justified in exacting a price for her pains. Nature and people owe her acquiescence for her hardship. When her due is not forthcoming, she demands it. " 'All right, Mr. Greenleaf,' " she declares at her wit's end, " 'go get your gun. We're going to shoot that bull' " (47). Behind her command lies the assumption that she is the injured one trying to keep order and prosperity and a breeding schedule, while others are living on her industry and causing chaos. She sits in the judgment seat. The world and its freeloading inhabitants stand guilty before her. When taking matters into her already full hands, Mrs. May approaches the bull with the zeal of an exterminator on pest control. One does not trifle, of course, even with a scarecrow of a bull. Nor does one toy with imposing guilt on others. No one submits to Mrs. May's tactics. Mr. Greenleaf in particular ducks the false guilt that Mrs. May tries to place on him. The story of her fight to oust the bull is the story of her demands denounced and reversed until she takes the bull and her personal guilt for bullying others into her bosom.

Besides pushing people around with her property, Mrs. May assails them with debasing images. In her pale myopic eyes, Mr. Greenleaf is a charity case. His sons O. T. and E. T. have achieved much more in the world but are still wards of her beneficence. They could not have risen without Mrs. May's keeping their father on her payroll. Moreover, her taxes paid for the war in which they fought and supported the French wives they brought back, while the boys took advantage of the government's veteran benefits to study agriculture at the state-funded university. Their mother is worse yet. Mrs. Greenleaf is a prayer healer. Every day she clips newspaper reports of disasters—women raped, criminals escaped, children burned, movie stars divorced—and with her body and soul prays for their salvation. Her concern for these countless lost souls goes deep, for her self-giving in their behalf is ecstatic.

Whatever motivates Mrs. Greenleaf to intercede for unknown sufferers is of no interest to Mrs. May. She regards the woman's reckless passion as obscene. Rather than sprawling and screaming in the woods for people she does not know, Mrs. Greenleaf ought to be home washing her family's clothes. Mrs. Greenleaf's carrying-on about Jesus repels Mrs. May, who, to cite O'Connor's famous description, is "a good Christian woman with a large respect for religion, though she did not, of course, believe any of it was true" (31). Of course. Belief costs, and Mrs. May is unwilling to pay. Her violent dislike of Mrs. Greenleaf, whom O'Connor calls "a sympathetic character" (*Letters* 148), is part of Mrs. May's self-defense. Mrs. Greenleaf's abandonment is a reminder of the terrible price of love and faith. " 'Oh Jesus, stab me in the heart!' " she repeatedly shrieks (31). She loves by assuming the affliction of each victim. Mrs. Greenleaf is a scandal. As a living example of the sacrifice that Mrs. May tries to shun, Mrs. Greenleaf can best repay the good Christian woman for her largesse to the Greenleafs by staying out of her sight.

Mrs. May sees her own sons as traitors. They could at least lend an ear to her travails. After raising them through childhood and boarding both in adulthood (not to mention providing the special attention required by Wesley's salt-free diet), she has a right to ask that they be respectful and successful. At the very least, they should show her a grateful disposition. The price of filial piety, however, is so exorbitant that Scofield and Wesley go out of their way to mock her expectations. Scofield is a policy man, an embarrassment for whom Mrs. May must supply excuses. Wesley, the emaciated academic, strains her with his hateful temper. When the sons are not brawling, they can share in the fun of taunting their mother. Telling her that the detested bull belongs to the hated Greenleaf boys gives them particular delight. Mrs. May, in turn, shows a knowledge of their emotional immaturity in imagining that her sons will marry " 'trash' " (29) just to destroy everything that she has built up. Spite runs in the family. Even if Mrs. May's suspicion proves untrue, it justifies in advance her having the lawyer entail her property so that the spectral trash-wives will not inherit her farm.

Fearful at times to the point of personal cowardice, Mrs. May nevertheless demonstrates stubborn courage in acting openly to defend what she takes to be the principles of justice. She storms over to O. T. and E. T.'s place to leave a message ordering that they promptly remove the bull from her premises. However, as the grandiosity of her rage meets the reality of others' indifference over a lost scrub bull, her confidence dwindles. Before a jury of six nonplussed Greenleaf children,

Mrs. May's commotion dissipates into an impertinent scrutiny of how the Greenleafs live. They live well. Mrs. May snoops around their farm to find fault and discovers instead a showplace of efficiency. The advanced technology and spotless milking room distress her anew. Evidence that the Greenleaf boys, sons of her hired hand and that prayer healer, are rising above her lays bare the fear and envy behind her tenacity. More for others means less for her. Again, people have merely to be themselves for Mrs. May to feel used. The success of the Greenleaf boys drives Mrs. May into a self-lacerating reminiscence of all that she did for those ingrates—gave them her sons' old clothes, old toys, and old guns, gave them " 'my pond' " to swim in, " 'my birds' " to shoot, " 'my stream' " to fish in (46). Resentment takes its toll on her spirit. Mrs. May's egotism swells into a screech of Creation herself spurned by those to whom she distributes her bounty.

The more Mrs. May is ignored, the sooner her dictatorial impulse hardens into satanic resolve. Her last despairing effort at control is to order Mr. Greenleaf to kill his sons' bull. The excuse is the safety of the dry cow herd, but the motive is to get back at the Greenleaf boys for forgetting that Mrs. May remembered their birthdays and Christmases with gifts and for their temerity in surpassing her at managing a dairy farm. She does not hesitate to use Mr. Greenleaf for her end. The atonement of the bull through the father's hands for the sons' transgressions will be received with satisfaction by Mrs. May, who can disclaim responsibility for the sacrifice by ascribing her vengeance to the indifference of the Greenleaf boys: " 'If those boys cared a thing about you, Mr. Greenleaf,' she said, 'they would have come for that bull. I'm surprised at them' " (49).

A real surprise is in store for Mrs. May. When she accompanies Mr. Greenleaf to the slaughter, the black scrub bull that called on her that moonlit night frolics out of the woods "as if he were overjoyed to find her again." Before Mrs. May comprehends the danger, the "black streak" romps to her and buries "his head in her lap, like a wild tormented lover." The aroused gallant sinks one of his horns into his beloved's heart. His smooth kill drives into Mrs. May the truth about her culpability that reverses her relation to her struggle and to the cosmos. O'Connor captures the heroine's *retournement* through a shift in facial expression, by which the reader can detect the brightening of Mrs. May's inner awareness. As the animal bounds toward her, Mrs. May stares in "a freezing unbelief"; when the bull spears her heart, her face opens into a look of quaking illumination, which changes into a cooing repose when the bull, shot finally by Mr. Greenleaf for goring Mrs. May, pulls her head close to his ear. In the moment of death, Mrs. May's sight is "suddenly restored." For this restoration, she must endure an "unbearable" light (52).

The new vision is a dispossession. The light is unbearable for the proprietress because things are returned to their original perspective and ownership. With the black bull over her, the pastures Mrs. May claims and for which she would spill blood are blotted from her sight. Deposal reverses the value of her hard work. Whereas she expects nature to assist her in accumulating wealth, she should be helping to build the earth for a larger good. She wants to use the earth and to increase order, but succeeds only in isolating herself from others and separating others from their dignity. The new light of grace clarifies her selfishness to show that productive work gains value by sharing.

Perhaps the most notable feature of Mrs. May's restored sight is that it arises out of an erotic embrace with the bull. O'Connor discerns a connection between sexuality and death that is impressive for all its triteness. Here she equates the fact of love with the expression of death. One always follows the other. The Christian character of this fusion comes earlier in the story through Mrs. Greenleaf's petition, " 'Oh Jesus, stab me in the heart!' " In the dark woods she abandons herself to personal sacrifice for the anonymous hordes of victims of train wrecks, plane crashes, and human violence. Such self-donation bespeaks an unusual love. Mrs. Greenleaf believes that only a pierced heart communicates the strength of her mission, and so she asks to be pierced by a love that admits the world's disasters and that is pleased to conquer only in death. The response to Mrs. Greenleaf's plea, however, falls on Mrs. May. That it does is neither a technical expedience nor a literary irony. The displaced piercing incarnates O'Connor's belief that the growth of love building the earth toward convergence depends upon the response, willing or inadvertent, of one person for another. If others suffer because of Mrs. May's fear and oppression, then she too must bear anguish in the larger interest of charity.

Being subject to affliction should not take Mrs. May unawares, since she tells everyone that she has always been the victim. On the horns of the bull, she becomes the sufferer she claims to be. And for all its self-indulgence, the image of herself as the victim conveys the dignity of a woman who insists that her troubles count, who does work hard, and who does give. The problem, however, is her myopia. Her nearsighted eyes see material things as holding value and relief from jeopardy. Her final victimization reveals the loving truth hidden within the conception of herself as sufferer. The intimacy with the bull explains that the yearning and guilt that Mrs. May has felt all her life could have drawn others into union, as the bull comes to her, had she understood that those whom she injured shared in her desire for security and in her need to rise and prosper. The many real adversities of her life are not reasons for tyranny or causes for despair; her conflicts are the tribulations of ascent.

The amatory embrace tells us that love is the way of ascent. Along with loss and gore, the action gives definite signs of upsurge. Bloom lies in Mrs. May's name. It also abides in her dormant capacity for love, which is finally released through a refinement of her nature. Until her death, *May* underscores her magisterial manner of giving permission to do this or that; but the story ends by bringing out the May quality of spring-flowering. Here O'Connor's poetry asserts its quiet power as she allows nature to vivify her heroine's transformation. The sun, which manifests divine love as the source of physical life, shows how grace seeks out Mrs. May in the diurnal course of things. As the sun sets on the day before her death, it moves "down slowly as if it were descending a ladder" (45). Upon touching the ground, the solar energy seems to enter the bull, for the next day in the pasture the black animal appears to Mrs. May as the shadow of the sun. Then the sun infuses the whole earth to make the morning of Mrs. May's death a shimmering sapphire of a day. Birds are so much with song that they are "screaming everywhere." The grass is "almost too bright to look at," and the sky is "an even piercing blue." The glory of the day seizes Mrs. May. As she drives Mr. Greenleaf through the woods into the open field to kill the bull, she marvels, " 'Spring is here!' " (48).

Spring heralds the green-leafing of Mrs. May. Its ultimate power penetrates her when the bull, shadow emissary of the sun, pierces her heart. Spring not only coincides with the cycle of new life and with Lent; *Lent* means "spring." On the horns of the bull, Mrs. May enters the season of penance and rebirth. In fact, O'Connor's most striking development of the final scene is to embody one of the pleas for deliverance expressed in the psalm that epitomizes Passiontide. "My God, my God, why hast thou forsaken me? / Why art thou so far from helping me, from the words of my groaning?" begins Psalm 22; then, two-thirds (line 21) through the lament, the psalmist calls out: "Save me from the mouth of the lion, my afflicted soul from the horns of the wild oxen!"

Psalm 22 cries for release from misery. The oxen and other animals express to the sufferer the conduct of her or his enemies who see misery as a sign of God's abandonment, just as Mrs. May conversely sees prosperity as due reward for her troubles. The psalm gains its Christian character through Jesus' shouting of the dreadful first line at the hour of His death. While this momentous association would be congenial to Mrs. May's exaggerated notion of her lot, O'Connor does not use the psalm or the bull's horns to sum up a life's work in order to show how failure signals God's punishment or how success indicates God's blessing. Neither "Greenleaf" nor Psalm 22 concerns justice or prophecy. Both offer, rather, a presentation of the biblical precedent of the suffering servant, fulfilled in transcendent form for the Christian in Jesus, Who will find consolation in God. In the end, love requires that Mrs. May carry the suffering ideal in her heart.

The woman with a pierced heart is not a metaphor for Flannery O'Connor. Heart in O'Connor's writing is never a figure derived from an anatomical organ or an abstract code. In her fiction, heart retains the biblical designation of the inborn center of the human person where one stands before God as a bodily whole, the center where eternity dwells and occurs. Nor is the heart ever sweet. O'Connor knows it to be terrible in its dark death throes. The black bull plunges Mrs. May into a starker desolation than any poverty she has ever imagined. She is pierced by her own wretchedness and transience. Her heart feels her essential insufficiency. All of those years of toil, Mrs. May is threatened, usually vulnerable, and thus always guarded and lacking in any more real power than self-pity could generate. Fear makes her defy suffering by magnifying it. The bull breaks through this defensive stamina to real endurance, the strength to live through desolation. To surrender in her long, futile warfare is to prepare Mrs. May for lasting victory. What supernature calls for is performed by the scrub bull and, more than that, comes by his nature. Traced through the dramatic pattern of the story, the achieved union comes from above at the same time that it rises out of the ground. The cut of the bull's horn is the will of God that Lucette Carmody in *The Violent Bear It Away* calls love. The kindness of the Lord spares Mrs. May through violence. The woman with the pierced heart finds rest.

What gives Mrs. May peace does not come in return for her years of being put upon, as she supposes it would, but arises from the new way in which she is known. The bull's horn spiking Mrs. May's heart is O'Connor's way of showing that the bull knows the heroine as God knows her—as frail and needy and without the protective myths she spends her life cultivating. Such raw exposure of new self-knowledge would account for the intolerable light and would be ample reason to seek being spared the revelation that comes from the horn.

Still, mercy softens the puncture. Mrs. May is loved at last. Nothing, not even her ego, separates her from the love of God. She no longer needs to assault anyone who tries to compromise her vision of herself, because her felt lovableness is unassailable. The last words of "Greenleaf" describe a tremor of joy as Mrs. May seems "to be bent over whispering some last discovery into the animal's ear." As her blessed alarm passes, Mrs. May leans over, gently murmuring the heart's secret to the bull in grateful recognition of finding herself loved. Their attachment is the presence of God. Mrs. May brightens while we gaze horror-struck. The difference is that we look at the present; with restored sight she sees into the future.

"A View of the Woods" rounds out O'Connor's trio of widow-widower stories with a blow of grace that is more startling than the collapse of Julian's mother and more gruesome than the impalement of Mrs. May. The recipient here is Mark Fortune, age seventy-nine. Though he does not reach the 104 years of General Tennessee Flintrock Sash in *A Good Man Is Hard to Find,* Mr. Fortune is the oldest protagonist in the last volume who outlives a spouse and remains unmarried; he is also by far the richest of the three and indisputably the nastiest of them. He completes a pattern. Each of the first three stories of *Everything That Rises Must Converge* depicts greater wealth, more advanced age, deeper anxiety, fuller tyranny, and sharper mean-spiritedness. This progression permits O'Connor to consider the possible contribution or hindrance of material abundance to convergence. The delights are plain. What is dangerous about material goods for O'Connor is not what they are but what they replace. Money in this group comes to replace God and love.

In old Mr. Fortune's case, his estimable holdings in real estate bring notable emotional poverty. He owns 800 acres, and believes that he has access to affection by just that much; but the truth is that with all his land he is deprived of the basic entitlements of decency and respect. The source of Mr. Fortune's destitution is his quantifying of feelings and his treating his family as so many lots to which he has the deed. As landlord, he assumes the right to choose who will love him, a right that he exercises with arrogance heightened by delusion. He lives with and depends upon his daughter, but in his mind the woman amounts to a nameless third or fourth offspring in a vague line of descendants. Mr. Fortune has no use for her, her sullen husband Pitts, or, for that matter, any of their first six children. Only the seventh child suits the old man. Announced before birth as the grandfather's namesake, the last born is the family bribe to the landlord's ego. The infant turns out to be a girl and is named Mary Fortune Pitts, and the granddaughter of Mr. Fortune's old age becomes his child of fortune. Nine years old at the time of the story, Mary Fortune demonstrates the intelligent determination that her grandfather respects and finds lacking in the rest of the Pitts family. They become each other's closest friend. He takes her riding in his battered mulberry-colored Cadillac, buys her ice-cream cones, and will treat her to the legacy of his property. Then in his grave Mr. Fortune can rest confident that Mary Fortune will make her worthless family jump to her will, a will forged in the image and likeness of his own volition.

Economic prosperity encourages Mr. Fortune to dispense with God and evil and to place his hope in progress. Now that the electric company has dammed the river, his half-mile stretch along the new lake could command a good price. Things are moving so fast that there is talk of a paved road by his place and of a telephone line coming in. Mr. Fortune, a self-anointed "man of advanced vision," is obliged to build for the future by selling parcels of land. He imagines that from a new-car showroom, a supermarket, a gas station, a motel, and a drive-in movie theater, an eventual town will rise that should be called "Fortune, Georgia" (58). This wistful hodgepodge of newfangled petty enterprises may form a picture of patriotic development and community in Mr. Fortune's mind, but the effect of the scheme on the family is division and vengefulness. Economic power can, and here does, deprive its wielder of community with others. With the Pittses, acrimony is intentional. Mr. Fortune keeps the Pitts family in line with reminders of his lawful possession, so that each sale of land drives home that they are at his mercy. To tighten the rein, Mr. Fortune neither accepts rent nor allows Pitts to drill a deep well after the old one dries up. The family lives in hock; they may never own anything. If the old man allowed Pitts to pay for a drilled well and pump himself, Pitts could claim to own something on the place. Instead, water must be piped from the spring, and with each drop they drink, Pitts and his family must swallow their dependence on the stream that flows from the source of all life on the place, Mark Fortune.

The old man's latest lesson in captivity to the Pitts family is the crisis of the story. " 'I'm going to sell the lot right in front of the house for a gas station' " (62–63), Mr. Fortune gloatingly tells his granddaughter, as the pair watch a huge yellow bulldozer gouge the earth. With comparable ruthless force, Mr. Fortune intends to ram his newest cruelty through the family's life. Mrs. Pitts calls the location in front of the house "the lawn" because of the lovely view of the woods it affords from the house porch. The lawn is also where the children play and where their daddy's calves graze. Pleasure and beauty and usefulness to others, however, interest Mr. Fortune less than does the gratification of making the family feel his resentment. Business provides a smoke screen for wrath.

Mr. Fortune's anger boomerangs, however, by eliciting equal fury from his nine-year-old double. When called " 'Jezebel' " for condemning his scheme and then told to walk home, the young champion of the family's affection for the lawn scorns her grandfather's insult by refusing, as she puts it, to ride home in the Cadillac " 'with the Whore of Babylon' " (64). Mr. Fortune tries to parry the slur with a reminder that a whore is a woman, but the feeble technicality fails to salvage his pride. The child's denunciation hits home by describing what the place becomes under his rule. Babylon, the home of harlots and of earth's abominations, is the reservoir of adversity to God. It embodies the enslaving power of sin. Mr. Fortune's despotism places his acreage well within the spiritual boundaries of Babylon. When the new gas station planned by the local entrepreneur, Tilman, rises directly in front of the house, the family will be sealed in by the satanic wall that Babylon erects.

The gas station will give final shape to the Babylonian atmosphere that prevails on the place in the form of emotional violence and child abuse. Because Mr. Fortune designates Mary Fortune as his heiress apparent, Pitts sets his daughter apart for ritualized beatings. Pitts is the victim who takes on and extends the persecution of his captor. Too weak to confront his father-in-law, Pitts blames innocent Mary Fortune for the old man's arbitrariness and denies responsibility, as a coward must, for his own malevolence. The young girl lives in spiritual degradation and in fear of physical pain. Suffering in "A View of the Woods" results from the denial of guilt that drives so many O'Connor characters to lay their unexamined sinfulness upon another. Pitts, "a Christian and a sinner," is for O'Connor "a pathetic figure by virtue of the fact that he beats his child to ease his feelings about Mr. Fortune" (*Letters* 189).

Pathos is a kind word for Pitts's sadism. His conviction of personal righteousness leads to a harshness that rivals the pitiless treatment of captives by Babylonian rulers. " 'She's mine to whip,' " says Pitts to Mr. Fortune, the girl's puny protector, " 'and I'll whip her every day of the year if it suits me' " (62). When the urge comes, it suits him to lash his daughter with efficiency and without feeling. The flailing of Mary Fortune has the formulated action of institutionalized violence that loses its power to appall, and that emotional numbness is the real horror of Pitts's conduct. At the dinner table on the noon when Mr. Fortune announces his plan to sell the lawn to Tilman, Pitts resorts to prescribed brutality to vent his anger with the old man. He blames Mary Fortune for the sale and orders her to his truck, which takes them to the woods, with the rehearsed cold summons, " 'Come with me' " (65). The signal given, the grim rite unfolds to its inexorable end. Mary Fortune prepares herself for punishment and clings to a pine tree while Pitts lashes her ankles with his belt. For nearly three minutes she whimpers and jumps in place with stoical acceptance. Then she slides under the pine tree to hug her feet for comfort, as Pitts in serpentine silence coils back to the truck.

The flogging at the pine tree dramatizes the cruelty that is Mary Fortune's way of life. Even her benefactor torments her. On the one occasion when Mr. Fortune spies on the beating, he springs from behind a boulder to taunt the anguished child after her physical assailant leaves. Abuse follows abuse: " 'Why didn't you hit him back? Where's your spirit? Do you think I'd let him beat me?' " (61). The incitements are to camouflage Mr. Fortune's spirit, which Pitts has vanquished on the girl's body. The family may defer to Mr. Fortune's need to show his power by playing paterfamilias, and grant him the seat at the head of the table, but Mr. Fortune's emotional place remains under Pitts's thumb, where everyone is kept. Pitts retains the power of usurper, controlling the two persons whom the old man claims as his. Through marriage Pitts has taken Mr. Fortune's daughter, who was raised in the "duty to stay here and take care of Papa" (56); and through might he governs Mary Fortune, the old man's spiritual twin. Besides living in the house that Mr. Fortune owns, Pitts has his eye on making the entire place his home. Time is on his side, for he stands to gain from the old man's work and tactics. Pitts's power is so complete that Mr. Fortune directs all his energy toward undermining his son-in-law's sway. Even the old man's generosity with Mary Fortune serves as retaliation against Pitts.

Mary Fortune pays dearly for the punitive dishonesty of male parents of two generations. Mr. Fortune berates her for letting Pitts hit her without striking back, and to survive the girl must deny the wounds on her flesh. " 'Nobody beat me,' " she barks. When confronted with the old man's eyewitness proof, she twists contradiction into murderous determination, as though she has been waiting to settle scores for a long time: " 'Nobody's ever beat me in my life and if anybody did, I'd kill him' " (61). It is possible, as one reader says, that the girl blocks out the whipping because she knows that her grandfather is the person beaten through her image (Feeley 125). Cowards do enjoy private, indirect communication, and in this instance Mr. Fortune does feel that Pitts is also driving him "down the road to beat" (61–62); but psychological subtlety sidesteps the physical shock. O'Connor gives an unvarnished picture of a tearful, furious nine-year-old rocking herself into numbing comfort as a ranting grandfather approaches with love deformed into ire. Child and man are locked in pain.

O'Connor highlights the negative state of their bond in order that we discern in the depth of the entanglement the positive requirement of love that they suffer with and for each other. Each already feels the other's hurt. It is a question of voluntarily taking the ache upon themselves to absorb submission into their love. This mystery is unbearable for Mary Fortune and Mr. Fortune, as it is for all sufferers who stumble under the burden. Rebellion is the continuous and understandable response. Especially for this vulnerable child, vindictive denial makes life possible; but it also makes daily living more injurious, because dissembling severs experience from reality—and drives the physical cut into Mary Fortune's spirit. The welts on her ankles will heal long before the gash in her soul mends.

Mary Fortune does not recover from the hidden lesion. She dies of it. After her grandfather acts on his intention to sell the lawn, she acts on her threat to kill anyone who lays a hand on her. The sequence takes two sinister turns. As Mr. Fortune and Tilman close the deal to sell the lawn, Mary Fortune hurls bottles at them. Loss of the lawn is intolerable, and the girl uses the violence she has learned from her father to obliterate the reality she cannot stand. To teach the hellion a lesson, Mr. Fortune adopts the tactics she respects and takes her to the woods. Reversal causes reversal. In becoming Pitts the flogger, Mr. Fortune precipitates and receives the blow, which for him is fatal, that he wanted the girl to give Pitts. She bites, kicks, and punches. He wheezes, protests, and in one final burst of fury strangles her while cracking her head against a rock.

The earlier picture of humiliating grief in the woods darkens into an exhibition of jumbled hatred and destruction. Twisted pleasure and warped economic obsession create a contorted heap in diabolic union. Not only do Pitts and Mr. Fortune, archenemies, become one, the human fuses with the mechanical demon that it emulates. The story begins with grandfather and granddaughter watching the earthmover eat red holes in the clay for the new lake that heralds progress; at the end, the same monstrous yellow machine watches over the carcasses left by rapacious humanity gorging itself on bloody human clay. Egotistical devouring consumes the human organism.

Though the "ugly red bald spot" secluded half a mile back in the woods is deserted, the long thin pine trees "appeared to be gathered there to witness anything that would take place in such a clearing" (78). In her answer to the inevitable question about Christ figures in her stories, O'Connor tells a correspondent who wondered if Pitts fits the role that the pine trees in "A View of the Woods" represent Christ. "I had that role cut out for the woods," she says (*Letters* 189). We need no anthropological explanation of a cosmic tree to appreciate O'Connor's assigning the pines a redemptive purpose. On this count, Christology squares with her early presentation of guilt and transcendence. *Wise Blood* acquaints us with the ragged figure of Jesus moving from tree to tree in Hazel Motes's mind to show him the route to sanctity. For those condemned to death, as are Mary Fortune (who is scourged by her father at a pine tree) and Mark Fortune, the trees reveal how a curse becomes a deliverance when one takes upon oneself, as Jesus does, the curse of others. The tree of the cross becomes "the wood by which righteousness comes" (Wisdom 14:7).[1]

O'Connor's strategy at the end of the story follows the request in the liturgical hymn *"Christe Sanctorum,"* which asks: "May we whenever tempted to dejection/Strongly recapture thoughts of resurrection" (*Worship* #739). The pines display the power to give doomed life meaning. Their saving life is present for all to see, and death gives Mark Fortune a glimpse of it. As his convulsing heart throws him on his back, the dying man can look beyond the blood-stained clay out of which he wanted the town of Fortune, Georgia, to rise, to contemplate the tall pines "thickened into mysterious dark files that were marching across the water and away into the distance" (81). The pines elude the claims of ego to rescue life from economic supremacy. Secure in their cosmic freedom, the trees offer a vision of their own, unclouded by human desire. Below lies the pit dug by covetousness and filled with pain; above climb the slender pines in life-redeeming bloom. Freestanding, they grow out of O'Connor's red Georgia earth to be ever green, as hope always can rise from dejection. Patient and firm and lean, the pines soar to the sky in convergence with the vast creation born of love and returning to love.[2]

Mary Fortune treasures the view of the woods enough to kill and die for it. The front porch looks out on natural loveliness revealing depths of wonder. Seen in and of themselves, the trees furnish a perspective that beautifully complicates the ending. For the defeated Mark Fortune, the horizon effects a *retournement* from the servile exploitation of the land to a redemptive obedience through losing it. He tries to buy love, but the *retournement* sends him into the world of guilt and sorrow, where he must pay for it. And for the reader, harrowed by the carnage and puzzled by pines striding on water, the woods accomplish a similar turnaround by palliating the spectacle of wretchedness with a premonition of hope. The woods are the Omega heart of the matter.

The ugly red spot where Mary Fortune returns for punishment and where her grandfather cracks her head on the rock is not, after all, the first site of execution associated with the cranium. "Skull" is the English equivalent for Golgotha (Calvary). The place of the skull bears patient witness to murder in order to lay a sacramental foundation for the saving power of love that O'Connor shows in the pine trees.

NOTES

1. The Latin liturgy has a hymn sung at Lauds of Good Friday that presents the saving drama in which O'Connor finds the role for the woods. The lines run:

> *Crux fidelis, inter omnes*
> *Arbor una nobilis:*

Nulla silva talem profert
Fronde, flore, germine:
Dulce lignum, dulces clavos,
Dulce pondus sustinet.

———

Hail, true cross, of beauty rarest,
King of all the forest trees;
Leaf and flower and fruit thou bearest
Medicine for a world's disease;
Fairest wood, and iron fairest—
Yet more fair, who hung on these.

Though the tree of Eden (Genesis 3:1–7) was treacherous, the tree of Calvary will bear foliage, flowers, and fruit of saving value. *The Hymns of the Dominican Missal and Breviary,* edited with Introduction and Notes by Aquinas Byrnes (St. Louis: B. Herder, 1943), p. 98.

2. Georgia's pines share the Lord's promise to Israel of guidance and sustenance: "It is I who answer and look after you. / I am like an evergreen cypress, from me comes your fruit" (Hosea 14:8).

6

Preparation

Indebtedness expresses the pathos of being human, an awareness of the
self as committed. Man cannot think of himself as human without
being conscious of his indebtedness. Thus it is not a mere feeling but
a constitutive feature of being human. To eradicate it would be to destroy
man's humanity.
Abraham Joshua Heschel, *A Passion for Truth*

The second trio of stories in *Everything That Rises Must Converge*
builds on the opening sequence of reversals. After turning around the
moral direction of evil in the first three stories, O'Connor now takes up
preparing her protagonists for the new. Whereas reversal depends upon
shock, preparation in "The Enduring Chill," "The Comforts of Home,"
and "The Lame Shall Enter First" involves knowledge. The pattern is
familiar in anagogical writing. The dramatic movement in *Everyman*
provides a classic example of such growth. Knowledge appears in
the play to signal Everyman's spiritual readiness to ascend Godward.
Acquaintance with new truth dramatizes the same beginning of upward
progress in O'Connor's modern moralities. The heroes of the middle
three stories receive the special understanding conferred by the Holy
Spirit, the source of Jesus' strength that Teilhard believes is the energy
propelling creation toward unity. The protagonists perceive an ordering
of the universe that places all they see and know within the transcendent whole of divine love.

The idea of a principle operating beyond their mental categories is the last thing the heroes of these stories expect to encounter. They have life figured out. All are confident that they know what is real and what is true. The existentialist writer in "The Enduring Chill" believes God to be a notion created by the human mind; the dedicated social worker in "The Lame Shall Enter First" comprehends the defense mechanisms that determine human character; and the historian in "The Comforts of Home" grasps the rational causation giving order and virtue to the human story. If there is one thing they can dispense with, it is spirit, whether sanctifying or perverse. But awareness of inexplicable reality is what these Everymen gain, and the unexpected teacher is the Holy Spirit they deny. Immersed in the Spirit's milieu, O'Connor's highbrows learn the most intimate mystery of all, the mystery of love.

The lesson is plain, and complements the discovery made earlier in the volume. "Everything That Rises Must Converge," "Greenleaf," and "A View of the Woods" show how felt experience of personal responsibility—summarized in the pierced heart—plunges the protagonists into the world of guilt and sorrow that they try to evade. The second trio of stories approaches that domain from another direction. As the moral center moves from the heart to the head in this group, so the heroes are thrust into the realm of cleansing grief when the divine presence invades their minds. The shift in anatomical emphasis expands O'Connor's insight into how guilt advances different sensibilities on their journey to God. It is not simply fear or blame that the protagonists of these middle stories put onto others. O'Connor's intellectuals are too smart for that common evasion. They compound the tactic by ascribing virtue to the wrong source. Both displacements distort responsibility, but the habit of mind that confuses virtue with evil acts not out of ignorance but in malice. To impute to evil the power of good, moreover, is to attack the Holy Spirit (Mark 3:28–30). The result is an enduring blasphemy. A person who does not accept the working of the Spirit makes it impossible for herself or himself to recognize the word and work of God.

Throughout "The Enduring Chill," "The Comforts of Home," and "The Lame Shall Enter First," the obstacles to knowledge are raised by the heroes themselves. They are always free to affirm the Spirit, Whose physical manifestations abound, but their superior training gets in the way of heeding the obvious. Education brings them to see that God is a nonentity. In asserting the sufficiency of their contemporary way of knowing, these men of learning isolate themselves both from knowl-

edge of the spiritual world and from contact with the domestic world of
a child or parent they love. It is this separation from the desire to love
that exposes the failure of mind, when severed from feeling, to grasp
reality. No theory or book can effect the reconciliation of desire and act.
Abstract thought might explain alienation and guilt, but it cannot
make the heroes love. Love begins with a recognition of God's love for
the human person and develops through an interior transformation by
an invisible power. So it is that the Spirit takes the initiative to assert
the divine principle and energy in the lives of O'Connor's spirit-defiers.
The Spirit leads them to feel their loss of love, and that deprivation
prepares them to discover that to love is to participate in the divine
action they reject. O'Connor's intellectual can no more escape guilt and
God through thought than her landowner can shirk responsibility to
God by claiming property rights.

The first know-it-all is Asbury Porter Fox in "The Enduring Chill."
He is an aspiring writer from the backwater southern junction of
Timberboro who struggles in his fifth-floor walk-up apartment in New
York City to make his mark as a serious artist. Little comes of his
determined work. A couple of "lifeless" novels, a half-dozen "stationary"
plays, assorted "prosy" poems, and some "sketchy" (92) stories litter his
path. If these discarded fragments do not point to success, they do guide
Asbury to a partial awareness of his nature. He feels that he lacks the
imagination to create. The description of his inert language expresses
his state of being. At twenty-five, he is desperate. His only joy, real
enough, lies in his desire for art and for the life that he fancies goes with
artistic creation. And now, to make the crisis worse, he is seriously ill
with a fever of unknown origin that persists for four months, debilitates
him, and drives him back to the "insufferableness of life at home" (98)
in Timberboro, where Art, the unforgiving god he served and failed,
remands him to die.

"The Enduring Chill" begins with Asbury's arrival home on the
train from New York. He carries back all the personal remains of his
artistic pilgrimage—two suitcases of belongings and two notebooks
addressed to his mother after the fashion of Kafka's accusatory letter to
his overmastering father. Reminiscing about the future from the grave
inspires Asbury to confess his hope to break the shackles of home. Anger
makes his inner life illuminative. Looking back, he sees that his mother's
oppression doomed his plan to write, and the two black notebooks
will give the woman an account of her destruction of Asbury. In this

psychodrama, Everyman plays Messenger, God, Death, Kindred, Confession, and Angel. Dying is Asbury's communication, wholly negative of course. Emotion charges his notes toward a supreme vendetta to the degree that they will make his sixty-year-old mother feel the "enduring chill" (92) of self-judgment. Mrs. Fox will pay for her artist-son's defeat by feeling the dispiriting effect that her Philistine nature casts on his lifework.

Such is Asbury Porter Fox's view of his career; now we may inquire into the true cause of his failure. He totes it back with him to Timberboro packed in the baggage of his mind. "He had always relied on himself and had never been a sniveler after the ineffable," he reflects while confined to bed. Asbury's self-worship enervates his writing. As with the epistolary reprisal, his words are about himself. His mind sets the margins of reality. More and more of himself means less and less life in his words. Even his affinity for art serves narcissistic ends that cut language off from fuller meaning. Art-as-temperament does not demand craft but thrives on holding mirrors up to self-worth or, now with Asbury, self-loathing. Mary George, his older sister, says to a carnival pitchman when Asbury is five that he is " 'a real stinker and too big for his britches' " (109). He remains spoiled at twenty-five; now, however, life is too small for him. He imagines himself morally larger than Timberboro and yearns for a world to confirm his image. Whatever does not gloss his mythology of Artist, he mocks. Home is a cage. Mrs. Fox's staunch care is an imposition. Medicine is useless. Religion deludes. And since such folly does not go without saying, Asbury wants to say that " 'God is an idea created by man' " (106). Art made from these convictions can only be lifeless, since it excludes God and creation, the source and evolving affirmation of life. O'Connor shows that unbelief, not mother or environment, inhibits creativity.

Asbury wears the garb of modern philosophical integrity over the ancient posture of blasphemy. As expounded to the priest who visits him on his deathbed, Asbury's ethic is a contemporary version of self-idolatry that, in the name of intellectual valor, converts the precepts of common sense to nothing. The achievement left to Asbury is to make his vanishing life imitate the art that might have been. His personal end enacts an episode in the total existential drama of our age. Death will be a physician, coming "as a gift" (99) that Asbury accepts with equanimity. He makes the stoic's obeisance to suicide as the honorable way to shorten the futile torment in Timberboro, but in deference to his mother's social standing he decides to spare her the embarrassment that a son's suicide would bring. The two black notebooks in the manila envelope locked in the desk drawer will be revelation enough to her limited mind. Personal affairs arranged, Asbury can take up dying in this desert with a composure that forges "victory" (99) out of waiting for the end. Accordingly, he needs no " 'spiritual aid to die' " (100). Accepting extinction affords a "mystical clarity" (103) with which he can gaze "down into the crater of death" (104).

"The Enduring Chill" is not simply about an aspiring writer who denies the presence of the Spirit in the world; it concerns how he inflates blasphemy into heroic endeavor. Asbury's last days for him partake of high drama. Death summons Everyman to a general reckoning that can vindicate twenty-five years of struggle. The plays Asbury writes may be static, but the one he lives out makes him the hero of his vital script. The action of the story unfolds in the routine of life in Timberboro, whose inhabitants parade before the dying writer as so many minor figures of inadequacy. The contrast is telling. Asbury approaches the art of dying with the same enervating disposition that brings death to his art. His denials of spirit continue to dispose him to protest against his ultimate being. Those around him, who are less burdened with unappreciated sensitivity, react soberly to his histrionics. They are his foils, through whom a hidden power works to transform Asbury's spiritual resistance into a reception of love. This love first comes to him in the affection of those caring for his needs, and then as a gift from the Spirit to put aright the virtue and evil that Asbury confounds.

All the minor characters in the passing show provide comic relief from Asbury's gravity. His thirty-two-year-old sister Mary George, who is a principal of a county grammar school, cuts through Asbury's morbidity to put his homecoming at the elementary level on which his self-pity operates. " 'The artist arrives at the gas chamber' " (90), the indignant schoolmarm in Girl Scout shoes chortles at the front door of the house. Mrs. Fox also addresses the little boy in Asbury, who gets attention through sickness; but the child to whom Mrs. Fox speaks is to be excused from growing up. She is delighted to have her boy home. She plans to fix up " 'a little studio' " where he " 'can write plays' " (93). Since smart people with artistic temperaments do have nervous breakdowns, Mrs. Fox can nurse Asbury through his crisis with the confidence that sunshine and dairy work will snap him out of it. She has always been both mother-comforter and father-protector. She defends her boy against Mary George and against his own artistic excesses. Mrs. Fox also stands guard over any spiritual encroachment. When the visit with Father Finn, who comes at Mrs. Fox's invitation, turns honest and the priest tells Asbury that he is " 'a lazy ignorant conceited youth' " (107), Mrs. Fox bursts through the door, where she stands guard, to spare her poor sick child the truth he has needed all his life.

If Mrs. Fox does an inadequate job of preparing Asbury for life, her maternal instinct provides a service in not taking Asbury as solemnly as he takes himself. She has the good sense to call Doctor Block. Block is a country physician with an affection for his patients and a solid understanding of his work. He views Asbury's illness neither as metaphor nor as void. Disease for Block is a degenerative organic process against which he dedicates himself to fight. As an enemy of sickness and death, he knows when to go forward and when to hold back. The phenomenon of the body commands his respect for its mystery. His advice rests on a profound respect for the irreducible duality of life. The mark of his medical intelligence is his healthy admission of ignorance before hidden changes. When Asbury presents what he claims to be a unique disease that lies beyond a country doctor's competence, the large-eyed playful physician owns, " 'Most things are beyond me. . . . I ain't found anything yet that I thoroughly understood' " (95). Asbury's rare ailment, it turns out, is one mystery that the backwater practitioner thoroughly understands. Blood tests indicate brucellosis, or undulant fever, a chronic bacterial infection common to dairy animals, and a condition from which Asbury will recover but with which he will experience intermittent fever and weakness his entire life.

Block's medical art not only impedes disease, it also blocks Asbury's death-affirming arrogance by locating the real cause of illness as physical. There is no pathogenic specter that singles out Asbury for attack. Block correctly thinks that agent is from some unpasteurized milk, and with local pride assumes that he got the infected milk up north, but the reader knows that Asbury picked up the disease at home because of his foolish vanity. To show the two black dairymen, Morgan and Randall, that his mother's authority over them is dispensable, he breaks her rule and drinks warm milk in the dairy. The unpasteurized milk carries the bacterium. Asbury uses Morgan and Randall in his own frustrated effort to break free from his mother's power and contracts disease. His displaced anger comes back to him when he summons the black men to play out his final good-bye. Mrs. Fox ushers Morgan and Randall to Mister Asbury's deathbed as her surrogates who, rather than serving as an audience for the dying artist, mouth lies about his looking well that Mrs. Fox wants her son to hear.

What Asbury wants is for his death to have meaning. The best way he can think of finding it is by dramatizing his plight through enlightened conversation. As a final wish, he asks that a Jesuit pay him a call. And so a Jesuit is invited as part of the entertainment for the playwright's farewell performance. The Jesuit's role is to bring the fresh air of culture to the desert. Again actuality falls short of Asbury's theatricality. The priest who arrives is the plainspoken " 'Fahther Finn— from Purrgatory' " (105). Finn is Block's double, the spiritual ally of life who furthers the work of the medical enemy of death. The hearty, red-faced Father Finn even mirrors the round, baby-faced Doctor Block. Both are cherubic because they are, just as Mrs. Fox hopes Block will be, angels found "on the rooftop and brought . . . in for her little boy" (93).

Divine messengers they are; and sturdy they are too, like the large black-eyed woman behind whom huge wings might have folded who greets Francis Marion Tarwater on the way home in *The Violent Bear It Away.* As with the woman, sass will not do with Block and Finn. These two visiting healers are loving through their serious regard for Asbury. They deliver their message with an ultimatum for contrition. The priest in particular issues the demand in the down-to-earth manner used by all of O'Connor's angels. After exposing Asbury's ignorance of rudimentary catechistic lessons, Father Finn charges him to pray that the Holy Ghost will come to him. Insulted that the Jesuit does not evoke more suitable confidants from *The Golden Bough* or James Joyce, Asbury blurts, " 'The Holy Ghost?' " and asserts his self-sufficiency without the Spirit. Fashionable nihilism is sheer blasphemy to Father Finn, who pounds his fist on the bedside table and confronts him with the horror that he has tried to spare Asbury: " 'Do you want to suffer the pain of loss for all eternity?' " (107). This caring messenger bears another bit of news. When Mrs. Fox comes to Asbury's defense, Father Finn exposes the coddling and disregard in her not teaching her child his daily prayers—an upbringing which Mrs. Fox believes was virtuous. But Finn's judgment melts into affability. He lays his hands on Asbury's head. The visit ends with a blessing for Asbury and a comfort to Mrs. Fox that her son is " 'a good lad at heart but very ignorant' " (108).

The angelic service of Block and Finn attempts to correct Asbury's ignorance so that his goodness can develop. Their way is to remove the medical and spiritual delusions that keep Asbury from the truth that he has been seeking. The obstacle to the Spirit's approach is Asbury's swelled head. As his mother is not his oppressor, Art is not his goal. His real work is his life; his quest is for the experience of the Spirit. And his desire is as common as his ailment, and just as persistent. Asbury Porter Fox shares in the primary human instinct to seek freedom from the limiting conditions of the material universe. His yearning is so strong that it outfoxes his inveterate self-pity. He tells himself that he is coming home to die, but on arrival "a startling white-gold sun" communicates imperceptibly with his hope of witnessing "a majestic transformation" (82) among the shacks of dilapidated Timberboro. Even Asbury's contrived friendliness with Morgan and Randall expresses a real desire for communion with others he sees as oppressed.

The truest unfolding of Asbury's search comes in the natural affinity he feels for Ignatius Vogle, S.J., the polite, disinterested priest he meets in New York City after a lecture on Buddhism. The gaunt, bespectacled Vogle is a stand-in for Pierre Teilhard, whose work not only gives the title and impetus to O'Connor's final book but also credits the unitive transformation or convergence of creation to the intervention of the Holy Spirit in evolution (*Christianity and Evolution* 237–43). O'Connor names Vogle ("bird") for the dove that heralds the coming of the Spirit of God upon Jesus to announce this curious Jesuit bird as the advocate or Paraclete of the Spirit's activity. Vogle listens to the profound negations of nascent bodhisattvas dismissing salvation as the destruction of various illusions; and when asked by Asbury for his thoughts on the enlightened exchange, Vogle cuts through the weary celebrations of universal oblivion with a cheerful expectation of " 'the New Man, assisted, of course . . . by the Third Person of the Trinity' " (86).

Though the idea of personal resurrection seems ridiculous to the seekers awakened to meaninglessness, Asbury warms to the "icy clarity" (86) of Vogle's smiling disposition. The Jesuit acknowledges the rapport by handing Asbury a card with his address on it. But more than a calling card passes between them. The charisma of the encounter in New York spreads through the entire action of "The Enduring Chill." Though Vogle and Asbury do not meet again, the bird dwelling in Vogle's name and inspiring his voice and wry smile furthers their relationship by flying south to Timberboro, where it moves toward mystical intimacy with the ailing youth.

The bird approaches Asbury in several forms. Besides its human namesake, Vogle, two other species haunt Asbury. One is the hawk resembling the falcon of Yeats's poetry, which spirals in widening gyres of anarchic release. The falcon of Timberboro, however, does not break away from the falconer's control into chaos. Asbury writes in his notebook of the hawk as the soaring energy of his imagination which fails to escape his mother's domestication.

The other winged creature is the water stain on his bedroom ceiling. This ordinary mark is the rarest of all birds. Its beak carries an icicle, and its wings and tail drop finer icy streaks. Only the divine Artist could have etched this "fierce bird with spread wings" (93) from a leaky roof, and only the human artist whose gaze does offices of truth for the Spirit's hidden work could detect the bird's wondrous outpourings through the weathered plaster. O'Connor sees the mystery and presents Asbury's bedroom as a sanctuary. The water-stained bird on the ceiling forms a canopy over a sacred enclosure in which Asbury has slept since childhood. *Tabernacle* means dwelling, the sacred place where God dwells and reveals Himself; and that presence exerts an odd pressure of disturbing beneficence on Asbury. As an adult he feels the old irritation of childhood that the mark caused. Through the intervening years the obstinate bird has waited to drop the icicle from its bill and thereby manifest the full presence in the place. The suspended shoot menaces Asbury in illness, as it bothered him before; yet the tendril, if nourished by his good heart, will make Asbury the New Man that Vogle believes will come.

The habitation of this bird does not have the elaborate materials specified for the tabernacle in Exodus, but O'Connor does provide one structural feature that richly expresses the dwelling as the place of holy presence. She decorates the headboard of Asbury's bed with a carving of a garlanded cornucopia overflowing with fruit. The bird has gifts of love and union to bring, and Asbury has offerings to make in preparation for the bird's coming. The store on the headboard indicates the voluntary gifts out of which the tabernacle of Asbury's life is to be erected. Theologically, the abundant fruit expresses the generosity through which the human person approaches God and through which God approaches humanity; psychologically, the fruit represents the rewards that will come from the humility and suffering that Asbury has to offer.

The fierce bird bestows its gift the moment Asbury is strong enough to receive it. His acknowledgment of guilt confesses his spiritual readiness. The first thing Asbury does after Block gives him the news that the fever is not fatal is to retrieve the key to the drawer containing the notebooks so that his words do not hurt his mother. As a terminal victim of existential angst, Asbury could excuse his anger by denying his need for medical and spiritual help, but as a chronically sick person who will need help, he will have to accept the kindness and love of others. It is easier for him to feel anger than to feel his guilt. Guilt demands change. Still, the discomfort of guilt opens a way to restore the bonds he has broken. His frail and racked body can atone for the wrath he displaces onto others.

O'Connor concludes "The Enduring Chill" by dramatizing two gifts of sight that will help Asbury endure the raw purgation that Father Finn stokes in him. The first is the new perspective on nature that O'Connor gives to all those who are jolted out of their specious autonomy to clarify their new life. Asbury stares out his bedroom window as a red-gold sun glides from under a purple cloud. The blinding sun is about to break through the black treeline beneath the crimson sky. When the sun does shine forth, the brittle black wall of treeline dissolves into a burning bush. And so with Asbury, whose defenses against the Spirit also melt. Nature assures him that it is inevitable and wonderful that his resistance perish. The result is the enduring warmth of flame from the bush through which Moses becomes aware of God's presence (Exodus 3:2–4).

The second gift of sight is Asbury's watching that natural wonder alive in the Spirit's invasion of his life. The charisma makes the little world of the bedroom converge with the vast process of outer nature. First, the blazing sun stuns Asbury into throwing his head back on the pillow, from which his eyes fix on the ceiling's brooding bird. Asbury feels depleted: "The old life in him was exhausted. He awaited the coming of new." To stress the rejuvenation of the hero, O'Connor calls him "boy." Then a peculiar chill numbs and sensitizes him. The boy is now disposed to feel the hint of spring as someone living close to the cold could. The ceiling bird, which constitutes the sky over Asbury's sphere, appears to move. With nourishment suspended from its beak, the bird descends as an adult would to feed a newborn chick. As knowledge promotes growth of spirit, so the staff of life supplied by the bird nourishes the sick boy by teaching him that sickness has value and can offer a way to others and to God. The lesson makes Asbury blanch.

The falling bird sheds a blinding light, showing Asbury that surrender to infirmity and free acceptance of responsibility for his deceptions can lead him out of his hated confinement. The Spirit opens the way. In a blink, before Asbury's instinctive resistance to truth can check him, "the last film of illusion was torn as if by a whirlwind from his eyes" (114).

The "as if" does not soften the explosive effect of Asbury's restored vision. What is accomplished is the real transformation promised by the "mighty wind" in Acts 2:2 when it rushes from heaven into the house of Jesus' followers to fill everyone present with the Holy Spirit. The blast prepares for new growth. For Asbury, development lies in expiation. Making amends will offer the hero the opportunity to make the gifts of will out of which he can furnish the spare tabernacle he discovers at home. Moreover, the guilt that he once denied will have the cool and sanctifying benefit of making him welcome the whirlwind as a preparation for the purifying terror before him in the future. Not even the prospect of a diminished life need daunt the boy who has looked to the panorama of New York City for fulfillment. In the Gospels, the Spirit seems to show itself only in extreme situations; and so Asbury in his new era can count on the Spirit each day to be with him in the tabernacle of adversity.

Such a promise of the Spirit points up a crucial distinction drawn throughout O'Connor's fiction between healing and curing. Grace can help heal Asbury, but it cannot cure him. O'Connor further understands healing to be a two-edged sword. Only a power like steel tempered in icy water, as the emblazoned ceiling bird is forged, can lay bare the guilt tucked deep in Asbury's soul. And yet, if mighty and surprising, the pendant icicle is also tender, as are the bull's horns in "Greenleaf." The violent cut of love makes room for the bird to sow the seed of maturity in Asbury. Love is the gift presented in his utter abandonment, and it is for Asbury to make the new his own, his own place where the Spirit can dwell. The last words of "The Enduring Chill" are an infinitive, *to descend,* to announce the eternal activity of the Holy Spirit cutting a way to God through the Spirit's own self.

The way to God in "The Comforts of Home" opens by means of an altogether different wind than that which inspirits Asbury. A countercurrent of evil sweeps through "The Comforts of Home." As its source is not heaven but hell, the wind scorches rather than braces the protagonist. The fiery gust arrives in the form of Sarah Ham—check-forger, pathological liar, drunk, parasite, schemer, temptress, and nymphomaniac. At nineteen Sarah Ham is a maelstrom of lawlessness. Even when she is not inebriated or plotting to ensnare, her shaggy hair, hysterical voice, and eyes glaring from broad cheeks that pinch to a pointed chin give the impression of turmoil. The image of agitation materializes when Sarah insinuates herself into the life of Thomas, the hero of the story. The impact disturbs Thomas to the degree that he feels "as if he had seen a tornado pass a hundred yards away and had an intimation that it would return again and head directly for him" (128). The hint comes true. The violent whirlwind returns at the end of the story when Sarah Ham slinks down the staircase just as Thomas tries to plant a gun in her pocketbook. With each thrust of her bare legs out of her kimono, the tornado builds, for her sudden appearance sears Thomas's face with "an ugly dull red" of sexual shame heightened by being caught red-handed trying to frame her for one crime she does not commit. Her salacious laugh bounces down the staircase to make way for her provocative advance to the hero. "Thomas whirled" (140). Compromised by his sexual exposure and legal culpability, which pull him into the vortex of turmoil, the bewildered Thomas accidentally fires the gun and kills the one person he loves, his mother.

Before Sarah Ham intrudes on their life, the love between Thomas and his mother sustains a cozy universe of two. She keeps an orderly house and prepares delicious meals. Her domestic devotion makes a dwelling in which home and workshop and church are one. After thirty-five years of such comfort, Thomas has no desire to leave or to have the routine upset. His work as historian provides all the excursions away from home that he will take. He can venture into the lives of first settlers (local, of course) through articles for the Historical Society while he stays put at his desk. Life for Thomas is a matter of large and small entrenchments. His typewriter is stationary, and his luggage lies in some forgotten place. To his way of thinking, everything that comforts must stay put.

Thomas surrounds the enjoyments made by his mother with emotional fortification. Both strongholds are designed for the security of the other person. Thomas may seem too preoccupied with his historical essays to care about his old mother, but he does respond to her welfare with concern. Fine cuisine and tidy rooms are not his motives, either. The narrator of the story claims for Thomas the same good heart that Father Finn sees buried in the ashes of Asbury's self-absorption:

"Thomas loved his mother. He loved her because it was his nature to do so . . . " (118). The intellectual cast of his nature molds his affection in such a way that protectiveness takes the form of repelling any challenge to their tranquility. Thomas loves his mother as a child loves. If his trained mind can handle ambiguities of the past, his inexperienced heart cannot cope with displeasure in the present.

At thirty-five, the midpoint of life, the hero has yet to grapple with evil. His consciousness needs the security blanket of denial to function as much as his body requires his electric blanket to sleep. Immaturity, then, constrains Thomas to live in a world removed from sin and vexation; and misguided filial service calls him to guarantee that ideal for his mother as well. Were it within his ability, Thomas "would have spared her all unpleasant sights" (120). The power to control the behavior of all those around him seems within reach. Thomas maintains his domain of agreeable appearances with a mental housekeeping rivaling his mother's saner fastidiousness. The two labors—hers of physical care and his of emotional management—produce the comforts of home.

The very comforts of this home make its inhabitants vulnerable by weakening their capacity to deal with the discomforting reality they shut out. The more confident they are about accommodating the unpleasant, the more inept they become. The old mother, a lady, tries to domesticate evil and suffering with lessons in respectability. Armed with the *"nice thing to do"* (118), Thomas's mother goes forth on missions of benevolence. The folly of her indiscriminate good will alarms Thomas, who, sheltered by home and work, fears having to safeguard his mother from perils engendered by "her daredevil charity" (116). Yet though he wants to help her, he cannot. Abstraction robs him of his virility with Sarah Ham and of action in his mother's interest. For Thomas, evil exists in the mind, which can moderate any excess. His reliance on reason rather than a box of candy, which his mother trusts, to tame evil may sound mature; but the events prove that sophistry is as naive as and more dangerous than unthinking charity. It is wiser in O'Connor's world to assume that the devil has a sweet tooth than to think he has no bite at all.

No one would be more shocked than Thomas to learn that rationalism is merely another version of his mother's sentimentalizing evil. O'Connor is happy to supply the lesson. The jolt of recognition explains Sarah Ham's purpose in "The Comforts of Home." She brings cynical self-acceptance to a world of prim denial. Tornado that she is, Sarah demolishes everything in her path with her harshness. The story begins with her getting out of the old lady's car by sliding her long legs out from under a dress pulled above the knees. During her stay, the girl's behavior is no less overt than her entrance. She uses people and destroys order. The cheerful mother of the house, however, sees her charge as a helpless unfortunate sent to jail by congenital tendencies beyond the girl's control. Genes and social hostility compel her to break laws; Sarah, according to Thomas's mother, does not choose to do it. If a box of candy does not reform her, a job or a friend or, without fail, the comforts of home will do the trick. Social work, however, is laughable to Sarah, who is schooled in volunteer reformism. Charity as practiced through doing something nice calls attention to the self-image of the doer and trivializes the sense of responsibility in the recipient. Sarah regards Thomas's mother as a silly old windbag; and since Sarah is held cheap to begin with, she remains free to manipulate the lady.

Thomas depersonalizes Sarah in more subtle ways and, accordingly, receives a more stinging rebuke. He judges Sarah culpable for her action, yet he applies his mother's alibi of helplessness to Sarah's predicament. When the old lady excuses Sarah's nymphomania as " 'something she can't help,' " Thomas, out of the need to suppress his sexual interest in the visitor's legs, reduces Sarah's excessive sexual desires to mechanistic flaw. " 'She's a moral moron,' " he says fiercely. " 'Born without the moral faculty—like somebody else would be born without a kidney or a leg' " (117–18). Creation is to blame for bringing forth an incomplete human.

Thomas scorns Sarah Ham in the same way that the citizens of Taulkinham in *Wise Blood* abuse Enoch Emery and that George Rayber disdains little Bishop in *The Violent Bear It Away*. All look down on a human person whom they fear or cannot control, and think of the person as a form of life without spirit. "The Comforts of Home" takes the reader deeper into the effects of contempt on the scorner. Now we have a loving son fearful of his own love for his mother. Unlike Rayber, Thomas struggles to protect the person he loves; but he goes about it with a selfishness that defeats love. To justify himself, Thomas turns Sarah Ham into pure evil, "the very stuff of corruption, but blameless corruption because there was no responsible faculty behind it" (124). Sarah Ham becomes a slut. Being a slut makes her radically different from Thomas and his virtuous, if irksome, mother; "slut" in the hero's economy embodies a subspecies of humanity without spirit. Sarah Ham and vice are one kind of life; Thomas, his mother, and the comforts of home are another. Such dualism blasphemes the Spirit because designating Sarah a moral numskull places her beyond the Spirit's reach and therefore beyond repentance. In effect, Thomas tries to limit God's purpose to forgive.

Though this Thomas doubts the Spirit's rule over evil, the Spirit approaches Thomas through the very stuff of depravity. For one thing, Sarah Ham schools Thomas in guilt. There is no doubt in her mind that she must pay for her crimes, and she wants Tomsee, as she calls him to tease his stupid innocence, to know that her felonies count. She may hoodwink others, but she does not deceive herself. Jail and hell are realities to her. Beneath her histrionic shriek that even hell would reject her if she committed suicide (which she bluffs with superficial slashes of her wrists) lies a plea to be taken seriously as a moral person. She flaunts hysteria for the same purpose that she parades her sexuality: to reclaim for sin the importance that softheaded thinkers and do-gooders try to obliterate. Her extreme actions measure the world's stubborn refusal to see her as she is. Vice does not fit into the respectable order of the universe. " 'Nobody wants me anywhere,' " wails pure evil. " 'They didn't even want me in jail' " (131). Without guilt, Sarah Ham has neither place nor dignity.

The wanton woman also serves the Spirit by showing the guardian of virtue the value of self-esteem when he lies about discovering the pistol he planted in her purse. " 'Found it my eye!' " (141), she yells just before she lunges for Thomas's throat. Justice demands that Sarah pay for her crimes and also that Thomas be accountable for his. The criminal slut retains the moral sense that the idealist loses. Sarah's truthful presence condemns Thomas. He covers his shame by projecting it onto the cosmos, damning "not only the girl but the entire order of the universe that made her possible" (140). Having sloughed off personal responsibility, Thomas falls prey to the hissing voice in his mind of his father, which incites wrath; and the possessed hero censures Sarah: " 'The dirty criminal slut stole my gun!' " A whirlwind of furious accusation causes Thomas further to heed his father's satanic command to murder. And Thomas fires the gun. The shot is meant to annihilate once and for all the "evil in the world" (141), but the bullet kills his mother.

The old lady pays the ultimate price because Thomas refuses to accept guilt when he is caught framing Sarah for arrest. Next to Thomas the serene, Sarah the tornado is a refreshing breeze. Her threat is physical and comic, while his disturbance is intellectual and fatal. When incommoded, his obsession with mental comfort bursts into a rage for "the peace of perfect order" (141). He sets out to make the world safe for himself and his mother and finishes by bringing down upon himself guilt for his mother's death. The outcome lays bare the deeper guilt at the origin of his dualistic thinking. Evil may endanger human relations, but self-righteous perfectionism excludes the Spirit by denying the possibility of grace to restore broken bonds.

The eruption of matricide in the humdrum lives of respectable citizens concludes "The Comforts of Home," and the old lady's corpse lies between the dutiful son she loved and the outcast girl she took in. This lurid disaster, however, does not mark the end of things. O'Connor gives the story a twist by turning both killer and accomplice over to Sheriff Farebrother for his old-fashioned exposition of motives. The sheriff embodies the dark half of Thomas's mind. Farebrother's brain calculates facts down to their inexorable doom: the killer and the slut are about to embrace over the mother, whose death the son contrives to pin on the girl—until he, the shrewd officer of the law, catches them *flagrante delicto.* Farebrother is not only wrong but, having consented to Thomas's frame-up of Sarah Ham in the first place, is corrupt. His deductions bespeak a hard-boiled fatalism that looks to evil for explanation. From his perfectly logical untruths, the reader must discern the workings of the Spirit.

Farebrother seems to have surprised readers as much as he does Thomas. Two persuasive discussions of "The Comforts of Home" cannot make clear sense of the ending. One goes deep into the psychic recesses of Thomas's Oedipal crisis to explain that unexamined erotic attraction to Sarah seals his mother's fate. Obliged to incorporate Farebrother's verdict into its psychology, the analysis discounts the sheriff's tabloid sensationalism as O'Connor's reduction of Thomas to the moral level of Sarah Ham. The disreputable cop sees through malice to expose Thomas's "mock Apocalypse" (Asals 115). If Farebrother's pat solution fits the inverted revelation that one critic finds, that same formulaic language for another reader fits neither the affirming theology nor the taut craft that we expect of O'Connor. In this reading, Farebrother's version of the killing is a lapse in technique which indicts all the characters and rejects all courses of action, the effect of which is to deprive "The Comforts of Home" of a "moral center." What remains is an untypical O'Connor narrative in which we have "irony stripped of its anagogical implications" (Walters 145).

There is mystery in the story, and the solemnity with which these critical misgivings are delivered suggests that we look to the comic aspect of the tale to understand how the concluding fillip fulfills a hidden plan. In fact, "The Comforts of Home" calls attention to the contrast between the tumultuous passions of the principal characters and the smart-aleck idiom of Farebrother. The sheriff's mind operates like a projector illuminating the last frames of a B-movie thriller, with himself as hero and everyone else as supernumerary. The mechanical mind finds comfort in the melodramatic simplicities of the old B-format. Matters come to a neat legalistic resolution as the cop gets his man. Frantic action and grim retribution—staples for Saturday afternoon thrillers—provide the rigid moral lenses through which Farebrother reads and distorts the accident. Earlier in the story, Sarah Ham even puts in a word for MGM's famous Crime Does Not Pay series. For O'Connor, the Hollywood suspense film amuses in a different way. She turns its cheap effects into exposures of the modern sensibility that claims to know reality well while lacking a sense of virtue and mystery.

Like the sadistic enforcers of the law in *Wise Blood,* Farebrother is vicious. He arrives on the death scene not because he is clever or preserves justice but because he agreed to let the law be used by Thomas to railroad Sarah Ham. Years of dealing with crime teaches Farebrother that people are base and selfish and brutish, given to substituting law for cowardice as Thomas does; and the automatic calculations of the sheriff's brain reveal the working of Thomas's mind in hatching the plot. Matricide and the double cross, gaily observed, act out the malevolence that the cynic expects. Farebrother's brain draws connections that presuppose evil to be controlling human nature.

Where evil rules, loss and death and destruction are foregone conclusions. The moment Thomas abstracts Sarah Ham into pure evil, he implicates himself in the sinister process. Matters worsen when he thinks that he is the exponent of the law which, he reasons, must protect his perfect domestic order. It is expedient for Thomas to retreat from life into abstraction, and Satan is eager to supply a scenario to make moral escape heroic. In not opposing evil, Thomas falls into the role assigned by the devil and thereby becomes a minor character in the drama of evil battling good in which the lord of evil, writer and director, stars. The ending of "The Comforts of Home" flashes before us the B-script slam-bang finale in which senseless death overtakes daily life. The sheriff's attitude conveys the callous acceptance of humanity brought low in violence.

The spiritual dimensions of Farebrother's view run deep. He offers fantasy as macho truth with proud grit that is blind to a vast universe of experience. There is the love of Thomas for his mother that makes her death grievous, and there is the staircase (borrowed from the *Miss Lonelyhearts* set) that leads upward to hope as well as downward to the dead body. But Farebrother's deadpan fatalism defines a puny moral order of life. A throng of menaces and brutalities weaves its cloud above his brain as he presents a world shaped by the vilest conception of human nature. Such a world is desperate. Thomas crosses into despair when he covers his guilt by blaming Sarah and the cosmos. To curse the universe is to rationalize violating it. Like The Misfit in "A Good Man Is Hard to Find" and the platoon of self-loathers that follows, Thomas must destroy what he cannot endure. Death, premeditated or accidental, marks the triumph of mental order over reality.

Amid this collapse, nevertheless, the little apocalypse at the foot of the staircase provides a focus to correct Farebrother's distortions. *Thomas* means "twin"; and this Thomas, the scribe who feels unique, sees his twinship to all—to his mother in her love of virtue, to his father in his cruel rationality, to Sarah in her sexuality and evil and being scorned by the law, and to Farebrother in his exanimate cynicism. All converge in Thomas. Like molecules opening, the characters enter into a new combination through Thomas, who admits them into himself. All rise toward a future of convergence through the lessons of this new unity. The reality of evil and the truth of guilt are the messages of the Spirit. The horrible death that comes to the woman at the hands of her adoring son is a devastating exposure of the illusion of immunity that the son seeks. Out of this desolation the Spirit points to another response. The acceptance of one's own evil liberates one by opening the way to repentance.

My language here may not do justice to O'Connor's craft. The ending of "The Comforts of Home" is a horror happening like a torturous dream. The B-thriller overlay neither alters nor accounts for the pain; instead, it hints of another way to feel the loss before our eyes. The contrary lesson that O'Connor brings home teaches that sin and guilt can deepen and nurture love. The tie between Thomas and his mother has power and a long history, but their love lacks depth and growth because they cannot deal with evil and then build on guilt. Their immature preoccupation with pure good and the nice thing to do stunts a thirty-five-year-old man and a middle-aged woman into a boy and a boy's mother. By submerging guilt in pious charity or mental gesture, mother and son make it impossible to recognize in each other the common blame that brings one to be forgiven. In their loyalty to each other, Thomas and his mother try to make a perfect little place for themselves outside of the work of God. The final joining of the characters in evil does express, however, the need for mercy. Mercy is a part of the future that Farebrother's dark "expectations" (142) cannot embrace. Consolation is nevertheless present, for the Spirit partakes, as the title of the story guarantees, of the commonplace. The experience of the Spirit is the comfort underlying all the comforts of home, the Omega comfort.

— "The Lame Shall Enter First" describes the effort of a young widower, Sheppard, to succeed where Thomas fails in furnishing a home with the comfort of spiritual value. The good of another comes first for Sheppard. Selflessness allows him to stand beyond reproach, and he wants to instill the same ideal in his ten-year-old son Norton. The model for goodness is social casework. Sheppard, who is the City Recreational Director, spends his free time helping the boys at the local reformatory. One young offender, Rufus Johnson, who has an I.Q. of 140, catches Sheppard's attention. He sees that he can help Johnson, and Johnson in turn can help teach Norton to be good and generous. Though Johnson has a record of indiscriminate destructiveness that lowers his moral quotient to a level at which he brags that Satan controls him, Sheppard still gives Johnson the key to his home. Social psychology explains this daredevil kindness. By giving Johnson the comforts of home, Sheppard can make Norton grateful for what he has. No longer the only child, Norton will have to compete for affection and learn to share. Also, he will feel guilt for being so involved with himself.

Sheppard is not smart enough, however, to foresee the outcome of his enlightened plan. Johnson's intelligence proves to be the genius of death as he shrewdly leads little Norton to kill himself. The story ends with the child hanging himself from a beam in the attic. Just a moment before dashing up the stairs, Sheppard realizes that he uses Norton to fill his vanity with false charity. At the top of the stairs, the father who plays God by controlling others—for their own good, of course—must confront the price his son pays for his father's egoism. The virtue of selflessness turns out to be a self-conscious absolute that overshadows paternal love. Whereas the death of the old lady in "The Comforts of Home" brings to light the blasphemy of Thomas's denying the power of God to forgive, the death of the little boy in "The Lame Shall Enter First" exposes in Sheppard the sin of attributing the power of good to the evil spirit.

Sheppard violates the Holy Spirit not by being unprincipled or unloving but by being so highly principled that his precept of love never needs to be made flesh. The opening scene shows the disparity between Sheppard's ideal and practice. Father and son are having breakfast; like the first meal in the other all-male household of Mr. Head and Nelson in "The Artificial Nigger," their breaking fast holds the essence of their relationship. Bright and early, Sheppard turns his mind to Norton's future, which looms unpromisingly because of the boy's mental slowness. While Sheppard muses on Norton's faults, Norton fends for himself to make breakfast. He lumps together chocolate cake, peanut butter, and ketchup. Sheppard makes the pap more indigestible by serving up a hefty portion of food for thought, topped with sickly sweet self-congratulation: " 'Norton,' Sheppard said, 'do you have any idea what it means to share?' " (144). He then lists Johnson's deprivations to point up all the blessings that Norton has at his disposal to share with others. Father rears son from the book of good parenting; but we already know from Mason Tarwater, the best parent of them all, that one can no more nurture a child with ideas than one can change a diaper in one's mind.

Sheppard's instruction backfires. When he tells Norton to be thankful that his mother is not in the state penitentiary, the bereft boy howls in grief over his mother, who died more than a year earlier. Her absence cuts so deep that Norton welcomes the idea of her being in a penitentiary because then he " 'could go to seeeeee her' " (146). The timetable that Sheppard follows for sorrow tells him that the period of mourning is past and that selfishness accounts for Norton's crying in this awful way. After all, Sheppard misses his wife, but helping others allows him to forget his loneliness. Norton's misery forces Sheppard to remember the pain of love lost. Unwilling to experience his soul's coming to terms with loss, Sheppard berates his son for abandoning himself to sorrow. His father's reproach and his own desolation, with help from chocolate cake and ketchup, make Norton vomit.

Breakfast in the house had not always been a sociology class or discipline session; nor had Norton's behavior previously struck Sheppard as selfish. When Sheppard's wife was alive, meals were joyous. By glancing out the kitchen window, Sheppard can recall the time when he and his wife and their child took meals, including breakfast, outside on the fifty-foot grassy slope leading down to the woods. That pleasure ended over a year ago. His wife is the missing ingredient of love. Her death makes a great difference in the survivors' lives. Sheppard's fleeting picture of familial bounty tells us that he feels the loss of his wife, but his mind forbids him to dwell on the permanent separation from the woman he loves. The heart of her ten-year-old son, however, has no schedule. His mother's death remains a fresh privation. If Sheppard allowed his sense of loss to rise to consciousness, he might understand just how alone Norton feels. The boy's mother was the family's primary source of emotional sustenance, and her death diminishes her son by the measure of human meaning provided by her love. The stocky boy tries to eat his way back to comfort, but food does not help. He also sells seeds for nickels and dimes, which he counts every few days with the hope that money will sprout a prize, a consoling affirmation that his life has meaning even though his mother is dead.

If we keep in mind that "The Lame Shall Enter First" treats the soul's attempt to assimilate loss by recovering that love which gives meaning to life, then we can appreciate that O'Connor is at once more gentle and more exacting with Sheppard, a protagonist who lies outside her sympathy (*Letters* 491). The story shows that even an altruistic social scientist who manages emotion by abstraction depends on love to survive. Sheppard's clinical categories and posture of control do not fill the void in his heart left by the death of his "good" wife (*Letters* 498). A palpable emptiness prevents him from sleeping in the bedroom that he and his wife shared before her death. Sheppard felt deeply for his wife, and now cares very much for Norton; but at the moment he is too fearful to confront the absence of the woman he loves. Volunteer work provides an escape from sorrow, but avoidance is the solution of the weak. Because Sheppard does not mourn, he is unable to help Norton through grief, a pain that Sheppard feels himself. His speech on suffering while Norton suffers amounts to a lame request that Norton feel better so that Sheppard can feel better.

The harsh side of O'Connor's development of the hero comes out in the explanatory sequence going back one year to Sheppard's first interview with Johnson in the reformatory and their subsequent conferences. These Saturday sessions give a wacky definition of counseling, for the ego of the counselor is presented for shrinkage to the hard-bitten young counselee. Johnson's "monstrous club foot" (149) focuses the strange process. Sheppard turns the deformed foot into a symbol that explains away Johnson's mischief. Angered that his criminal record does not matter, Johnson tries to shock the Saturday therapist: " 'Satan,' he said. 'He has me in his power' " (150). It is a sinful life, but it is his. The contempt of the prideful sinner, however, does not touch the swollen confidence of the rationalist. The human mind can decipher everything. " 'Maybe I can explain your devil to you,' " Sheppard says (151). The improvidence of his remark defines itself, but the timing of his promise bears noting. That Sheppard's thoughts of commitment to Johnson occur at the moment when Norton goes to bed sick to his stomach and hurt in his heart tells us that Sheppard uses Johnson to dodge loving Norton.

While Norton is alone in the house trying to ease the pain of his father's rejection by counting seed packages, a heavy thunderstorm suddenly stops; out of the hush Johnson arrives, opens the door with the key that Sheppard gave him, and storms into the kitchen. Hunger drives this ominous presence. He thumps straight to the refrigerator, standing in his wet black suit like a drenched crow surveying for edibles. The flower seeds on Norton's bedroom floor clearly will not satisfy this scavenger. When he finishes with the garbage cans that he ordinarily prefers, this bird turns to whatever is on hand. He will try feasting on humanity as well. His rapacity with people takes the form of humiliation. At Johnson's command, Norton becomes first a waiter, serving the intruder a sandwich and an orange, and then a slave, whose subjugation titillates the glutton's taste. Even Leola, the black housekeeper, becomes on arrival an object for control. The orgy of destruction climaxes with Johnson's ransacking the room and clothes of Norton's dead mother. Dressed in the woman's red blouse, green silk kerchief, and corset, Johnson whirls in a macabre rock 'n' roll dance down the hall toward the kitchen (for still more gratification?). Norton hides mortified in a closet until his father returns home.

The sexuality of the invasion suggests the intimate hold Johnson has on Sheppard, and warns of the ravisher's power over Norton. Johnson is an incubus or is possessed by one. Sheppard will even allow the stranger to occupy the dead woman's bed. The destroyer will cling to his living victim until the victim dies. But the charm of Johnson's intelligence numbs Sheppard to his danger. When tearful Norton reports the truth about Johnson's rampage, Sheppard scolds the child for tattling and asks the desecrator to help teach Norton about sharing. Norton's misery has no effect. Not even contempt from Johnson breaks the spell; it serves, instead, to add embarrassment to Norton's confused feelings toward his father, who remains aloof. " 'I'm above and beyond simple pettiness' " (161), Sheppard says, confident of immunity precisely at the moment he is ensnared by the demonic intruder and his son stands rejected.

Sheppard's superiority grows from a belief that he lives by truth. Illusion does not take him in. When Rufus Johnson invokes Jesus and Satan to explain getting into trouble with the law, Sheppard seizes the chance to enlighten the youth: " 'Rubbish!' he snorted. 'We're living in the space age!' " (151). New knowledge frees the mind from sentimental prejudices. On a later occasion, Norton, after hearing Johnson speak of eternal darkness, asks about where his dead mother might be; his question meets the same cool, didactic detachment in his father: " 'Your mother isn't anywhere. She's not unhappy. She just isn't' " (164). Neither heaven nor hell awaits the space age. Death no longer reveals human destiny. Removed from life and put into Sheppard's mind, death is an image of the void. Sheppard takes science into his heart as an idol and passes it on to Norton as comfort. Sheppard's truth, however, consoles Norton less than does Johnson's vivid picture of hell, because hell holds out to the lost boy the possibility of seeing his mother again.

If truth is confirmed by dispassion, then Sheppard's agitation proves his truth to be false. The moment Johnson moves into the house, Sheppard becomes cruel. That night he whips Norton for making a scene over Johnson's sleeping in his mother's bed. Paternal discipline is not a function of love or judgment but is an expedient to condition behavior. Right and wrong are beside the point. So too with Sheppard's relation to the law. The police come three times for Johnson, and each time Sheppard distorts facts to suit himself. The first time, the police want to arrest Johnson for vandalism. He is innocent of the charge and appeals to his guardian for honest support. Sheppard, not knowing if Johnson is guilty, acts on a private "twinge of guilt" (167) for being lenient with the youth and for being overly concerned with winning Johnson's approval. To show firmness while really punishing Johnson for withholding gratitude, Sheppard decides that a night in jail will teach the hoodlum to value someone who is kind to him. Johnson pays for Sheppard's ego and hates the man for it. When the police come again, this time about a break-in on the corner of Shelton and Mills, Johnson is guilty of the offense; once again Sheppard twists the issue, but now to show how loyal he can be. The charade fails. Johnson knows the difference between trust and self-serving opportunism, and he holds the man in contempt. On the third police visit, the upstanding Sheppard reduces himself to a sycophantic accomplice covering up for the young felon. The more Sheppard compromises himself to curry Johnson's favor, the less aware Sheppard is of his destructive hypocrisy. What characterizes evil in this " 'dirty atheist' " (188), as Johnson calls him at the end, is Sheppard's imperviousness to both truth and guilt.

Johnson seeks no such separation. Whereas Sheppard's conception of evil is psychological, Johnson's is sacral. Johnson tries to duck paying for his crimes, but he knows that he must pay for his sins. In fact, he insists upon doing so, and preserves a sharp distinction between society's law and God's command, between human desire and ultimate necessity. Science propels its faithful to galactic heights; guilt drives Johnson to divine judgment. " 'I ain't going to the moon,' " he snaps to Sheppard, the true believer in space travel, " 'and when I die I'm going to hell.' " The lunar beam drawing the astronaut does not hold a candle to the " 'everlasting darkness' " (164) seen by Johnson's grandfather. Johnson anticipates damnation as a guarantee that his action is important enough to fall within God's final consummation of history. When Sheppard offers excuses for his criminal activity, Johnson counts for less; when science denies the reality of hell, he counts not at all. Johnson's insistence that hell is real goes beyond denouncing the atheist's obtuseness; his claim is the sinner's assertion of integrity. He is not a case; he is a creature of God. Johnson helps Sheppard by opposing him, defying him. The criminal unmakes the good citizen and leads him to discover remorse.

In the battle of nerves that ensues, Sheppard's defeat is a foregone conclusion. He fails, as his opponent explains, because the good can triumph only if the good is true—that is, if virtue conforms to the essential reality beyond the ego of the doer of good. In such a reality, there is evil to overcome and not mere tendencies of the psyche to offset. Sheppard " 'ain't *right*' " (155) and his uprightness " 'ain't true' " (180) because his good works refer to himself as giver in order to obligate others to his ego. When Johnson introduces his hillbilly respect for hell to the city house of scientific clarity, he sets a higher standard of generosity and personal debt. " 'Nobody can save me but Jesus' " (180), he reminds Sheppard. Johnson owes repentance to the one Who gave His life to keep others from burning and thrashing in hell. This "Jesus business" (182) upsets the good Sheppard, who is not accustomed to doubting his uprightness. Contention erupts into attack on the final evening of the story, when Sheppard arrives home to find Johnson dressed in his grandfather's black preacher's suit, reading from a Bible stolen from a dime store. Instead of acting on his desire to evict Johnson, Sheppard suffers a face-off. The brazen boy makes the virtuous Sheppard feel like "the guilty one" (182). The three never sit down at the table for supper. Their meal is a sacrifice of blame. Johnson tears a page from the Bible and eats it with Ezekiel's zeal and the prophet's aim to declare himself on God's side; leaving the house, he tells Sheppard that the devil has him in his power.

Though the small black herald of doom exposes " 'that big tin Jesus' " (187), Johnson is not the master of events. His defeat of Sheppard is preparatory to a deeper outcome. His accusation is accurate; his refusing a new orthopedic shoe insults the man's generosity; and his felonies bring the reformer to admit his hatred of Johnson. These retaliations entrench Sheppard in the feeling of being beyond reproach; they do not change him. Only Johnson's influence on Norton pierces the tin Jesus' godliness. The shrewd boy gains control over Norton by addressing his desire to know his dead mother's whereabouts. Having staked out his place in hell, Johnson is brought to testify to the possibility of heaven. If Norton's mother believed in Jesus, Johnson says, then " 'She's saved.' " Whereas Sheppard talks of the moon and stars, Johnson guides his pupil to thoughts of his mother's being " 'On high' " (165), which, he explains, requires that one be dead to get there. The next day, the boys enter the baseball field with Johnson's hand on Norton's shoulder, the older boy hissing into the enthralled child's ear. The image of ominous dependency sharpens several days later when Norton rests his cheek against the sleeve of the boy's black suit. We never hear the instructions, but the mortal confusion caused by Johnson becomes known in Norton's suicide. Convinced that Mamma waves to him from the twinkling star clusters at the end of the telescope, Norton hangs himself so that death, the access to on high he has just discovered, will shuttle him to his supernal mother. And upon reaching the stars, the lost son will find at last his father's approval for being the space cadet that good boys should be.

The little astronaut's body dangles from an attic beam like a demand for reparation that cannot be completed in all the time left to those responsible. Norton's suspended corpse accuses Johnson, whose vindictiveness and warping counsel provided the means; and the child's body accuses Sheppard, whose coldness and false science provided the motivation for his son's suicide. Both are guilty, but each accepts guilt differently. Johnson excuses himself in advance when he announces that he is going to hell and, therefore, is beyond remorse. Sheppard, however, touches depths of responsibility. It is his ending, his story of receiving the gift of guilt to spare him from the satanic fate of unfeeling.

O'Connor prepares her hero for rescue by administering her usual jolt of love. After sending Norton to bed as punishment for insisting that Mamma lives in the stars, Sheppard hears the siren of a patrol car. The police arrive with Johnson handcuffed to tell his guardian that he is going to jail for stealing. The legal formality occasions Johnson's moral identification of evil in himself, in the world, and in Sheppard as well. Sheppard can rely on his rationalizations to deny his culpability, but the cold he feels "on his shoulders" as if cast by an "icy cloak" (187) is not so easily removed. The garment is God's will. Its weight immerses Sheppard in responsibility both for his sins and for his love of Norton. Lucette Carmody, the lame child-healer in *The Violent Bear It Away*, explains the strange cold that gusts into the ending of "The Enduring Chill" and of "The Lame Shall Enter First" as the climate of divine love. The coldness is the promise that in return for obedience God's love is with and by the protagonist.

The truth that comes to Sheppard is cold: he did more for the boy he disliked than for his own son. When repeated in silence, words of contrition pass into his blood to enter his heart, which, softened by grief, strengthens Sheppard to stare directly into his abysmal vanity and to acknowledge "his own emptiness." Love for Norton makes Sheppard rush to hug and kiss the boy, who by this time has left his bed to fly to his star-mother. The last sentence of the story describes Sheppard beholding "the child hung in the jungle of shadows" (190). Already burdened by the icy mantle, already repentant for his selfishness and agonized by his revived love, Sheppard takes in a searing vision.

O'Connor's poetry at the end of "The Lame Shall Enter First" is twice poetic because of the immoderateness of Norton's act. The details resonate to one of her radical images. The seeds Norton played with earlier sprout into the tree of life on which he dies, suggesting the offering of another son Who hangs ragged in the trees of the hero's mental forest in *Wise Blood*. The gentle ghost of Norton will inhabit Sheppard's conscience with the same persistence that the tattered figure stalks Hazel Motes. Norton has paid for his father's sins. The tripod and telescope on the attic floor under Norton's body betoken the new vision transferred to Sheppard, who now sees the marvel in the debt of love he owes his son.

A world with guilt is also a universe with wonder. Guilt brings Sheppard to see things anew. In the beginning, he buys the telescope and microscope to instruct the two boys about the enormous and minute aspects of the cosmos, in the belief that everything there is can be seen and everything that can be seen is explainable. The moon hovers as the final destination for his future cosmonauts. The two boys, however, with their opposing wisdoms teach the instructor about invisible extensions of the firmament. Their lessons provide two remedies for pride. Angered by Sheppard's trivial excuses for sin and bored by his scientific toys, Johnson trains Sheppard's eyes on hell, a lasting place that is more vital than a mere lunar satellite of earth. Then Norton's sacrifice blows Johnson's fatal doctrine and Sheppard's scientism sky-high.

Norton's death displaces all systems of knowledge with mystery. He lives the truth stated in the title of the story. The principle of the lame entering the kingdom of God first is not a biblical prescription but an attitude toward transcendence. In "The Lame Shall Enter First" there are the physically impaired and those who are otherwise handicapped; and the lamest does enter first. Norton, who is slow and responds "lamely" (145) to his father's gestures, leads the way to life by virtue of his mental handicaps. He can approach life and God by no other means than the direct way of love.

Norton's lameness defines the human condition. All the characters are spiritually disabled before God; all are enfeebled by being free without grace. At one extreme stomps Johnson, whose clubfoot marks a moral nihilism that derives not from his anatomy but from his sinning with prideful exhilaration. Sheppard hobbles at the other end. "Like a lame man's legs, which hang useless," we read in Proverbs 26:7, "is a proverb in the mouth of fools." Sheppard is one such fool. His inability to put his knowledge and his love to use is his lameness. When Sheppard reels back from the sight of his dead son, he feels his deficiency and falters in grief.

The surest sign of spiritual progress in O'Connor's fiction is a character's recognition of her or his wretchedness. Seeing his pitifulness brings Sheppard to the abyss of mercy, which unites him with his wife, son, and adopted son. All are lame yet capable of rising out of their ruins into convergence. Norton, who knows that love exacts its toll in tears, leads the way and pilots Sheppard into a vast continuum of passion where he will live both his life and his death. Guilt burns in Sheppard's spirit like a supernova luminous with love.

7

Fulfillment

A house for wisdom; a field for revelation.
Speak to the stones, and the stars answer.
At first the visible obscures:
Go where light is.
Theodore Roethke, "Unfold! Unfold!"

The final three stories of *Everything That Rises Must Converge* are the most audacious and most tender of Flannery O'Connor's raids on the ineffable. "Revelation," "Parker's Back," and "Judgement Day" show as fully as she dared the mysterious fulfillment of her comedies in the divine plan. All are forged during the enfeebling months of terminal lupus leading to O'Connor's death on 3 August 1964, and celebrate the power that sustains O'Connor in bringing the stories to completion. "You have to be without energy," O'Connor writes on 23 November 1963 to a friend, "to gauge whatall it takes" (*Letters* 549). Writing fiction when physically diminished takes humor and excitement about what comes next. What is in store is the end. Death for O'Connor demands verve; and her last stories reconceive destiny in defeat, demonstrating mirthful confrontation with absolute reality.

This farewell builds through each of the final stories, but "Judgement Day" caps the sequence with a special magnitude of vision. For her last protagonist in the last predicament, O'Connor returns to her earliest material. The result is a canonical tale. The retrospective reach of "Judgement Day" offers an ideal way to examine the evolution of

O'Connor's fiction. In the concluding chapter, I have taken advantage of the story's scope to discuss "Judgement Day" along with its antecedents in order to suggest how O'Connor's first thoughts lead to her final design.

The moral strength of "Judgement Day" also informs "Revelation" and "Parker's Back." In all three stories, the potential for disaster lurks in the protagonist's way of being in the world. "Revelation" depicts a righteous matron who puts down everyone in sight; "Parker's Back" portrays an indefatigable sensualist who tries to get his wife's attention and to count for himself by having his entire body tattooed. A sudden illumination, however, changes their attitudes and spares them from the self-destruction their habits can cause. A new understanding of their desire redirects a narrow aim into a loving cosmic recognition, and the longing of each character turns in harmony with the infinite. The *retournement* dazes both heroine and hero. Their confusion gaily points out the disparity between how little they wanted and how much more they are freely given. A certain bewilderment and humor are proper to the marvel felt at the journey's end in these two stories. Confused joy crowns each action with an exalted finale.

The amiability of "Revelation" and "Parker's Back" comes not merely from the characters making headway to ultimate consolation. Progress toward God underlies every O'Connor story. Having looked to charity for explanation, O'Connor in maturity finds the hidden God in evil desire itself. The negative theophanies of *A Good Man Is Hard to Find* and *Wise Blood* are replaced by emanations of the infinite. A deepening perception of the world makes the characters not only questers for love but also partners with the absolute. Where human life crosses the threshold of divine life, there is a passage that Teilhard describes as attaining the "peak of ourselves, the acme of originality" (*Phenomenon of Man* 263). In his scheme, self-discovery signals the individual's contacting the Omega Point, which lies somewhere ahead in the consummation of history. Teilhard's Omega becomes O'Connor's Everything. *Everything* in the title of the last collection embraces the actual variegated stuff of the characters' battered bodies and geographical displacements, unified through the transcendent focus inherent in matter awaiting completion in spirit. Teilhard's Omega marks the end of the world—the end, he speculates, as it recomposes into the noosphere.

For all her admiration of Teilhard's supreme poetics, O'Connor would never bring her narratives to rest in a huge abstract denouement.

Truth in her world comes enfleshed; it is never grasped aesthetically. "Revelation" concludes with the heroine seeing a rapturous swarm of souls shouting hallelujah as they rumble skyward. "Parker's Back" ends with the hero receiving in his consciousness the image of Christ tattooed on his back. Material nature affirms inner unveilings. What the characters' eyes and backs take in is a communiqué directing their attention beyond their present distress to the future goal.

The future for O'Connor is the message of freedom. Freedom brings the future into view. When emancipated from self-centeredness, the protagonists see their rightful place in the pattern of the whole. Their new view is intimately linked to the present human relations in which the characters find themselves at the end of "Revelation" and "Parker's Back." Besides not canceling their awakening with death, as is her way, O'Connor leaves the protagonists alive and married. Loyal attachments call attention to themselves in a fiction that posits the characters' essential relationship to be with God and that as a rule depicts a lack of substantial relationships in human dealings. Marital ties in "Revelation" and "Parker's Back" seem to go with the new future. The hero and heroine have a domestic partner to test their revealed partnership with God. Duty to another will impart not only a recognition of the conscious pride that the human spirit feels but also a sense of guilt for the inescapable pride involved in every human enterprise, particularly in the undertaking of love. The alpha of self-understanding leads to the Omega of divine communication.

II

Mrs. Ruby Turpin of "Revelation" could use new information from any source. She is a closed circuit of intolerances that pass for social distinctions. The signals of new knowledge trace the pattern expected of a woman with a little bit of everything, who does for the church and who would not lounge around the sidewalks drinking root beer. The message sent to Ruby Turpin is to uphold virtue, and she takes on the role of God's deputy on earth bearing the sword of heaven to keep social order. Everyone's place is established. Black people retain their historical assignment to the bottom, poor whites occupy a separate but equal rung near the bottom; and as Ruby scans society upward, she finds home owners, home-and-land owners—among whom Ruby and her husband Claud number—and on top, richer versions of the Turpins.

Exceptions to the hierarchy do not modify it. When Ruby tries to account for the black dentist with two red Lincolns and a swimming pool on a farm with white-faced cattle, she disregards the facts to preserve the abstract system. The result is mental turmoil as the connections break down into an entropic horror of the classes hauled off in a boxcar to a gas oven. Ruby is anxious to protect her moral and economic standing by trashing others.

Critical judgment repays Ruby Turpin in kind. The picture of her to one reader is "unrelieved by any redeeming qualities." Her prejudices and conduct "reveal her as a negative moral agent, unaware of her own absurdity because she is so attached to an inauthentic existence" (Muller 47). Other responses change the focus to Ruby's last vision but alter neither the dismissal of her nor the critical consensus that the bigoted woman receives the social comeuppance she deserves. The usual reading finds Ruby Turpin at the end pondering the secular implications of her racism. The revelation completes "the message of ill-founded self-esteem," for which O'Connor's "language and image of theology" do not serve a spiritual purpose but create an emotional epiphany that exposes "the most self-respecting people" as the most perilous (Shloss 112–13).

The observations seem true, and yet they would render Ruby Turpin unrecognizable to O'Connor. "If the story is taken to be one designed to make fun of Ruby," O'Connor writes to an attentive reader, "then it's worse than venal" (*Letters* 552). With a more charitable grasp of human malice than shown by some readers, O'Connor appreciates that it takes a mighty big woman to give God a piece of her mind from across a pigpen, as Ruby does at the end. "She's a country female Jacob," O'Connor explains to an old friend (*Letters* 577). Behavior that would make a parson swear brings an admiring smile to O'Connor.

"Revelation" makes no more effort to gloss over the defects of Ruby Turpin than Genesis tries to hide the weaknesses of Jacob. Rude outspokenness can express depth of conviction. "I like Mrs. Turpin as well as Mary Grace," states O'Connor (*Letters* 577). Mary Grace is a tough Wellesley student in the story who has her fill of Ruby in a doctor's waiting room and throws a book at her. The indignation of both women sets a high law for their own reckoning. The younger woman is downright offensive. Mary Grace is "so ugly" for the simple reason that " 'Flannery loves her,' " explains the author, borrowing the response of another friend (*Letters* 578); and Ruby Turpin is so beastly because

O'Connor has amazing things in store for her. Jacob receives from God the help available to one who is essentially good and who can be used by Him for a great destiny. Jacob wrestles with God, and God gives Jacob insights into the future (Genesis 49:2–27). The blessings of Jacob fall on both Mary Grace and Ruby. Mary Grace receives knowledge as an intermediary that she hurls at Ruby in the form of a curse. The malediction turns out to bless Ruby with an eventual prevision of what will befall her and everyone else in days to come.

The message has been coming to Ruby Turpin for some time, but she picks up only what suits her. The events on one hot summer day, from morning in the physician's office to sunset back home at the farm, break through Ruby's prejudgments to confer "some abysmal life-giving knowledge" (217). The usual reading of this new awareness equates it with Ruby's seeing her arrogance in subjecting others to her power. While she does feel the effect of her insolence, she also perceives the benefit of submitting to the power controlling all things. The revelation, then, concerns an exposure of Ruby's vice as part of the disclosure of the righteousness of God. The message comes from and goes back to divine mystery, which, more than psychology for O'Connor, is life-giving, and which accounts for the affectionate presentation of Ruby Turpin.

If we regard Ruby Turpin from the Omega perspective given to her, we can see that, far from the monster critics make her out to be, Ruby is a classic example of a person who is ignorant of God's righteousness and who therefore goes about establishing her own just order. She has, to cite Paul, "a zeal for God, but it is not enlightened" (Romans 10:2). *Zealot* is the word for Ruby. On arrival in the doctor's waiting room, she wastes no time sizing up the ridiculously inadequate space. It bulges with violations of her personal fantasy of how people ought to be. There are the boy with the runny nose in a dirty blue romper, his white-trashy mother with bedroom slippers, the gum-smacking redheaded woman, and a stringy old man with rusty hands. Also, she finds the fat and acned Mary Grace, accompanied by her well-dressed mother, who is the notable exception to the offending rule. Finally, there is the doctor's secretary, who pays more attention to the gospel music on the radio than to the ashtrays filled with cigarette butts and bloody cotton swabs.

Indignation regulates Ruby's first impressions and subsequent deportment. Respectable even when piqued, she uses cordiality to remind offenders of their transgressions. Ruby singles out the proper lady to be the ally through whom she can rebuke others and laugh at their expense. " 'I wish I could reduce' " (193), Ruby says brightly to the modish mother of Mary Grace in order to call attention to a woman lumbering into the physician's examination room. Here is Ruby Turpin, who sees herself as the soul of charm and virtue, unable to endear herself to the strangers who are collectively diminished by her black eyes staring out of her 180-pound bulk. A chatterbox, a complainer, a classist, and a racist, Ruby Turpin combines so many attributes repugnant to readers that O'Connor's fondness for her female country Jacob challenges us to feel our way through "Revelation" anew (Gordon 41–45).

O'Connor's improbable sympathy again derails the reader with the reminder that in spiritual writing one must reverse the ordinary way of thinking about human evil in order to recognize social strife as the result, not the cause, of inner turmoil. With Ruby Turpin, the source of unrest is her mistaking social mores for the order of grace, which, to her credit, she is eager to obey. Fervid for divine respect, she pays scrupulous attention to matters ranging from the hygiene of her pigpen to the tidiness of the people forming the Doomsday extravaganza. Ruby confounds her need for propriety and desire to be an attractive female with being the good woman cherished by God. Her injurious behavior reflects the same desire to be worthy before God. God's favor, to her way of thinking, is a matter of fairness. Rendering people their due is important enough to Ruby for her to quarrel with God. Ruby's cruelty to others and the harm she brings upon herself are prompted by her need to believe that the world is just.

Her severe sense of justice makes damnation a vivid reality. The threat of God's wrath directed toward Ruby keeps her on guard against any condemnation. Fear dominates her emotions. Too submissive to reject conventional oppressions, and too proud to see her complicity in them, Ruby allows regional prejudice to serve as the regime of grace by calling racism "God-given" (218). She can see herself as Christian while looking down on others by believing that they have brought on their plight and therefore deserve what happens to them. Low status justifies further scorn. Disdain also helps to mask Ruby's fear of judgment by elevating vanity to divine acceptance. Her heart rises when she thinks gratefully, as she frequently does, that God "had not made her a nigger or white-trash or ugly!" (203).

Ruby believes that she has only to present herself before God as a church-going and law-abiding landowner, and she will be saved. The supposition is so common to human thought that her attitude can go unquestioned. The error lies not in trying to treat others and God in a just way; rather, Ruby's mistake appears in her belief that she can be justified by her own virtue and power. Though she is right in seeing justice as the highest moral virtue, she is wrong in separating justice from love. More is required of Ruby to be a good Christian woman than respect for other people's rights to things and feelings. Justice in its Christian form makes everyone stand as a debtor before the law of love.

Ruby's limited interpretation of justice pervades "Revelation." When she arrives at the doctor's office with Claud, there are two vacant places, a chair and a sofa seat; and so her decision to stand is a complaint about not being offered a proper place next to her husband. Sick people in a doctor's office do not necessarily function as they would at a social gathering. The condition of others is secondary to Ruby. She needs respect at every turn to bolster her notion of justice. Those below her provide the deference that guarantees that in God's economy she is saved. She may think herself the source of justice, but the slightest human encounter entails renewed proof of her moral standing. The crisis occurs when Ruby's need for justice fills the waiting room with recrimination and boasting to the point at which the fat and ugly Mary Grace throws the book she is reading at Ruby. Then, like a vampire fiend, Mary Grace crashes across the table to grab Ruby's neck. When finally sedated by the physician, Mary Grace whispers in a low voice the possible truth that Ruby has spent a lifetime trying to avoid: " 'Go back to hell where you came from, you old wart hog' " (207). After being examined by the gray-haired physician, Ruby goes home.

During the afternoon of recovery back at her farm, Ruby Turpin tries to find solace in herself, in her conscience where she has always found righteousness. She proceeds with her case before God with the anger that Job feels should bring his cause to victory: " 'How am I a hog and me both? How am I saved and from hell too?' " (215). Her denials of sinfulness become more strident before the divine bar, but lose their force of persuasion. For all her pleading, she cannot convince herself that she is entirely in the right. Ruby's essential virtue arises from her deep-seated desire not to be lied to, not even by herself. Resting on the bed, she raises her fist in small stabbing motions "as if she was defending her innocence to invisible guests who were like the comforters of Job, reasonable-seeming but wrong" (210). Tears dried, Ruby orders Claud to kiss her; but the loud buss does not divert her attention from the ceiling with mysterious handwriting on it, a secret that she wants divulged. But the proud woman also wants respect again, for which she turns to the black workers. The three black women patronize Ruby with cheap consolation and flattery. Their lies increase Ruby's rage.

It is after dismissing Claud and the workers that the infuriated Ruby takes her suit to God, Who she knows is just and Who therefore can be confronted without fear. While hosing down the pig parlor with more than her usual zeal, the litigious heroine recites her obedient good works as actions warranting a message more in keeping with His promise than with the one issued by Mary Grace. Self-praise fails to bring relief, and God lets her dare pass. Ruby soars to accusation: " 'Who do you think you are?' " (216). Like O'Connor, God must admire Ruby's temerity, because the affront shouted into the air is immediately picked up by a wind and carried over the pasture and the highway and the cotton fields and back to her "like an answer from beyond the wood" (217). The quick *tour d'horizon* not only marks off the confines of Ruby's property, it also prepares her to see within the limited purview the message that she refuses to hear and the secret on the ceiling that she wants to decipher. The blend of lovely and didactic touches in the sunset contains the essence of Ruby's day. The setting sun reddens the wood. For Ruby, the wood turns deep red to match her very wrathful eyes burning with pride and her precious self and name. With "a mysterious hue" suffusing everything, including the sow and her seven shoats, revelation is unmistakably in the air and on the ground. The heroine's shaking her fist at God creates in the rubescent sky "a watery snake" (216) to indicate, as the serpent's reappearance in the Book of Revelation does, that the day of divine messages is at hand. God's dispatch to Ruby Turpin comes in reducing her to silence. The irrepressible jabberer is lost for words: "She opened her mouth but no sound came out of it" (217).

Ruby's joyful humor arises through O'Connor's delicate crafting of the ending. If God's humbling Ruby to speechlessness convicts her of folly, it does not say that she is wrong to want to appear justified before Him. In fact, the vision of salvation troops storming the sky suggests that justification before God is the state for which everyone has been created. Ruby's distress comes from her reliance on social sentiment elevated to holy writ. Law alone—in this instance Christian legalism overlayed with spiritual materialism—cannot accomplish the glorious approval that Ruby admirably seeks.

The difference between how Ruby and her tribe of respectable people believe justice operates and how it actually fulfills God's purpose can be seen in their place of honor bringing up the rear of the apocalyptic march in the sky. The first are last. Ruby sees that she has turned things upside down. Her misinterpretation of the Day of the Lord severs law from promise. She sees doing what is right as the way to be saved and forgets that redemption can only be the work of God. Moreover, O'Connor presents deliverance more as a medley than as a tidy bit of Ruby's housekeeping. The purple streak in the sky across the crimson field in which clean blacks and poor whites are decked out in the white robes of Revelation (7:13–17), followed by "freaks and lunatics shouting and clapping and leaping like frogs" (217), is a boisterous exhibition of Jesus' promise in the vineyard parable (Matthew 20:1–16) that the last shall be first. But we should not be at all sedate about the motley pageant. If we are, we risk joining in step with the prim, respectable marchers whose starchiness excludes them from the carnival fun. O'Connor's festive concreteness carries the theological day in "Revelation." The multicolored spectacle is the peacock's plumage fanning out in human liturgical form.

The display is more than a passing show of God's justice and mercy. The end of "Revelation" fleshes out Ruby Turpin's new knowledge into felt obligation. After the vision fades, she continues to hear voices of the happy souls shouting hallelujah. Their unabashed praise for divine mercy throws into relief Ruby's petty obsession over not being black or poor or ugly, attributes which she might well envy, since the proprieties she values are impediments to grace. Such virtues must be burned away, and they are before her eyes. Feeling that she has nothing besides profitless rectitude to take to God, the good woman is shamed in her own sight. Nevertheless, exposure sets her course right. She must make her way slowly back to the house along "the darkening path." At forty-seven, twelve years more than Dante required, Ruby meets up with the honorable sinners making their way toward God. Union comes at the close of day. Dusk falls on the ground as Ruby's guilt falls on her. The shadow of sin may tone down her arrogance, but it cannot eclipse her zest. Ruby Turpin remains one of those country women "who just sort of springs to life," O'Connor explains to a friend; "you can't hold them down or shut their mouths" (*Letters* 546). Brashness will serve her well now that the future goal is clear. Her eyes "fixed unblinkingly on what lay ahead" (218). Festival eyes are Omega eyes. They can see God's sense of humor.

Over the realm of cosmic time, humankind creates a mortal span of wonder, an insistent rumpus, which the Spirit alone can endow with new life. Earlier in the story, on the radio in the doctor's office, a hint of something majestic in the offing comes to Ruby. A gospel hymn plays, " 'When I looked up and He looked down.' " Knowing the song well, Ruby mentally fills out the last line of the lyric, " 'And wona these days I know I'll we-eara crown' " (194). When she looks up from the hog pen as the story concludes, a visionary light comes to rest in her eyes; and she sees herself and everyone else rising to the peak of existence on a bright streak. The wonder opening before Ruby is the coronation of spirit, the "new way to sanctity" that O'Connor, following Teilhard, understands to be "that of spiritualizing matter" (*Presence of Grace* 88).

The piecemeal procession shows that union embraces diversity but precludes singularity, the benefits of which Ruby extols unreservedly. Loss of her distinctiveness brings a greater justice than any reward she bargained for. She can see in the spree of the celestial trippers that chastisement reveals the depths of God's love wherein each feels divine readiness to pardon. Stunned by the unexpected changes wrought by purgation, Ruby gets down from the hog pen and turns off the faucet in a moving defeat. The deputy surrenders her sword of righteousness. The last picture of Ruby gives the impression of estrangement and strength, tried and annealed strength. She needs it, for she has much to bear. Claud is, by his name and by the cow's kick, a lame person; Ruby, she learns to her amazement, also numbers among the halt. She lumbers back to the house from the wound of guilt (*homo claudus*).

"Some rise by sin," says the wise lord Escalus in *Measure for Measure,* a serious comedy that is close to "Revelation" in its preoccupation with justice, "and some by virtue fall" (II, i, 38). O'Connor so cherishes Ruby Turpin that she submits her country female Jacob to both inequalities of temporal justice so that she can create in Ruby the sense of eternal justice. By knowing the clay from which she is made, Ruby prepares for the union that divine forgiveness unfolds before her. The swinging bridge of light extending from dark earth through field of fire to starry sky also spans inner zones of guilt, expiation, and the fullness of communion. As night falls and the crickets strike up around her small yellow frame house, Ruby Turpin approaches the heart of the mystery of God. He, not she, is just.

III

A vision with a message comes twice to O. E. Parker in "Parker's Back" during his twenty-eight years. The first comes when he is fourteen and neatly divides his history in half. At a fair he sees a sideshow performer tattooed from head to foot with pictures that jump alive as the man flexes his muscles. Drawings of people and animals and flowers move as a single intricate dance of creation before the gaping young hero. The next fourteen years become a search for the awe Parker felt at the fair. His quest for excitation ends, as it began, with a vision. Parker is operating a tractor that crashes into an enormous tree; on impact, his shoes and the tree and the tractor burst into a Mosaic theophany so intense that Parker feels the fiery breath of the burning tree on his face.

The biblical character of these visions escapes Parker. Religion is useless to him. Rugged confidence in himself requires that he dismiss any thought of divine influence. " 'A man can't save his self from whatever it is he don't deserve none of my sympathy' " (238), he says to the tattooist, who asks Parker if he is saved. Parker's disregard for religion exists side by side with his powerful sense of mystery. The vivid concreteness of the performer's tattoos and the scorching picture of the burning tree stir him to act and search and feel in new ways. He grasps their emotional force with clarity while remaining baffled by what, if anything, they mean to him.

To a person of faith, everything is miraculous insofar as it is touched by the hand of God, but the unbeliever must sort things out by her or his own devices. "Parker's Back," like *Wise Blood,* has an accidental vision throw the hero for a loop so that he can go back through his personal negations to the source of power that arouses him in the first place. Like Hazel Motes, O. E. Parker responds to an indomitable presence with his full being. He habitually stands before the world with his mouth hanging open. When he joins the navy, his mouth closes; but five years of naval hardening no more stamp out Parker's desire for ecstatic excitement than a four-year hitch in the army alters Hazel's decision to avoid Jesus. Life on a drab mechanical ship cannot dim Parker's oceanic eyes, which reflect in miniature the immense "mysterious sea" (224). He is spiritual without being religious. Astonishment remains Parker's talent, and his capacity for wonderment in the physical world leads him to God.

Parker's sensuality assists him in his movement Godward. He likes his women fleshy, amiable, and numerous. His adolescent delight in tattoos serves his manly pleasure with women, since he "had never yet met a woman who was not attracted to them" (222). Yet beneath his swelling ego, there lies the nagging sense of feeling ordinary. This unformed feeling disposes Parker to the aggressive female, who can direct and shape his desire. When his truck breaks down on the highway, he meets Sarah Ruth Cates, who is skinny and bossy and indifferent enough to his sexual stance that he marries her to meet the challenge of her libidinal coldness. Parker is another Chantecleer whose favorite is a henpecking Pertelote. Sarah Ruth is to the core the strict, God-fearing daughter of a Straight Gospel preacher. Try as he may, Parker cannot get Sarah Ruth's approval, even though her pregnancy suggests that her body and heart have not totally surrendered to her mind. The hero's last and desperate attempt to break through her rigidity takes the form of having a Byzantine Christ tattooed on his back. Instead of winning Sarah Ruth over, the tattooed Christ becomes another vision, the decisive one. This vision embeds into Parker's body and spirit the message seen but vaguely understood on the performer's body and in the burning tree.

Without Sarah Ruth, Parker could not decipher what is on his back and what comes before his eyes in the tree. Marriage sharpens his ambivalent feelings about himself and the world into creative opposition to the drabness around him. If he is "puzzled and ashamed of himself" (219) for staying with his ruthless wife, Parker also seeks out the very discipline that Sarah Ruth embodies. Her gray eyes that are sharpened into two icepicks resemble the iodine pencils used for tattooing. He appreciates her eyes as instruments to outline her moral prohibitions on him. Her bans against whiskey, tobacco, bad language, lies, and color are less important to Parker than the rigor of submitting to a pattern of order, the very quality he sees in the performer's tattoos and feels lacking in his random body pictures.

Sarah Ruth's cutting speech serves as the electric tattooing implement. Her words strike with piercing exclamations. " 'You don't talk no filth here!' " (221) are her first clawing words. Once pinned, Parker accepts her stinging indictments, usually honed into scriptural shibboleths, until his rebellious body is riddled with warnings against the sins he enjoys. Sarah Ruth's last words cut him to the quick with the punishing stiletto of expulsion. The Byzantine Christ exceeds the allowance she makes for his habitual vices of lies and vanity. " 'I don't want no idolator in this house!' " she cries. After she beats him senseless with the broom, her "eyes hardened still more" (244) to prod her sentence into her stunned husband, now leaning against a pecan tree. O'Connor portrays a country female version of Kafka's Commandant, who reigns in his story, "In the Penal Colony." Brandishing the broom as her scepter of control, Sarah Ruth runs a substation of Kafka's punitive province, where, as the officer in his story explains, guilt is never to be doubted. Sarah Ruth's Christian duty is to supervise the judicial rite of inscribing the suitable punishment into the body of the accused. The sinner must learn it on his body.

Gaining knowledge through flesh does not frighten Parker. However unfit he is for Sarah Ruth's home rule, Parker's unconscious desire is for a total authority to which he can subject his mind. His initial thrill over the performer's tattoos is the feeling of integration between inner and outer order. The problem for Parker arises in the authorities to which he looks for meaning. He quits high school at sixteen, then quits trade school and works for six months at a garage to pay for tattoos. Revels of idle young manhood ensue; beer, women, and brawls sink Parker into a dissoluteness that incites his mother to drag him to a revival for correction. Parker naturally flees. He lies about his age to join the navy. In the navy he goes AWOL, is locked up in the brig, and is dishonorably discharged. Marriage follows, and Sarah Ruth becomes the last imposition of regimentation that fails to control Parker or to provide him with inner wholeness. The institutions are neither improbable choices nor inherently corrupt; they simply are inadequate for the man of wonder.

Only tattoos break Parker's cycle of discontent. The satisfaction from a new tattoo lasts no longer than a month, but for that time he feels excited. The high also creates in Parker a physiological dependency. After the contentment wears off, each tattoo exacerbates his sense of emptiness, and he craves another tattoo to alleviate his depression. Finally, all of his body except his back is tapestried. At first, static sentimentalities, such as the eagle perched on a cannon and his mother's name, do the trick. These inert images soon give way to drawings of dynamic pursuit in a panther and a tiger. Then the figures soar with hawks and lofty royal personages. Each tantalizes and betrays. As much as the progression in the designs indicates Parker's ascendent desire, the intensity exposes the impossibility of his ever finding satisfaction in lifeless pictures. He wants not the image but the actual stuff of wonder in himself. Without this vital feeling, his body remains a hodgepodge of disconnected pictures, lumpish sketches awaiting a power to bring them together as real.[1]

Parker does well to despair in social, ecclesiastical, and military formalism. Obedience for obedience's sake is worthless, and he knows it. Given his simple desire to take part here and now in a harmony beyond himself, obedience makes sense only if it opens a way to actual and timeless life. He intuits that the vibrancy of the absolute pulsates in the rhythm of matter, in things as they are. The people around the hero belong to a Gnostic world that holds flesh in contempt. For his quest, Parker must stay with his instinct to celebrate the body, his body, which his would-be captors disparage and try to subdue through one abstract stricture or another. Matter remains for Parker the sustaining ground of the ecstasy that first inspires him at the fair. The more he decorates his body, the more fully he receives wonder, until, after intervals of dejection, the mystery of the divine figure stenciled on his back becomes manifest and fills him with the Spirit.

The incarnational cast of Parker's temperament shines forth at the end of the story, and one is inclined to pave the way to the ending with theological cement. "Parker's Back," however, shows the truth about physical life that Parker feels through blunt physical action; and the reader can appreciate Parker's sensibility by observing O'Connor's skill in showing how God has use for the man who has no use for Him. Defeat at the hands of Sarah Ruth, for whom Parker longs, denunciations and all, drives Parker to act in order to be recognized. Pregnancy no more softens her scorn for the sexual pleasure he needs than the marriage ceremony at the County Ordinary's office stops her incessant attacks, on Jesus' behalf, of Parker's profligacy. There is nothing left for him to do but to overcome his reluctance to decorate his back, which requires a mirror to admire, with a picture that would break through Sarah Ruth's prudery. A religious subject alone, he concludes, could seduce a wife whose love for God impugns love for her husband. At first, the idea of an opened Bible strikes Parker as a way to open Sarah Ruth's heart, but then he realizes that the tattoo would merely duplicate the real Bible that she already reads from: "He needed something better even than the Bible!" (231).

His frustration shows good sense, for he and Sarah Ruth do need something more than the Book to live by. What he is fighting against in

Sarah Ruth, the archbiblicist in O'Connor's fiction, is her habit of approaching life through the Bible, a false wisdom that deprives the Bible of its revelatory character and removes from life its essential goodness. Just thinking about this last-ditch effort to master a woman who is saved exacts a physical price. He is losing flesh from insomnia without getting any strength from his wife's bad cooking to fight the new terror that someone is trailing him.

Parker need not worry about the paranoid hallucinations that sent his grandfather to the state mental hospital. The shadow stalking Parker is real. O'Connor has been tracking this figure's constant and uninterrupted pursuit through the trees of Hazel Motes's conscience, across the dirt road that Tarwater takes back to Powderhead, and into the old woman's clearing, where the stalker ambushes Parker with a hot gust from the burning tree. The theophanic blast puts the fear of God into Parker without his knowing who hit him. He knows only that a tattoo is like oxygen, a breath of freedom. He runs fifty miles to the city to satisfy his obsession for a picture of God. While the flight strains Parker, his thirst and body ache indicate that the hunter is closing the gap between them. The indefatigable someone who is trailing Parker has something to lay on his bare back.

The pursuer transfers the consignment at the tattooist's studio. To arrive at the decision already willed for him, Parker must stay on the backward course set by the hunter at the burning tree. In the fashion of reading a Hebrew text, Parker scans the tattoo artist's picture book from back to front for a suitable image of God. Reverse chronology takes him from modern sentimental representations through older daunting portraits to the ordained one that commands in silent firmness that Parker "GO BACK" after passing it by. He flips the pages back to "the haloed head of a flat stern Byzantine Christ" (235) awaiting him. The icon blares like an unveiling of itself and of Parker's inner need. Here, behind the feeble Christologies born of humanity's search for a pat on the back, there lies the one authority strong enough to compel Parker's obedience; and the face-to-face contact brings the hero out of himself. The will of God and the response of Parker are becoming one.

The source of power in this Christ is the eyes. Their "all-demanding" and "subtle power" (235) seizes Parker from the printed page. Parker senses that the peculiar technique of the picture's little blocks creates the effect, and to preserve that force he insists that the artist stencil all the little blocks giving this Christ mysterious reality. The extraordinary pain of shouldering such stippled detail is not too high a price for Parker. To the artist's astonishment, Parker will pay with money and time and anguish to receive this riveting figure. Parker's demand that the tattooist copy the Christ exactly bespeaks an emotional consciousness of an aesthetic fact. The visual effect of a Byzantine mosaic derives from block lines. These mosaics are designed to be seen in the hazy light of lamps and candles. To heighten the light's play, the tiles are set in varying angles to create shimmering surfaces of movement akin to the intricate arabesque of brilliant colors on the performer's tattooed body that dazzles young Parker at the fair.

The eyes of the Byzantine Christ yanking Parker to life would be liquid and pale, like Parker's own slate-colored eyes—reflections of an unearthly realm far removed from the nearby alley and pool hall that Parker frequents when in the city. The mosaic composition in the hands of Byzantine artists works imaginatively around the piercing eyes. When the tattooist quits at midnight without completing the job, Parker feels cheated because the eyes are missing. The eyes complete the design, and they complete the work of the pursuer. After the Christ is finished, Parker looks into a mirror to see his back; he turns white and moves away from the reflection. The eyes in the mirrored face, however, continue to stare at Parker. Everything now rises to converge in these eyes. Not only do the eyes drive Parker to the eastern pole of Christendom, Byzantium, they absorb the disparate parts of Parker's tattooed body and marked soul into a harmonious unity.

The eyes of the Byzantine Christ are the Omega for all the optical energy emitted in O'Connor's world. The eyes train on Hazel Motes, her first Christian *malgré lui,* from the long silver streaks of stars over Taulkinham and from the back of Hazel's mind. The eyes confront Francis Marion Tarwater, the reluctant prophet, from the crooked trees at Powderhead and from the sunken sockets of Bishop's face. And the eyes glare at O. E. Parker, the spiritual sensualist, from the burning tree and from his back. O'Connor unfailingly registers authorial wonder at God's enduring watchfulness over human affairs. *Ha zi əl* is Hebrew for "God sees." Besides adapting the biblical name *Hazael* for the hero of *Wise Blood,* O'Connor develops this divine seeing through various stages of aggressiveness needed for her belligerent protagonists. God does not let them out of sight up to and through the final pinpoint of light, the apex of self-contemplation. "Parker's Back" offers O'Connor's fullest consideration of God's keen visual attention. Parker's icon is one remnant from ancient Byzantium that is more lasting than the fine, perishable "artifice of eternity" of which Yeats sings. O'Connor's artifact from Byzantium is eternity alive. The unfading eyes incised in Parker's back still see, see through him. The Omega gaze is irrevocable.

Like the horns of the bull in "Greenleaf," the sharp eyes embed in Parker the precedent for obedience that gives permanent meaning to the picture of Christ he freely chooses. O'Connor's use of the tattoo epitomizes her theology of matter. The Word made flesh communicates the Son's self-donation in service to the Father's plan for humankind. The divine Logos takes human form to pay for Adam's sin of disobedience by hanging on the cross. Christ's incarnation and crucifixion, His first and last acts, embrace the most thoroughgoing obedience to God's dictum. The Son's obedient death flows into the culminating event of the resurrection. The inauguration of universal judgment when humans are initiated into the divine reaffirms the dignity of flesh, as Christ's humanity becomes a permanent part of one world.

Without any notion or need of such theological commentary, Parker participates in God's promise of fulfillment. Parker is a simple man, obsessed by the necessity of getting a tattoo of God that will bring Sarah Ruth to heel and that will recapture joy. He wants rapture; and in reaching above and beyond himself, he learns that fullness must come from a greater-than-human source. However inarticulate, this awareness expresses a spiritual hope in O'Connor's world; and O'Connor makes use of whatever talent the character has to attain this possibility. With her sensualist, she will have to use his body to bring Parker to God. Since Christianity is a material religion in proclaiming that the Word is made flesh, O'Connor finds no impediment to showing how Parker's transcendence inheres in his body. Parker's yearning to feel the activity of God in his flesh confesses the basic Christian hope. Matter provides union with God.

Once Parker is like a lump of wax receiving every impression of Christ's countenance, the all-demanding eyes waste no time making their demands known. Parker must communicate God's presence to others as God has communicated His self to Parker. Obedience to this will always costs, and Parker's toughness will be needed. So too will his unbelief be called into service. He can carry the face of Christ to places otherwise closed to professed witnesses.

Parker accomplishes just this feat after the tattoo is finished. Fortified by a pint of whiskey, Parker goes off to the pool hall he frequents when in town. The effect of his appearance is amazing. Mocked, and ashamed about being shamed, Parker can stand before flouters of the Spirit, uttering a denial of God to his fellow deprecators while wearing the truth on his back in silence. When the brawlers pull off Parker's shirt to see the tattoo, silence falls around them until it extends like a beam of light from the basement of the pool hall to the roof. The foundations shake. The frightened louts break the silence by cursing Parker, who, with Mary Grace's indignant wrath, responds by lunging at the tormentors from hell. A free-for-all erupts, and Parker lands in the alley.

O'Connor compares the dumping of Parker with the casting of Jonah into the sea. Both suffer abuse for defending God before pagans. Punishment clarifies Parker's identity. He is a worshipper of God, albeit a disobedient one. His rebellion, therefore, deceives only himself. Intoxication and willfulness, which make up his last fourteen years, play into God's hands. As when Jonah hops a ship to Tarshish to escape God's order to go to Nineveh, Parker, in making haste to the barroom to shake off the all-demanding stare on his back, ends up being a scapegoat for the mocking pagans.

The sign of Jonah is his preaching; if he says nothing, he remains safe from physical harm. The sign of Parker, however, is his tattooed back. Given his vanity and the habit of infidels to rend garments, it is unlikely that Parker can keep his shirt on. He is a walking tabernacle. Remove his shirt, and the visible manifestation of God blinds its beholders. Parker's bizarre body will remain alluring in its truthfulness. As a bearer of this petrifying sight, Parker can expect to suffer for the panic that comes from bringing unruly humanity face-to-face with the countenance that brooks no defiance. Parker's back gives one answer to the question posed by O'Connor's unfinished manuscript, *Why Do the Heathens Rage?:* they rage to escape the terrifying intensity of God's demand for obedient self-conquest.

Before "Parker's Back" ends, God gives the hero an intimate experience of the great cost as well as the privilege of bearing the sacred face to the heathens. After the fight, Parker speeds home to Sarah Ruth, who, he believes, understands God and will comfort him in the confusion created by the tattoo. Befuddled as ever in seeking consolation for his spiritual anxiety in the sexual, Parker nevertheless feels a newness in and around himself. The familiar surroundings of the ride home seem to be part of "a new country" (241). The dawn rises like an ally. Several yellow streaks flicker as he pounds on the door to be admitted to his house. Suddenly, a tree blazes with the light from the morning sun; the bright ally declares himself. Again, the ally rises to prod Parker into battle by reminding him of the all-demanding will that controls him. A long shaft of light nails him against the locked door, and the pain promised by this lance of light comes in the form of Sarah Ruth. Her cold unfeeling voice, insisting that Parker identify himself, pins the hero to the truth about himself that he has buried beneath twenty-eight years of denial. He whispers the watchword, his names, " 'Obadiah Elihue!' " (243).

Obadiah means "servant of God." The title designates how Parker must conduct himself in the new country that he has entered. Performing duties to the absolute will lead to the rapture he seeks. After he murmurs his first name, light pours through his body as a promise of joy. The entangled web of his soul, imprinted with his disconnected tattoos, fuses into an arabesque of creation—"a garden of trees and birds and beasts" (243). Parker's body, like the colorful hallelujah parade concluding "Revelation," presents a version of the peacock's splendor displayed. Having become a paradise of wonder, Obadiah freely gives his second name, Elihue, which affirms the God he serves. *Elihue* means "my God is he." With the initials O. E. acquiring substance, Parker's flesh is now made word. He feels himself to be the visible dwelling of glory.

Though Obadiah Elihue Parker is bathed in light, Sarah Ruth sees only a liar who will have to pay every penny to the old woman whose tractor he smashed. She bursts into hellish fury upon seeing the tattooed Christ. Another heathen, this time a Christian heathen who is scandalized by an enfleshed God, rages. " 'He's a spirit. No man shall see his face' " (244), she says. Revulsion toward matter in Sarah Ruth is not confined to food and sexuality. To release her Gnostic yearning, Sarah Ruth thrashes her offending husband so severely that welts appear on the face of the Byzantine Christ. Her scourging is the familiar reaction of fear and spiritual blindness. It repeats the gruesome anger that caused the pain expressed in the agonized features of the tattoo.

Beaten senseless, Parker staggers out of the house to recover from the lacerations. "Crying like a baby" (244), he leans against the pecan tree, the bower in which to await God's next move. Certain aspects of God's will are already clear. The pool hall and the house mark the poles of the pagan world in which Parker must serve God. To the heathens, who can only experience the abstract concretely, the icon displays the spirit-being; to the Christian heathens, who can only experience the concrete abstractly, Parker's back manifests the divine embodiment. Parker's mission is to bring the naked truth of God's mysterious double nature to a world that separates matter from spirit, evil from good. At once enfleshed and tortured, the tattooed Christ sends people flying; and as the outlandish exception to the Manichean rule, Parker can expect to be abused in the skirmish. He is a reproach to those living in a comfortable world of abstractions.

The icon of truth imposes a greater burden on Parker than his being theological sport for heathens. The eyes of the Byzantine Christ force Parker into "examining his soul," a process that will cauterize Parker's ego until he experiences the ultimate odium of guilt that he must acknowledge as his own before the avenging face of God. Though there may be detours, there is no turning back from the road of abandonment to divine providence: "The eyes that were now forever on his back were eyes to be obeyed" (241). The eyes are like hands laid on him with a pressure to seize and to guide him. Parker is ready. Having received the sacrament of the incarnation, he can be carnal; his affair of the libido inevitably turns into an affair of his whole being.

Parker also gains heart. The bruiser has always been afraid, afraid of challenge to his image of himself as conqueror and freeman. The challenges to that autonomy, however, pale before the challenges of the icon. Christ's eyes, the ultimate summons, are the orders Parker heeds. Weeping like a baby against the tree at the end of the story expresses his response to God's revelation of His self in Christ. Parker's breakdown is neither a spasm of defense nor a cry of pain from Sarah Ruth's beating. Rather, the shattering of Parker's false manhood opens the way into spiritual childhood and dependence on Christ. He has entered the world of guilt and sorrow, where each day, little by little, he will realize that his old life is breaking loose and falling off.

Parker the newborn has taken the final redeeming plunge to make himself whole according to his deepest obligations. Integrity in O'Connor's art is never purchased at the expense of passion. Rather, passion is the price of integrity. Parker already knows that liberty involves a different kind of pain than that imposed by prison. He is aware too that the most intimate of all human experiences is also the most vulnerable and exposed. The hidden love of his life—a love that others do not see and that he tries to hide yet displays—spills out. In this adventure of mystery, Parker will be living through the eyes on his back.

NOTE

1. *The Flannery O'Connor Bulletin* has maintained a running account of the sources of Parker's tattoos. Karl-Heinz Westarp's " 'Parker's Back': A Curious Crux Concerning Its Sources," 11 (1982): 1–9, shows that George Burchett's *Memoirs of a Tattooist* gave O'Connor the technical details of the art. Westarp, in "Teilhard de Chardin's Impact on Flannery O'Connor: A Reading of 'Parker's Back,' " 12 (1983): 93–113, compares the tattoos to Teilhard's process of convergence. In the same issue of *The Flannery O'Connor Bulletin,* James F. Farnham's "Further Evidence for the Sources of 'Parker's Back,' " 12 (1983): 114–16, cites an article in the *Augusta Chronicle* as a possible source for the Christ tattoo. To these proposals, I would add Kafka's "In the Penal Colony," which is in the O'Connor Collection at Georgia College. See Kinney, entry 556.

CHAPTER

8

First and Last Things

Upon your heads—is nothing but heart's sorrow,
And a clear life ensuing.
Ariel, *The Tempest* (III, iii)

Among Flannery O'Connor's literary remains housed at Georgia College, there is a noteworthy fragment of an unpublished lecture. It is part of a talk O'Connor gave in 1956. The passage holds no new evidence of her thinking, but it does crystallize O'Connor's view of artistic integrity and intensify its implication for her own art. Speaking as a writer to readers, O'Connor is making the point that the artist must present the truth as she or he sees it firsthand in concrete, human particulars. She then cites the example of James Joyce: "At the end of 'A Portrait of the Artist as a Young Man' Joyce has Stephen Dedalus say that he intends to go out and 'forge in the smithy of my soul the uncreated conscience of my race,' but in the next book that's not what we find him doing." Rather, "we find him meeting Mr. Leopold Bloom, and instead of creating a new pattern, discovering a very ancient one."[1]

O'Connor's sympathy for Stephen's backward progress derives from the lesson that shapes her development. She too learns to submit aspiration to experience. When she begins to write, Eliot's poetry hovers as her ideal of craft infused with knowledgeable witness to Christian faith. Early drafts of *Wise Blood* (1952), her first novel, depict a youthful yet depleted American Tiresias suffering all as he roams the Tennessee byways of the wasteland. Again, O'Connor's early story "The Geranium" (*Accent,* 1946), as Sally Fitzgerald so well argues in "The Owl and the Nightingale" (44–58), uses Eliot's "Gerontion" to portray the old hero's isolation. But whatever fascinates O'Connor about the rural American conscience forged in the workshop of high modernism quickly becomes transformed by the act of writing hammered on the anvil of fact. Mr. Leopold Bloom, emissary of the everyday, takes the form of good American country people to modify the O'Connor-Dedalus grand scheme.

In *Wise Blood* we find O'Connor grappling with Hazel Motes, a nihilist Protestant saint, and later in *The Violent Bear It Away* (1960) with Francis Marion Tarwater, a teenage murderer called to be a prophet. Through the trials of these and many other footsore and vehement questers, O'Connor, like Stephen, discovers an old pattern instead of making a new one. The tracks of O'Connor's adventurers through Tennessee and Georgia, as it turns out, follow an even older route than does the homeward voyage of Homer's pilgrim. Their itineraries cover the thoroughfares of wickedness and evil, movements between time and eternity that encompass absolute fulfillment. The more truthfully O'Connor as storyteller renders what she sees and not what she ought to see, the more vividly emerges the most ancient path of all—the biblical pattern of guilt and transcendence.

"The Geranium" provides a convenient shortcut to O'Connor's discovery of the pattern that reveals what the heart is and what it feels. "The Geranium" is her first published story (1946) and one year later becomes the title story of O'Connor's Iowa M.F.A. thesis (1947). Since the publication of *The Complete Stories of Flannery O'Connor* (1971), readers have known that her first story is the basis of her last, entitled "Judgement Day," which concludes her posthumous volume *Everything That Rises Must Converge* (1965). The parallel between the beginning and the end of O'Connor's career also has intermediate ties. Jan Gretlund has explained the relation of "An Exile in the East," which *The South Carolina Review* (1978) printed along with Gretlund's findings, to these pivotal stories (12–21). There is a still finer link. Absorbed by the need to get this material just right, O'Connor revised "An Exile in the East" into an unpublished story called "Getting Home." The changes in "Getting Home" take final form in "Judgement Day," which O'Connor sent to her publisher four weeks before her death.

What we have is a canonical story in four versions taking us from O'Connor's first thoughts to her final design. Again, one of the intermediate versions, "An Exile in the East," is now available; the other, "Getting Home," remains in typescript in The Flannery O'Connor Collection. If we consider the signal features of the first three drafts, and then examine the distinctive moral force of the last version, we can appreciate the odyssey that O'Connor undertakes.

Archival details and textual revisions can outline growth, but they cannot unravel the creative process effecting the transformation. By the same token, coming last does assign "Judgement Day" a privileged place, but that position does not guarantee artistic distinction. While "Judgement Day" gains richness from O'Connor's lifelong involvement with a single predicament—that of a dying man's trials—what distinguishes her culminating story is the way in which the essential drama fulfills the requirements of form as molded by an enlarged moral vision. With the four versions before us, we can see that as O'Connor goes beyond influence and styles to feel through the romance and anguish of her old hero's isolation, she is able to perceive its possible contribution to the saving plan of God.

Only in the final version of the story does the old man's plight yield dignity, and that grace comes through O'Connor's reversal of the usual way of thinking about the pain of estrangement and the responsibility of the hostile world for that hardship. Being cut off can bring one to know what one owes the world; and, in paying such an unexpected debt, the outcast can release the energy of love that raises the rejecting world to the Omega. In her shift of attention from the need to be loved to the need to love, O'Connor finds a new order of creation within personal loss and recovery. The pattern beneath all patterns turns out to be for her a death and a resurrection. The duty to suffer, in O'Connor's mature imagination, affirms the mysterious power of guilt to accomplish transcendence. What the sufferer gives in gratitude, God receives in grace; and what is divinely accepted is redeemed and made holy and set free in love.

II

The basic situation in all the versions of O'Connor's canonical story is simple: a disabled old man lives outside his native Georgia in New York City with his daughter and son-in-law. "The Geranium" names the displaced widower Old Dudley, and has him stuck sharing a bedroom with an indifferent sixteen-year-old grandson in a cramped walk-up apartment on the sixth floor. The tenement and its altitude frighten the countryman. Concrete separates him from solid earth, and the dog-run of a hallway looms as an extension of the cavernous railroad tunnels that coil underground and spew trains overhead onto platforms of perilous height. But Old Dudley's true acrophobia is geographical. Up north he can topple any minute to his death, whereas down south he stands on safe ground. Memory gauges the distance between mortal danger and secure life. He recalls Coa County's slow, red river which he fished with Rabie, his black friend, every Wednesday; and he thinks back on the quail and opossum that they hunted. The river and the woods, however, have shriveled into a grimy urban alley, which he can fish from his sixth-floor window with his eyes and his regrets. The best Old Dudley can do to recapture the old feeling of manly freedom is to pretend to shoot quail as he lumbers up the steps in the dark stairwell.

In New York, Old Dudley lives by rural southern values. When a black man rents the adjacent apartment, the old southerner assumes that the new neighbor, like all blacks, will know a place where they can hunt and fish. That this black man sports a pinstripe suit and shiny shoes does not preclude his knowing where to find a good stream. Old Dudley trusts blacks, Sunday suit and all; but he soon learns that northern blacks can be as cold and hostile as northern whites. Though he expresses a defensive dislike of " 'Yankee niggers' " (*Complete Stories* 10), Old Dudley comes to need the haughty black neighbor to help him back to his daughter's flat when he becomes weak in the hall while playing quail hunter. He needs the black New Yorker just as much as he needed Rabie back home to help him feel that he was a vigorous outdoorsman.

O'Connor's treatment of the relations between white and black in "The Geranium" is not political. Her interest is spiritual. The old man's ambivalence toward blacks—affection mingled with mindless condescension—results from an ambiguity in himself. Old Dudley resents his infirmity and his dependency, and he fights against these inevitabilities by blaming New York and its inhabitants, black and white, for his natural losses. He once lived in a "good place," he rationalizes after the black man helps him back to his apartment; but now he is stranded in a bad place where a black person can presume to call him " 'old-timer' " (*Complete Stories* 13). Prejudice masks fear of dying. To deny the suffering of old age, Old Dudley puts the onus onto the black man on whom he leans.

Though "The Geranium" leaves no doubt in the reader's mind that O'Connor shares Old Dudley's disgust with hellish New York, she is careful to shade his chauvinistic anger with culpability. He chooses to come north. When the prospect of spending his last years in a decayed Georgia boarding house full of old women strikes him, he sees the New York apartment of his daughter as a refuge. An endearing egoism justifies his decision. New York is bigger than Atlanta, he reasons, and therefore is the right size to accommodate him: "It was an important place and it had room for him! He'd said yes, he'd go" (*Complete Stories* 4).

The thought that there is no place for him is intolerable. When New York betrays the expectation that the hero formed from the picture show, he indicts the city to protect the recollection of Coa County as home, the place of dignity. As disapproval masks his fear of approaching death, so pride erases the fact that it was his idea to come north, and blinds him to whatever care his daughter provides. He makes her responsible for his disquiet. She is at fault for having been so taken up with her own idea of tending to her old father's needs that she coerced him to leave Georgia.

At the young age of twenty-two, O'Connor appreciates so well the attachment to roots that she grasps the emotional dodges expressing it. The lot of advanced years brings her without temporizing to explore the last hope to belong and the dislocation of its fulfillment in death. Old Dudley wants power in his decrepitude and mistakes inner shambles for outer decay. During this period of her admiration for Eliot, O'Connor supplies an objective correlative for the hero's plight in the form of a potted geranium. Every day from his window, the old southerner watches a pink, mangy flower (not the vivid kind that thrives in fertile Georgia dirt) that a neighbor puts out for air around ten in the morning and takes in at five-thirty in the evening. The plant reflects Old Dudley's crocked life in foreign soil. Framed by the window, he is an infirm and all-too-human stray, stuck yet stuck-up in pride. An old dud sits forlorn in a moving helplessness, staring at a pink geranium that he does not think much of. Here is youthful O'Connor's first protagonist, an old man in a sterile place.

Old Dudley is the Nestor of the Dedalus-O'Connor adventure. He is neither Homer's retired warrior, who enjoys tranquillity in the bosom of his daughters' families, nor Joyce's bigoted Mr. Deasey, who dispenses sententious wisdom about the past. Old Dudley, in sum, is neither the flower nor the daisy of old age. O'Connor's Nestor is an ordinary geranium that manages to remain alive in the common clay between epic romance and its parody. That ordinary soil is the province of guilt and yearning in which O'Connor enacts her spiritual comedies.

On the day of the story, Old Dudley waits in tears for the geranium to appear. The plant eventually comes into his sight in the alley below, shattered, its roots exposed to the killing city air. Beneath the sympathy for her Nestor's loneliness, O'Connor uncovers the source of alienation that lies deeper than locale. We see in the human soulscape the roots of pride, the origin of estrangement to which all of O'Connor's fiction returns. Though pride can be transcended, and though there is a city of hope beyond the New York of exile, these possibilities lie in the future of O'Connor's search. "The Geranium" ends with an indictment of the pernicious urban world and with the portrait of the emigré as a wounded wreck of a man.

To find a way out of the old man's lostness, O'Connor goes deeper into his deracination when she revises the story. The very title of the next version, "An Exile in the East," indicates that the hero's banishment from home becomes the critical issue. The symbol of the geranium gives way to nuanced differences between the congenial ways of Georgia and the harshness of New York. O'Connor worsens certain features of the hero's face to stress the dispiriting effect of New York on him. A face marked with red and purple spots changes into a sickly yellow visage with brown blotches. The New York climate is pathogenic. Also, the old man has a new name, Franklyn R. T. Tanner, to go with his new aspect. And the daughter acquires a big square face (but not a name) to embody the air of "righteous exhaustion" that comes from putting up with her difficult father. Despite the importance of her care for Old Tanner, the daughter has no impact on the events of the story. She, with duty-proud weariness, remains a function of the hero's sadness, a dejection that overshadows all of his connections except the one with his remembered Georgia. In evoking the past, "An Exile in the East" treats the racial emotions underlying the drama more fully than does "The Geranium," but the realistic details of "An Exile in the East" do not make it a significantly different story from "The Geranium." The old protagonist's destiny is the same in both versions. Both end with the ailing hero alone and at memory's gateway but not at the Spirit's access. The later story gives social perspective without adding dramatic depth.

The version of the story that we have only in manuscript, "Getting Home," does change the hero's fate. The common southern phrase that O'Connor uses for the title of this draft suggests her growing ease with the material, and that comfort comes through in the new tone and the conclusive ending. "Getting Home" makes the hero's place of rest at the journey's end more prominent than his exile, which he still endures. This old man longs for a home burial. Perhaps to underscore the ultimate propriety of a desire that might seem mere ranting to a Yankee daughter, O'Connor renames the old man F. T. Fairlee. Now fairness requires that Old Fairlee be put to rest back home. Getting home is a matter of deep urgency. If it means being cut up alive and thrown to the dogs, the price is worth paying for the peace of knowing that his body will be in native dirt. Rest means restoration; and getting home to rest is a manner of speaking that touches on the final act of living, since in this version the old hero dies.

His death prompts O'Connor to reconsider the position of the hero's daughter. Getting the old man home depends on a change in her will and sense of filial duty. In fact, from the manuscript we can see that the hero's death opens a double drama in the story as the crisis of the old man's death becomes a test of the daughter's character. As she is initially conceived, her reluctance to bother with a trip south to bury her father is a given of her urbanized nature; but as O'Connor works on the material, she approaches the daughter's resistance from the new possibility of conversion. "Getting Home" has the daughter argue with her Yankee trucker husband to justify the cranky old man's presence in their apartment. In the course of taking his side against her insensitive husband, the daughter manages to express a limited understanding of the aged Georgian's desire to get home.

There are several typescripts of "Getting Home" in the O'Connor archives. The one with the most extensive handwritten revisions has two endings. Taken together, they epitomize the moral expansion that results from O'Connor's careful remodeling of her Nestor episode. Both endings shift the narrative focus from the earlier concern for the old man to a new interest in his daughter. The first ending is typed as part of the manuscript, and it shows the woman achieving a matter-of-fact victory over her callous husband. The final paragraph runs: "She and her husband had an extended argument over the telephone about where he should be buried. He said here. She said at home. And she won. She wanted to rest at night, and if she didn't follow his instructions to the letter, he was just the kind, she said, who would haunt her the rest of her life" (Folder 194d). In seeing F. T. Fairlee to his Georgia grave in "Getting Home," O'Connor momentarily considers the way in which his life marks a decisive turn in the conscience of a surviving relative. This adjustment seems more to quicken O'Connor's mind than to satisfy her requirements of form. The new direction, once opened, widens the horizon of O'Connor's imagination. She deletes by hand the paragraph quoted above, and writes in the following ending: "She buried him in N. Y. C. but after she had done it, she could not sleep at night, so she had him dug up and shipped the body to Corinth. And now she rests well at night, which at her time of life is essential" (Folder 194d).

The changes are telling. Ghosts in O'Connor's world are instructive, and so she discards the petty spat between wife and husband in favor of the fierce grappling with a revenging spirit. It does not matter that self-interest calls the daughter to undo her father's hasty burial. What counts is Old Fairlee's getting home. He gets home at the same time that home gets the name *Corinth*. The daughter gets to sleep at night. O'Connor, for her part, gets her story: she crosses out the title "Getting Home" and in the large rheumatic scrawl of her terminal illness writes the words "Judgement Day" across the top of the title page. The reader gets a masterpiece.

III

O'Connor in the end writes about her displaced old man from an inwardness that unlocks his depths. She keeps the essential drama behind his brows by setting the story abstemiously. "Judgement Day" embraces no more of the physical world than a seriously impaired stroke victim can negotiate. The locale is the short distance from the old man's chair to the staircase where he dies. The time is a winter morning in New York. But a few hours are sufficient for the Day of the Lord to dawn in the life of T. C. Tanner, and several yards are expanse enough in O'Connor's austere world for the hero to reach his Omega destiny. In making his way to the banister, Old Tanner gets home by forging his way to God.

This final tale of loss displays O'Connor's genius for conveying full life in a partial world. The depth that she finds within the deficits of the here and now lies in the meaning ordinary things hold for the dying man. Without restricting her wisdom to his perception, and without imposing her understanding on his bafflement, O'Connor explores the invisible through the interplay of the hero's consciousness and circumstance. His failing vision, his failed health, the falling snow, and his waiting for God are the diminishments that shape "Judgement Day." O'Connor seats Tanner at his window to look at the brick wall that sinks into a fetid alley, and she stirs his inner vision to review the past that led him to the grim present and that will also lead him all the way back to his future in Corinth. Then she has him hobble to his death, an ignominious death. Tanner's recollecting and stumbling constitute the last trial of his life.

Tanner's final mental and physical acts dramatize the intense state of his heart that his infirmity can barely make known. Above all, what his heart feels is that his life is in danger. The peril is neither dying nor death. Rather, he has a holy fear of being buried in a profane place. He wants to rest in earth set aside for the service of God. Corinth, by name and by virtue of Tanner's personal history, is consecrated to carry out the plan of God, whereas New York is ordained for the use of cats and garbage. A proper burial to Tanner is more than a pious ceremony. Consecrated ground is the necessary material provision for the world that Tanner believes will come, and he wants to be ready for it. His daughter's indifference to his burial instructions amounts to her opposition to the approaching reign of God, and arouses an irate warning from the frail old bear: " 'Bury me here and burn in hell!' he cried and fell back into his chair" (248). His bodily fear and trembling communicate the terrible judgment that his thin voice hardly enunciates.

The daughter dismisses hell as " 'a lot of hardshell Baptist hooey' " (248), but Tanner sees damnation as a hard reality that the soft-minded may deny but nevertheless will confront. The more the daughter recommends the distraction of television to mollify the " 'morbid stuff' " that grips her father's mind, the more vividly do death and hell and judgment preoccupy him. Her refusal to feel the dire changes that are apparent in her father's body and spirit makes him more assertive about the truths by which he lives: " 'The Judgement is coming,' he muttered. 'The sheep'll be separated from the goats. Them that kept their promises from them that didn't' " (258).

The fear of not being in God's favor goes deeper than a last-minute desire to make amends. It has been in Tanner since childhood. Over the years, the fear of God humanizes Tanner by checking his strong instinct to settle accounts with those who threaten him by seizing his gun or knife. Fear of divine retribution weakens his emotional violence by making him feel the ultimate responsibility incurred by his actions. During his final exilic days in New York, fear becomes the basis for a more positive relation to God. The dread of never getting home to Corinth makes Tanner value home and hometown cronies as part of God's scheme; and deprived of his cherished vitality and autonomy, he recognizes his utter dependence on God. Even anxiety over his daughter's trustworthiness turns his heart to God. He realizes that divine readiness to help those in need, as he now is, outbalances everything else. Fear of God, then, is negative in word only. Tanner's fear contains his confident love of God, Who is recognized and loved because Tanner feels the total difference between his helplessness and guilt and God's absolute justice and mercy.

Two waves of memory enact Tanner's conversion. Both center upon his departure from Georgia, where he enjoyed the friendship of Coleman, whom he left behind. After he overhears his daughter conceding to her husband's insistence that Tanner be buried in New York, Tanner puts up his emotional dukes to fight for dignity and tries to deny that he wanted to come to New York in the first place. Only after the land he and Coleman lived on was sold to the black Doctor Foley did Tanner agree to his daughter's demand that he come north. To stay on the property, Tanner would have been obliged to run his still for Foley, whose terms encroach on Tanner's self-esteem. Rather than work for an uppity black doctor, Tanner heads north. Racism, then, props up his tottering honor. As pride drives him from Corinth, humiliation sends thoughts back to Corinth in contrition. Had he known that he would be stuck "in this no-place" of New York because of his daughter's treachery, he "would have been a nigger's white nigger any day" (257).

Tanner has a more cogent reason to stand in service and in gratitude before a black person. For thirty years he shares a life with Coleman, a black man. Though they live as partners in poverty in a shack on a forsaken lot, Tanner's pride requires him to believe that his wit gives him the upper hand with Coleman. After all, Tanner is "known to have a way with niggers" (252). There is an art to his dealing with Coleman, but it has nothing to do with Tanner's keen mind or very sharp penknife. The secret of their friendship is each man's open need for the other. Both are uprooted and settle on land not their own; each has an instinct for violence that holds the other's brute force in respectful control. Because the penknife of each could easily be directed by some intruding intelligence into the other's gut, the threat keeps both vulnerable. Black and white bruiser can grin in direct, even tender, recognition of the other's radical similarity. After thirty years, Tanner still cannot decipher his initial sensation on meeting Coleman. He has only a vague perception of "seeing before him a negative image of himself, as if clownishness and captivity had been their common lot" (255). The dimness of Tanner's memory, however, is clear enough for the reader, who can detect in the image a love born of respect and need and apprehension that allows rowdy, outcast black and white to live with honor in their exclusion.

Incarceration in New York sensitizes Tanner to feel what it is like to be marked, as the black person is, to suffer the evil of others. Burial in hellish New York means that Tanner, in the words that he would know from the famous fifty-third chapter of Isaiah, will be the one who "has borne our griefs and carried our sorrows" (53:4). By oppression "he was taken away" and "cut off out of the land of the living," and now Tanner must contemplate the disgrace of his daughter's making "his grave with the wicked" (Isaiah 53:8–9). Tanner at the end of his life bears the burden that Coleman shoulders from birth. By virtue of being black, Coleman must endure the accumulated injustices of the community. The common lot of clown and captive is that of the scapegoat, which biblical reflection exalts to the calling of the suffering servant.

The approach of Judgment Day hallows their bond. When they first meet, Coleman needs Tanner for a job at the sawmill; but at the end Tanner needs Coleman for the gathering of crosses. Coleman becomes the minister of the last days. Like a lost child, Tanner has a note to an anonymous assistant pinned in his pocket: "IF FOUND DEAD SHIP EXPRESS COLLECT TO COLEMAN PARRUM, CORINTH, GEORGIA." Coleman will take care of his body. Below this message, Tanner writes his last will and testament: "COLEMAN SELL MY BELONGINGS AND PAY THE FREIGHT ON ME & THE UNDERTAKER. ANYTHING LEFT OVER YOU CAN KEEP. YOURS TRULY T. C. TANNER. P.S. STAY WHERE YOU ARE. DON'T LET THEM TALK YOU INTO COMING UP HERE. ITS NO KIND OF PLACE" (246). The effect of the message, spelled out in capital letters on the printed page, is to pound out the definitive hold of God's judgment on the old man.

Tanner's advice to his fellow Corinthian acquires its full force in light of the hero's recent experience with another black person, this one an actor who rents the apartment next to Tanner's daughter. Tanner tries to befriend the new neighbor. " 'Good morning, Preacher' " (262), he calls out to the actor. Then Tanner asks if the man knows of a pond nearby. Tanner assumes that the black man fishes and that he witnesses for God, assumptions that he does not make about his white son-in-law. The worldly actor, however, misconstrues "Preacher" to be a racist slur; and he reacts by slamming the " 'wool-hat red-neck son-of-a-bitch peckerwood old bastard' " through the apartment door. So that there is no confusion with the stereotype of naive southern black, the actor blasphemes God before he assaults the old man: " 'I'm not even no Christian. I don't believe that crap. There ain't no Jesus and there ain't no God' " (263).

The black New Yorker's tantrum swells from some "unfathomable dead-cold rage" (262) that tells us that he is settling older scores than that of being addressed as a preacher. To dispel his historical anger for being the object of oppression, the black man displaces his wrath onto Tanner. Tanning the old southerner outweighs the affront of his country greeting. The injury is severe. Tanner's thick tongue, which stays frozen for days, indicates that he experiences a stroke. The disparity between Tanner's offense and his punishment is the spiritual portion of his trauma that pays for the abuses of the entire white race through the retribution of the furious black man. Tanner's affliction in this encounter reenacts the trouncing felt by those whom Isaiah sees as "wounded for our transgressions" (53:5).

The beating also pummels Tanner's heart. Now more than ever he must make his daughter understand his need to get home to Corinth. After wringing a promise from her that she will ship his body home, "he slept peacefully" (264). Rest brings a dream, and the dream buoys him up. An imagined voyage takes him from death-in-life in New York to life-in-death in Georgia. In the dream, a pine box carries him home. On arrival, the cold morning air of Corinth inspires him through the cracks of the coffin. Tanner sees Coleman and hears Hooten, the stationmaster, grumble about the latest of Tanner's tricks. When they are about to pry open the lid, the clown of captivity springs like Lazarus from the tomb: " 'Judgement Day! Judgement Day!' he cried. 'Don't you two fools know it's Judgement Day?' " (265). The dream of coming home comes to the dreamer.

Comic dream speaks to eschatological vision, for folly is one way of reaching the Omega. The wise person discerns the ways of God with clarity and can meet judgment with confidence. The fool, who is usually hot-tempered (Proverbs 14:17) and quarrelsome (Proverbs 20:3), comes by a different route; and though wisdom surpasses folly, the fool has a chance. The fool learns the hard way. The rod of discipline (Proverbs 10:13) must force the fool into God's plan. The fool's way is Tanner's way. His impulse is to reject God's law and to harm and control others, but fear of hell keeps him obedient. "The fear of the Lord," we read in Proverbs (1:7), "is the beginning of knowledge." In the end, Tanner's godly fear brings him home where he belongs; and he arrives through the dream as the fool of the apocalypse who heralds the new day.

The simple movement of the dream discloses the ancient pattern that O'Connor posits in everyday life. Tanner travels down south and rises up to celebrate a reunion. Grief ends in joy. This twofold pattern holds a momentous mystery. Descent and reascent, dejection followed by sudden exaltation, provide a rough sketch of death and resurrection (Durrwell 1–6).

From the high point of the dream there is a steady letdown in Tanner's confidence that he will get home. He senses the worthlessness of his daughter's promise and decides to get home on his own. This decision leads first to self-reproach and then to reconciliation. He knows that he is a nuisance and that his daughter is good to him: "He felt guilty" (265). As his daughter leaves for the store, Tanner extends himself: " 'I'm sorry if I've give you a lot of trouble getting sick.' " Contrition, however calculated, invites gentleness. " 'I wouldn't have you any other place' " (266), the daughter confesses, and she means it. The old man's apology turns into dread when he feels the physical difficulty of walking out of the apartment to embark on his trip home. When his body betrays him, he sinks into helplessness: "A sensation of terror and defeat swept over him" (267). The tide of darkness that sweeps over Julian, over Mrs. May, and over Thomas now overtakes Tanner with its irresistible force. He lumbers six feet beyond the apartment door before collapsing upside down on the flight of dark steps.

Downcast as he is, Tanner must fall still further in order to get home. The black actor finds the stricken old man on the steps and finishes him off by shoving his head and arms between the spokes of the banister. Tanner dies with his feet dangling over the stairwell like "a man in the stocks" (269). With a ritual gesture of good riddance to an old plague, the black actor assumes the role in the timeless drama of scapegoating and contemptuously pulls Tanner's hat over his head. Effaced, Tanner hangs from the spokes a cursed man. He must suffer not only the pangs of death but also the slings and arrows of the actor's impersonal wrath. The responsibility for the additional pain falls on the black man, who incurs the very racist guilt that he tries to expel by heaping it on Tanner. This violence, however, serves the higher purpose that the old man identifies with the consecrated ground of Corinth. Grievous rebuke humbles the proud old codger. Tanner at the end becomes the man of sorrows who, Isaiah says, must bear "the sin of many" (53:12).

The suffering servant embodies O'Connor's fullest recognition of human worth as achieved along the scriptural lines of falling and rising. The trials heaped on the servant, in both the Bible and O'Connor's fiction, plunge the servant into agony; but loving acceptance of the yoke exalts the servant. Surrender usually comes quietly, and that is how Tanner submits to divine providence. " 'The Lord is my shepherd,' " he mutters as he wobbles toward the sofa to embark on his journey, " 'I shall not want' " (267). The twenty-third psalm gathers together the various references to service in the story to show their ultimate importance.

Moreover, the way in which Psalm 23 celebrates reliance on the Lord and personal sacrifice parallels the technique of "Judgement Day." In the decline of life the psalmist looks back over the past to take heart in God's help through daily vicissitudes. That guidance assures the psalmist that God will be present for the final trials of the world. Two images portray divine help. The Lord is a caring shepherd and a generous host. The shepherd leads the flock through an arid desert and a dark valley to find green pastures; and the host provides shelter at the journey's end, where he festively anoints the wanderer's head with oil. The frank confession of trust that unifies Psalm 23 describes the shaping spirit of "Judgement Day." A simple habit of mind—recollection of help transposed into hope—conveys the faith evolved from commonplace experience. For O'Connor, with her biblical sensibility, what is usual is most unusual; what is done each day contains the stuff of eternity.

The arduous path through the valley of the shadow of death passes into the unlighted corridor of the New York building, through its alley, and down to Corinth. The steps on which Tanner stumbles in his effort to make a precipitous turn in the path serve as a bridge, like Jacob's ladder, from one world to the next. On the steps Tanner can even feel a way opening for him. Before the actor pushes him, Tanner lifts his hand, now "as light as a breath," to ask for help and, perhaps, to wave good-bye. The neighbor's scorn does not deter Tanner. He does not want. Everything about the clumsy, heavy man rises. Humor is part of his viaticum, his provision for the journey to eternal life. He utters his last words "in his jauntiest voice." He knows what he lacks and he knows where he is going: " 'Hep me up, Preacher. I'm on my way home!' " (269). The gesture is a prayer. Time for the old man presses on toward God and the Omega, not toward the past and destruction.

The story does not end in otherworldly triumph or in melodramatic death. O'Connor concludes "Judgement Day" by showing the effect of Tanner's death on his daughter, whose domestic preoccupations are the actuality in which she prepares for judgment. O'Connor lays down no rules, devises no theological categories for judgment. Common duty sets the terms: the daughter is obliged to bury her father in Georgia. Her initial response is to dispose of his body to suit her convenience, but conscience makes her worry about her betrayal. When she disinters the body for reburial at home, she too makes a descent into guilt; and she reascends when she does right by her father. The last sentence of the story reads: "Now she rests well at night and her good looks have mostly returned." O'Connor allows the eschatological aura to arise out of the poetic representation of the pattern of fall and ascent. The daughter, who has been a generous hostess, becomes the caring shepherdess.

The calm resolution makes "Judgement Day" something of an anomaly in O'Connor's work; but that unexpected narrative smoothness, arrived at over twenty years of attention, indicates where the heart of her total effort lies. Love and transcendence are O'Connor's true subject. The physical maiming and senseless killing and spiteful holocaust that regularly conclude her stories state negatively her theme by displaying how far humankind has strayed from the will of God, which is to obey His prompting to love. The shock in each story serves to remand the sinner back into the world of guilt and sorrow from which she or he tries to escape and in which wretchedness lays bare the duty to love. Violence in O'Connor's fiction exhibits the positive dimension of action and suffering. O'Connor's strategy is to make readers recoil from horror in order to embrace love. "Judgement Day" shows the benefit of acting to assuage suffering. With the return of the daughter's ability to sleep and of her good looks, the insoluble tangle of refusal and submission straightens out. Harmony prevails, and peace is the gift of God that O'Connor shows as a foretaste of glory. The repose concluding "Judgement Day" corresponds to a moving reflection in O'Connor's letters. "That's the sweetest thing I ever heard, now ain't it," she reassures a friend seven weeks before she dies about her resting comfortably. "Peaceful days & nights. My" (*Letters* 583).

"Judgement Day" does not pretend to dramatize the full mystery of redemptive peace. Instead, it shows how the new dispensation comes to each of us personally when the divine act of dying and rising reaches us through minor acts of love. The legacy of destitute Tanner is to bring his daughter out of her guilt to shepherd him from death to life. His need and her response align the here-and-now with the everywhere-and-always. Getting home is escaping from the narrow tenements of time to the house of the Lord (Psalm 23:6). The world of sin and death with its monstrous contingencies leads to the order of resurrection, which "Judgement Day" announces. The very detachment and coldness about which commentators all remark (Merton, "Prose Elegy" 37–44) produce an impression of grandeur in O'Connor's art.

O'Connor prepares her characters for elevation to a richer life by bringing them to the bedrock of experience: the awareness of limitation. This state of want is a sign that the last days have begun. Such poverty has nothing to do with economics. It has rather to do with mystery, and it is the central mystery of our position on earth as debtors to God in relation to one another. The poor in spirit can recognize their dependence on God and be amazed by the gracious result of their reliance. With midwinter in his heart and shadows closing around him, Tanner gives thanks.

O'Connor not only brings all her heroines and heroes to an astonishment born of utter want, she also writes from a similar position. "I work from such a basis of poverty that everything I do is a miracle to me" (*Letters* 127), she says to a friend. The gift of perceiving fulfillment in privation comes to the reader in the poetry of O'Connor's ideas about deliverance through guilt and love, of which the last story is the epitome. "Judgement Day" is Flannery O'Connor's *Nunc Dimittis,* a gathering up of her total experience of life within a final testament of acceptance.

IV

Nunc Dimittis

The transition from Old Dudley's imprisonment in New York in "The Geranium" (1946) to Tanner's joyful release in Corinth in "Judgement Day" (1965) maps the overarching adventure that articulates O'Connor's credo. Her basic story tells the struggle of getting home. Home, even for her sojourners who are not dying old men, remains God. Though the destination remains fixed and offers shelter, getting there is roundabout and risky. Suddenness rules the O'Connor pilgrimage. Fitful departures hurl reluctant wayfarers onto a wilderness road beset with snarls that lead to a deadly homestretch and explosive arrival.

Having explored the eerie and mighty deeds in the two novels and over twenty stories that produce this odyssey, I want to offer several reflections on the voyage's complexity. The overall pattern of the journey resembles a maze. Bafflement for both the travelers and the readers goes with the undertaking. There is no fixed entrance or point of departure. Each wayfarer approaches the common resting place from a direction that defines her or his special moral need. As O'Connor's art evolves, these diverse crossings complicate matters further by altering O'Connor's treatment of the passage home. All her tourists roam in darkness, but that gloom of sin becomes worthy of compassion as O'Connor comes to perceive that darkness too is created by the Creator. There are clues, for which an eagle eye is more useful than a guidebook, to lead us to this recognition. Each of O'Connor's novels and stories gleams with a light that goes into hiding, most frequently in darkness. The entourage of sinners gropes toward that light; in doing so, they lead O'Connor too into undiscovered sympathies that gradually transform her instinctive pugnacity about human dereliction into kindly humor.

O'Connor's response to *derelictio* —a being lost and abandoned— comes to the reader, then, under two aspects: the events that mark the return to God in the individual tales and the parallel progress toward compassion in O'Connor's mind. The fearsomeness of the narrative action is so well known that two decades after the publication of her last story, and despite conclusive evidence in her letters, essays, and reviews of a benevolent sensibility, horror continues to be the hallmark of O'Connor's writing. Not even the rising admiration of her mind and art changes this view. The perceptive studies now appearing (Brinkmeyer and Gentry, for example) deepen our understanding of the implied narrative personality responsible for the immediacy, passion, and seriousness of O'Connor's work. If we look within her imaginative grasp of reality—near yet distant, obvious yet mysterious—for the parturition of the moral craftswoman, we can also see that technique and dramatic harshness hide O'Connor's inner growth of the deepest tenderness.

Once again, O'Connor's response to another writer is an access to her mind. Her 1963 review of Barry Ulanov's *Seeds of Hope in the Modern World* praises the book for its ability to recover "the potential power of the modern world to lead a man closer to God" (*Presence of Grace* 159). The principle by which O'Connor evaluates this book and everything else that she reads is that of edification crafted in a spare and felt prose. In the case of an author like herself, who writes from deeply held religious convictions, O'Connor hastens to qualify the idea of seriousness by noting that the mere desire to bring people to God counts for little. It can even harm. Experience as an artist and familiarity with pietistic writing teach her that when the artist's belief is an unlived idea, or remains uninformed by craft and love of creation, the reader is turned away from God. J. F. Powers, to O'Connor's mind, numbers among the modern writers who know how to write and how to enflesh belief. His fiction brings O'Connor early in her reviewing career to formulate the guiding rule that belief must be honed and incarnated by love. Powers's work, "however much directed by his Faith, seems more directed by his charity" (*Presence of Grace* 15).

Charity for O'Connor amounts to discerning good within evil, and she possesses what she admires. Without blinking an eye before the desolation of our dark time, and without adopting its self-protecting detachment, O'Connor's compassion for God embraces in the end a love for all His relations in all His creatures in all their activities. Given the malice in her books, this claim may seem iconoclastic, even untenable. If so, a revision of our estimate of O'Connor is very much in order. Finding charity in her work depends upon the willingness of readers to see the characters with Omega eyes as worthy of the love that O'Connor accords them. Like survivors of torture who cannot recover their self-esteem long after the physical abuse stops, modern readers seem unable to accept stories of good hopes and renewal after withstanding O'Connor's battering documents of death and insignificance. Conditioned by a literature of expostulation, we miss the way in which O'Connor not only admonishes but also comforts. Her way is bold. The stories and novels assure us that even the routine dark business of this hour falls within the divine plan. Mass murder, self-extermination, sadism, and captivity open a way to God. The challenge of O'Connor's fiction is for the reader to find the saving purpose of evil.

Corinth is the right name for the Georgia backwoods where the last of O'Connor's derelicts transcends his moral suffering. Corinth is the legendary city of conversion. Once ruled by vice, Corinth put aside its sailor's-town debauchery to live by divine law. That turning to God to take Him in full seriousness is the climactic outcome toward which all of O'Connor's narratives move. "I have found," O'Connor makes plain in a famous declaration, "that my subject in fiction is the action of grace in territory held largely by the devil" (*Mystery and Manners* 118). Grace summons the sinner to rebel against rebellion. The sinner's acceptance of the call to participate in the divine plan dispossesses the enemy of God of one reserve under his vast jurisdiction. O'Connor describes this fractional but individually decisive victory as her "returning my characters to reality" (*Mystery and Manners* 112). Wherever her characters recapture what-is, there lies the Corinth of the heart.

V

To round off this overview of O'Connor's Corinth pilgrimage, I turn to the final reflections of the most important Protestant theologian of our century, Karl Barth. Barth's thought bears on O'Connor's thinking. His lectures on wonder, personal concern, and scriptural commitment in *Evangelical Theology: An Introduction* (1963) surmount five hundred years of doctrinal rupture in the Christian church to spur O'Connor's wonder, personal concern, and scriptural commitment. The Basel ecumenist incites the hermit novelist of Milledgeville to prod complacent Catholic readers of the local diocesan tabloid for which she reviews to deepen their faith through an intellectual *metanoia,* or change of outlook, by a scientific study of the Bible (*Presence of Grace* 164–65). For Roman Catholics not yet touched by the encouragement of Vatican Council II to approach the Bible critically, or for other Catholics who have settled for the *status quo* of unexamined dogma, O'Connor's call for an intelligent study of the God of the Gospels amounts to a reiteration of the scriptural rethinking of faith that Barth works out in his lectures in *Evangelical Theology.*

However inviting it is to explore fully the affinity between Barth's theology and O'Connor's art, their kinship must await the attention of another critic.[2] The connection I have in mind comes from a personal remark of Barth's rather than from his systematic analysis; and like O'Connor's "Judgement Day," Barth's statement arises during the last days of his life. Early in December 1968 he is preparing a sermon to be given in January 1969, when he is to address Swiss Roman Catholics and a reform group in Zurich on the subject of Christian unity. Barth died on 9 December 1968, before finishing the sermon. The text itself ends in mid-sentence, but the crucial idea is there to complete his final testimony. With those Christians who seek to obey their Master's will that they be one, Barth feels it necessary to discuss "starting out, turning round, and confessing" (*Final Testimonies* 54). On the night he dies, Barth is curious about where he could find best expressed the endless process of starting out, turning around, and confessing—the ancient pattern of guilt and transcendence.

He would find this reform in O'Connor's writing. Her fiction embodies the growth that Barth seeks. To begin with, her nearly exclusive attention to Protestant characters (passed over by critics as part of the Georgia scene where firebrand preaching is a cottage industry or misread as inadvertent spokespersons for Catholicism) expresses O'Connor's respect for those who take the Bible seriously (see Wood 15–26). Her strident fundamentalists bear witness to a biblical faith that O'Connor advocates and that Catholic dogma and ritual can obscure. She takes exception to the potential use of scripture for personal ends, but she respects the work of her preachers enough to supply through literary form the sacramental fulfillment that their scriptural emphasis tends to discount. The depth of O'Connor's vision lies in the union of the staunch Protestant commitment to the Bible with the strong Roman Catholic understanding of the sacraments.

O'Connor's pilgrimage home is the contemporary living out of biblical truths in a sacramental action. Barth would recognize the movement. O'Connor turns her nihilists and her believers and her indifferents around in their tracks to start them toward the new, the future good in relation to ultimate reality. Whatever her characters seek, she gives their desire its first true depth and meaning by bringing them to the desire under all desires; and she does so by leading even the most terrified, the most broken, and the most despairing to the brink of a deeper abyss than she or he imagined. Confronting the nadir, they learn that all of their previous yearning has been a preparation for a desire for God. The will to live by this yearning and the communication of grace to fulfill the decision constitute the sacrament, which in turn signifies the particular realization of Christian life in the character—a rebirth in spirit or an anointing for imminent death.

In the fiction, the awakening to consciousness of guilt and personal insufficiency provides the condition for reform. O'Connor's pilgrims begin to feel that something is owed, that something more than themselves is needed. Starting out in her narratives is the moment of desolation: when one is aware of guilt, when one is sick, when one is oppressed by enemies, when one is alive to a remoteness from God, and when one faces death. Social and moral training, however, discourages the very admission of guilt and need that opens the heart to accept the weakness that reveals God's strength. In fact, the charge that O'Connor brings against our age is that the propensity to deny the devil, sin, and guilt expresses the desire to be free from the need for God. O'Connor's books register the alarm that seizes her when she discovers the false transcendent world of dreams created by pietistic theology, science, social custom, and treacly art. These gods veil her characters from the reality to which she returns them.

Readers who do not grasp the love behind O'Connor's depiction of violent catastrophe will inevitably be perplexed by her protests against the modern flights from God. O'Connor herself is always respectful of the unbelief that prevents her audience from discerning the charity shaping her mortal comedies. But in the long run the opposing view of the modern temper serves O'Connor well. What is most courageous about her fiction (and about her letters and reviews too) is that her stories are written with a healthy affection for a hostile audience whose doubts become the terms through which the protagonists bring the reader to self-reform.

Like the Swiss theologian who changed the direction of Protestant thought by turning the study of theology back to the pastoral service of the church, O'Connor rescues the act of reading modern fiction from its self-referential cerebrations to restore the practice of fascination and instruction. The wonder arises from learning the eternal seriousness of human life in dark times. O'Connor's books insist that the anguish of this age counts. When Hazel Motes in *Wise Blood* pours out his disillusionment through self-mortification, he has in mind a grief with no end. Mason Tarwater in *The Violent Bear It Away* rants about sin with comparable belief in the ultimate importance of evil. The old prophet means neither the physiological compulsions nor the social deprivations that neurotically torment our age, but the sin of Adam with which we all are born and which we must bear until the crosses that Mason sees are gathered up.

O'Connor wants the reader to see that even in an age that presses for a purely individualistic and unique reckoning of the human condition, it is still the Lamb of God, not the laboratory, that takes away the sins of the world. To suffer in the O'Connor world means to suffer because of God or to live in absurdity; to sin is to sin against God or to live without the possibility of transcendence; and to be judged is to be judged by the hand of God or to despair of pardon.

Simply described, Flannery O'Connor's books present stories for a better world. To an age that trusts the latest technological finesse and psychotherapeutic technique to secure itself, her fiction offers the dignity of ultimateness, of needing no other but God. The journey home to Corinth provides inducements along the way to accept this measure of worth. Obedience to a mysterious infinity spares O'Connor's pilgrims from laying their unlived lives for very long on passing distractions and from remaining caught in traps. As with Tanner's stumbling the treacherous six feet from apartment door to stairwell, every step taken under the shepherd's protection is a victory. Reliance on the ultimate measure allows all the protagonists to accept the horror they cannot avoid, and brings them to affirm, as Tanner does from the jauntiest part of himself, things that cause weariness and disgust. Nothing is too paltry. Even more radical than the violent ending is the concomitant discovery by the hero and the reader that everything is turned to its good. Confessing leads the heroines and heroes out of desolation into consolation, the experience of being loved by God.

The benediction of our human reality is the Omega. Convergence begins in the characters' here-and-now with its sordid particulars. From the outset of the journey, the meanest incident must be seen as willed by God, Who, given the atrocities that erupt en route in the stories, takes drastic steps to bring humankind close to His plan. In the end, O'Connor cherishes the imperfect material world as the intended condition that restores creation to its Creator. Turning around and confessing take place in the fallen world because the eternal, she discerns, is in the world as the world is in the eternal. The dramatic pattern of O'Connor's Corinth pilgrimage bids the reader to recognize its turbulent rise and fall and reascent as the order of the God of holiness. Viewed as part of this mystery, to start, to turn around, and to confess become for Flannery O'Connor the way to love.

NOTES

1. From an unpublished lecture that O'Connor gave to the AAUW in Lansing, Michigan, in 1956. The passage is on page 6 of the typescript, which is in an unmarked folder in the O'Connor Collection at Georgia College.
2. We can now look forward to such a study. Ralph C. Wood's *The Comedy of Redemption: Christian Faith and Comic Vision in Four American Novelists* has been announced for publication by the University of Notre Dame Press. Wood uses Reinhold Niebuhr and Karl Barth to interpret the fiction of Flannery O'Connor, Walker Percy, John Updike, and Peter De Vries.

Appendix

Milledgeville
Georgia
27 August 62

Dear Mrs. Terry,

Thank you for your letter. I sympathize with your friend's feeling of repulsion at the episode of Tarwater and the man in the lavender and cream-colored car. It was a very necessary action to the meaning of the book, however, and one which I would not have used if I hadn't been obliged to. I think the reason he doesn't understand it is because he doesn't really understand the ending, doesn't understand that Tarwater's call is real, that his true vocation is to answer it. Tarwater is not sick or crazy but really called to be a prophet—a vocation which I take seriously, though the modern reader is not liable to. Only the strong are called in this way and only the strong can answer. It can only be understood in religious terms. The man who gives him the lift is the personification of the voice, the stranger who has been counseling him all along; in other words, he is the devil, and it takes this action of the devil's to make Tarwater see for the first time what evil is. He accepts the devil's liquor and he reaps what the devil has to give. Without this experience of evil, his acceptance of his vocation in the end would be merely a dishonest manipulation by me. Those who see and feel what the devil is turn to God. Tarwater learned the hard way but he has a hard head.

You can pass this answer on to your friend if you like, and I also enclose an essay on the novel, which I think is good. If you think it would help him, you can send it to him, but tell him to send it back to me when he's through with it. The one in Xavier Studies was a good one too—and I am wondering how it got as far north as Potsdam, New York.

I hope your virus is better. The peacocks have shed their tails for the season so I will send you a piece of the spoils.

Sincerely,

Flannery O'Connor

Bibliography

I. Works by Flannery O'Connor

The Complete Stories. New York: Farrar, Straus and Giroux, 1971.

The Correspondence of Flannery O'Connor and the Brainard Cheneys. Edited by C. Ralph Stephens. Jackson: University Press of Mississippi, 1986.

Everything That Rises Must Converge. Introduction by Robert Fitzgerald. New York: Farrar, Straus and Giroux, 1965; Noonday Press edition, 1968.

"An Exile in the East." *South Carolina Review* II (1978): 12–21.

A Good Man Is Hard to Find and Other Stories. New York: Harcourt, Brace, 1955; Harvest edition, 1977.

The Habit of Being: Letters of Flannery O'Connor. Selected and edited by Sally Fitzgerald. New York: Farrar, Straus and Giroux, 1979.

Mystery and Manners: Occasional Prose. Selected and edited by Sally and Robert Fitzgerald. New York: Farrar, Straus and Giroux, 1969.

O'Connor Collection, Georgia College, Milledgeville.

    Folder 194d, on "Getting Home."

    Letter to Mrs. Grace Terry, 27 August 1962.

    Unidentified folder, containing fragment of an unpublished lecture given to the AAUW in Lansing, Michigan, 1956.

The Presence of Grace and Other Book Reviews. Compiled by Leo J. Zuber. Edited with an Introduction by Carter W. Martin. Athens: University of Georgia Press, 1983.

The Violent Bear It Away. New York: Farrar, Straus and Cudahy, 1960; Noonday Press edition, Farrar, Straus and Giroux, 1980.

Wise Blood. 2nd edition. With an Introduction by the author. New York: Farrar,

Straus and Cudahy, 1962; Noonday Press edition, Farrar, Straus and Giroux, 1974.

II. Other Sources

Alighieri, Dante. *The Divine Comedy*. Translated with a commentary by Charles S. Singleton. 6 vols. Bollingen Series 80. Princeton, N.J.: Princeton University Press, 1977.

Asals, Frederick. *Flannery O'Connor: The Imagination of Extremity*. Athens: University of Georgia Press, 1982.

Balthasar, Hans Urs von. *Prayer*. Translated by A. V. Littledale. New York: Sheed and Ward, 1961.

Barth, Karl. *Evangelical Theology: An Introduction*. Translated by Grover Foley. New York: Holt, Rinehart and Winston, 1963.

——. *Final Testimonies*. Translated by G. W. Bromiley. Edited by Eberhard Busch. Grand Rapids, Mich.: William B. Eerdmans, 1977.

——. *The Word of God and the Word of Man*. Translated with a new Foreword by Douglas Horton. New York: Harper and Row, Harper Torchbooks, 1957.

Bornkamm, Günther. *Paul*. Translated by D. M. G. Stalker. New York: Harper and Row, 1971.

Brinkmeyer, Robert H., Jr. "Flannery O'Connor and Her Fundamentalist Narrator: A Narrative Interplay." Paper given at Flannery O'Connor Symposium, West Chester University, West Chester, Pa., October 8–9, 1987.

Browning, Preston M., Jr. *Flannery O'Connor*. Carbondale: Southern Illinois University Press, 1974.

Chadwick, Henry. *The Early Church*. Vol. 1 of *The Pelican History of the Church*. Baltimore: Penguin Books, 1967.

Coles, Robert. *Flannery O'Connor's South*. Baton Rouge: Louisiana State University Press, 1980.

Desmond, John F. *Risen Sons: Flannery O'Connor's Vision of History*. Athens: University of Georgia Press, 1987.

Drake, Robert. *Flannery O'Connor: A Critical Essay*. Grand Rapids, Mich.: William B. Eerdmans, 1966.

Driskell, Leon V., and Joan T. Brittain. *The Eternal Crossroads: The Art of Flannery O'Connor*. Lexington: University of Kentucky Press, 1971.

Durrwell, F. X. *The Resurrection: A Biblical Study*. Translated by Rosemary Sheed. Introduction by Charles Davis. New York: Sheed and Ward, 1960.

Eggenschwiler, David. *The Christian Humanism of Flannery O'Connor*. Detroit, Mich.: Wayne State University Press, 1972.

Farnham, James F. "Further Evidence for the Sources of 'Parker's Back.' " *The Flannery O'Connor Bulletin* 12 (1983): 114–16.

Feeley, Kathleen. *Flannery O'Connor: Voice of the Peacock.* 2nd edition. New York: Fordham University Press, 1982.

Fitzgerald, Sally. "A Master Class: From the Correspondence of Caroline Gordon and Flannery O'Connor." *Georgia Review* 33 (1979): 827–46.

——. "The Owl and the Nightingale." *The Flannery O'Connor Bulletin* 13 (1984): 44–58.

——. "Rooms with a View." *The Flannery O'Connor Bulletin* 10 (1981): 5–22.

Fitzmyer, Joseph A. *Pauline Theology: A Brief Sketch.* Englewood Cliffs, N.J.: Prentice-Hall, 1967.

St. Francis of Assisi: Writings and Early Biographies, English Omnibus of the Sources for the Life of St. Francis. Edited by Marion A. Habig. 4th revised edition. Chicago: Franciscan Herald Press, 1983.

Friedman, Melvin J., and Beverly Lyon Clark, eds. *Critical Essays on Flannery O'Connor.* Boston: G. K. Hall, 1985.

Friedman, Melvin J., and Lewis A. Lawson, eds. *The Added Dimension: The Art and Mind of Flannery O'Connor.* New York: Fordham University Press, 1966.

Gentry, Marshall Bruce. *Flannery O'Connor's Religion of the Grotesque.* Jackson: University Press of Mississippi, 1986.

Getz, Lorine M. *Flannery O'Connor: Her Life, Library and Book Reviews.* New York: Edwin Mellen Press, 1980.

Gordon, Sarah. "Flannery O'Connor and the Common Reader." *The Flannery O'Connor Bulletin* 10 (1981): 38–45.

Gretlund, Jan. "Flannery O'Connor's 'An Exile in the East': An Introduction." *The South Carolina Review* 2 (1978): 3–21.

Guardini, Romano. *The End of the Modern World: A Search for Orientation.* Translated by Joseph Theman and Herbert Burke. Edited with an Introduction by Frederick D. Wilhelmsen. New York: Sheed and Ward, 1956. Chicago: Henry Regnery, Logos edition, 1968.

——. *The Living God.* Translated by Stanley Godman. New York: Pantheon Books, 1957. Chicago: Henry Regnery, Logos edition, 1966.

——. *The Lord.* Translated by Elinor Castendyk Briefs. Chicago: Henry Regnery, 1954.

——. *Meditations before Mass.* Translated by Elinor Castendyk Briefs. Westminster, M.: Newman Press, 1956.

Hawkes, John. "Flannery O'Connor's Devil." *Sewanee Review* 70 (1962): 395–407.

Hawkins, Peter S. *The Language of Grace: Flannery O'Connor, Walker Percy, and Iris Murdoch.* Cambridge, Mass.: Cowley Publications, 1983.

Hendin, Josephine. *The World of Flannery O'Connor.* Bloomington: Indiana University Press, 1970.

Heschel, Abraham Joshua. *Man's Quest for God: Studies in Prayer and Symbolism.* New York: Charles Scribner's Sons, 1954.

——. *A Passion for Truth.* New York: Farrar, Straus and Giroux, 1973.

———. *The Prophets.* 2 vols. New York: Harper and Row, 1962; Harper Torchbooks, 1971.

Hopkins, Mary Frances. "Julian's Mother." *The Flannery O'Connor Bulletin* 7 (1978): 114–15.

Hyman, Stanley Edgar. *Flannery O'Connor.* Pamphlets on American Writers, Number 54. Minneapolis: University of Minnesota Press, 1966.

The Hymns of the Dominican Missal and Breviary. Edited with an Introduction and Notes by Aquinas Byrnes. St. Louis: B. Herder, 1943.

Kafka, Franz. *Selected Short Stories of Franz Kafka.* Translated by Willa Muir and Edwin Muir. Introduction by Philip Rahv. New York: Modern Library, 1952.

Kessler, Edward. *Flannery O'Connor and the Language of Apocalypse.* Princeton Essays in Literature. Princeton, N.J.: Princeton University Press, 1986.

Kinney, Arthur F. *Flannery O'Connor's Library: Resources of Being.* Athens: University of Georgia Press, 1985.

Lewis, C. S. *The Case for Christianity.* New York: Macmillan, 1944.

Lynd, Helen Merrell. *On Shame and the Search for Identity.* New York: Harcourt, Brace, 1958.

Mallon, Anne-Marie. "Mythic Quest in Flannery O'Connor's Fiction." Dissertation, University of Notre Dame, 1980.

Marcel, Gabriel. *The Mystery of Being.* Chicago: Henry Regnery, Gateway edition, 1960.

Martin, Carter W. *The True Country: Themes in the Fiction of Flannery O'Connor.* Nashville, Tenn.: Vanderbilt University Press, 1969.

May, John R. *The Pruning Word: The Parables of Flannery O'Connor.* Notre Dame, Ind.: University of Notre Dame Press, 1976.

Merton, Thomas. "Flannery O'Connor: A Prose Elegy." In *Raids on the Unspeakable.* New York: New Directions, 1966.

———. *The Seven Storey Mountain.* New York: Harcourt, Brace, 1948. New York: New American Library, Mentor Books, no date.

———. *The Wisdom of the Desert.* New York: New Directions, 1960.

Milton, John. *Paradise Lost.* Edited by Alastair Fowler. London: Longman, 1971.

Muller, Gilbert H. *Nightmares and Visions: Flannery O'Connor and the Catholic Grotesque.* Athens: University of Georgia Press, 1972.

Napier, James J. " 'The Artificial Nigger' and the Authorial Intention." *The Flannery O'Connor Bulletin* 10 (1981): 87–92.

The New Oxford Annotated Bible with the Apocrypha. Revised Standard Version. Edited by Herbert G. May and Bruce M. Metzger. New York: Oxford University Press, 1973.

Orvell, Miles. *Invisible Parade: The Fiction of Flannery O'Connor.* Philadelphia: Temple University Press, 1972.

Rahner, Karl. *Everyday Faith.* Translated by W. J. O'Hara. New York: Herder and Herder, 1968.

——. *Foundations of Christian Faith: An Introduction to the Idea of Christianity.* Translated by William V. Dych. New York: Crossroad, 1984.

——. *On the Theology of Death.* Translated with a Preface by Charles H. Henkey. New York: Herder and Herder, 1963.

Richter, Stephan. *Metanoia: Christian Penance and Confession.* Translated by Raymond T. Kelly. New York: Sheed and Ward, 1966.

Ridderbos, Herman. *Paul: An Outline of His Theology.* Translated by John Richard DeWitt. Grand Rapids, Mich.: William B. Eerdmans, 1975.

Rubin, Louis D., Jr. "Flannery O'Connor and the Bible Belt." In *The Added Dimension: The Art and Mind of Flannery O'Connor.* Edited by Melvin J. Friedman and Lewis A. Lawson. New York: Fordham University Press, 1966.

——. "Flannery O'Connor's Company of Southerners: or, 'The Artificial Nigger' Read as Fiction Rather Than Theology." *The Flannery O'Connor Bulletin* 6 (1977): 47–71.

Schillebeeckx, Edward. *Christ the Sacrament of the Encounter with God.* Translated by Paul Barrett and others. New York: Sheed and Ward, 1963.

——. *The Eucharist.* Translated by N. D. Smith. New York: Sheed and Ward, 1968.

Shakespeare, William. *The Riverside Shakespeare.* Edited by G. Blakemore Evans. Boston: Houghton Mifflin, 1974.

Shloss, Carol. *Flannery O'Connor's Dark Comedies: The Limits of Inference.* Baton Rouge: Louisiana State University Press, 1980.

Stephens, Martha. *The Question of Flannery O'Connor.* Baton Rouge: Louisiana State University Press, 1973.

Tate, J. O. "A Note on O'Connor's Use of Military Names." *The Flannery O'Connor Bulletin* 14 (1985): 99–102.

Teilhard de Chardin, Pierre. *Christianity and Evolution.* Translated by René Hague. New York: Harcourt Brace Jovanovich, Harvest edition, 1971.

——. *The Divine Milieu.* Translator unidentified. New York: Harper and Row, Harper Torchbooks, 1960.

——. *The Future of Man.* Translated by Norman Denny. New York: Harper and Row, Harper Torchbooks, 1964.

——. *The Heart of the Matter.* Translated by René Hague. New York: Harcourt Brace Jovanovich, 1979.

——. *Hymn of the Universe.* Translated by Gerald Vann. New York: Harper and Row, Colophon Books, 1965.

——. *The Phenomenon of Man.* Translated by Bernard Wall. Introduction by Sir Julian Huxley. New York: Harper and Row, Harper Torchbooks, 1961.

——. *The Prayer of the Universe.* Selected from *Writings in Time of War.*

Translated by René Hague. Introduction by Robert Speaight. New York: Harper and Row, Perennial Library, 1973.

Ulanov, Barry. *Seeds of Hope in the Modern World.* New York: Kenedy, 1962.

Underhill, Evelyn. *The Essentials of Mysticism.* New York: E. P. Dutton, 1920.

——. *Man and the Supernatural.* New York: E. P. Dutton, 1927.

——. *Mysticism: A Study in the Nature and Development of Man's Spiritual Consciousness.* 12th edition with Preface. New York: E. P. Dutton Paperback, 1961.

Walters, Dorothy. *Flannery O'Connor.* Twayne's United States Authors Series. New York: Twayne, 1973.

Westarp, Karl-Heinz. " 'Parker's Back': A Curious Crux Concerning Its Sources." *The Flannery O'Connor Bulletin* 11 (1982): 1–9.

——. "Teilhard de Chardin's Impact on Flannery O'Connor: A Reading of 'Parker's Back.' " *The Flannery O'Connor Bulletin* 12 (1983): 93–113.

Westling, Louise. *Sacred Groves and Ravaged Gardens: The Fiction of Eudora Welty, Carson McCullers, and Flannery O'Connor.* Athens: University of Georgia Press, 1985.

Wood, Ralph C. "The Catholic Faith of Flannery O'Connor's Protestant Characters: A Critique and Vindication." *The Flannery O'Connor Bulletin* 13 (1984): 15–25.

Worship: A Hymnal and Source Book for Roman Catholics. 3rd edition. Chicago: GIA, 1986.

Yeats, William Butler. *The Collected Poems of W. B. Yeats.* London: Macmillan, 1955.

Index to O'Connor's Works

General Index

A Note on the Author

Richard Giannone is Professor of English at Fordham University, Bronx, New York. He has previously published two books, *Music in Willa Cather's Fiction* and *Vonnegut: A Preface to His Novels,* and co-edited two anthologies. He has also published a number of essays on both English and American literature, including several on Flannery O'Connor.